Praise for The New Leaders

"A comprehensive study of our nation's multicultural workforce."
— HENRY CISNEROS,
U.S. Secretary of Housing and Urban Development

"A valuable contribution to our knowledge of what diversity work is happening in organizations and a useful guide to how such work can be undertaken. . . . Morrison's argument that white men must be deeply involved in the work is right on target."
— BUSINESS & THE CONTEMPORARY WORLD

"An insightful book."
— ETHICAL MANAGEMENT

"An excellent book that adds to our understanding of the issues and potential gains evolving from the diversification of our workforce."
— HR MAGAZINE

"If the United States wants to remain a top competitor in the global marketplace, employers must mine the rich potential of the diverse workforce. *The New Leader* offers practical insights into how American businesses can meet this all-important challenge."
— CHANG-LIN TIEN, chancellor,
University of California, Berkeley

"An inspirational practical approach to truly valuing diversity in America. . . . A clear blueprint for valuing diversity in the selection of leaders and the benefits that this brings to an organization. . . . Demands our attention."
— THE LEARNING CURVE,
AMERICAN SOCIETY FOR TRAINING AND DEVELOPMENT

The GOLD Research Team

Standing (left to right): Kay Iwata, Karen McNeil-Miller, Diane Ducat, Richard A. Morales, Kristen M. Crabtree, Karen M. Grabow, Judy A. Weir.

Seated (left to right): Nur D. Gryskiewicz, Ronald Stratten, Ann M. Morrison, Carol S. Y. García, Libby C. Keating, Edward W. Jones, Jr.

ANN M. MORRISON

LEADERSHIP
DIVERSITY
IN AMERICA

JOSSEY-BASS
A Wiley Company
www.josseybass.com

Published by

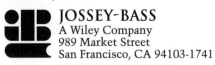

JOSSEY-BASS
A Wiley Company
989 Market Street
San Francisco, CA 94103-1741

www.josseybass.com

Copyright © 1992, 1996 by John Wiley & Sons, Inc. and Ann M. Morrison.

Jossey-Bass is a registered trademark of John Wiley & Sons, Inc.

Jossey-Bass books and products are available through most bookstores. To contact Jossey-Bass directly, call (888) 378-2537, fax to (800) 605-2665, or visit our website at www.josseybass.com.

Substantial discounts on bulk quantities of Jossey-Bass books are available to corporations, professional associations, and other organizations. For details and discount information, contact the special sales department at Jossey-Bass.

We at Jossey-Bass strive to use the most environmentally sensitive paper stocks available to us. Our publications are printed on acid-free recycled stock whenever possible, and our paper always meets or exceeds minimum GPO and EPA requirements.

Library of Congress Cataloging-in-Publication Data

Morrison, Ann M.
    The new leaders : guidelines on leadership diversity in America /
Ann M. Morrison. — 1st ed.
      p. cm. — (The Jossey-Bass management series)
    Includes bibliographical references and index.
    ISBN 1-55542-459-7 (alk. paper)
        0-7879-0184-9 (paperback)
     1. Executives—United States. 2. Women executives—United States.
  3. Minority executives—United States. 4. Affirmative action
programs—United States. I. Title. II. Series.
HD38.2.M67   1992
658.4'092—dc20   92-20107

FIRST EDITION
HB Printing   10 9 8 7 6 5 4
PB Printing   10 9 8 7 6 5 4 3 2

CONTENTS

FOREWORD

Ever since the Hudson Institute's 1987 report, *Workforce 2000,* detected a major shift in the demographics of the American workplace, U.S. companies have been grappling with questions of diversity. How will we integrate more women and minorities into our workforce? Can we attract the newly emerging workforce? Can we develop a more diverse company as U.S. companies are downsizing? And perhaps some have asked more cynically, isn't this just another wave of political correctness that is likely to blow over?

It seems like America's top corporations have moved in five hundred different directions all at once trying to answer those questions and others. Thus far, the results are less than satisfying. This is due in no small way to a lack of greater understanding about diversity, corporate cultures, the needs of talented men and women, and the marketplace.

In *The New Leaders,* Ann Morrison provides us with that greater understanding and so much more. She gives us practical guidelines and suggestions for getting started. She begins with the business case. Simply put: (1) diverse individuals give companies greater understanding of diverse markets and thereby enhance a company's marketing potential; and (2) valuing *everyone* within a corporation increases productivity. In order to meet the demands of a diverse marketplace, we need people who are of that marketplace, who understand it in all its cultural and economic dimensions, and who can provide a variety of perspectives on how to succeed in it. We also can no longer afford to discount the talents, skills, and contributions of any employee. We must instead create an environment where every person matters and every person is fully enabled to contribute to his or her maximum potential.

The New Leaders provides us with the background, support, and sound advice to not only value and manage diversity but to lead by building diversity as a competitive advantage. I say "sound advice" because I know firsthand that the approaches Morrison advocates work. When she and her former colleagues at the Center for Creative Leadership initiated their Guidelines on Leadership Diversity (GOLD) research project in the late eighties, I was proud that Motorola, the company I was leading as CEO at the time, was part of the experience. Then in October 1993 I was appointed chairman, president, and CEO of Eastman Kodak Company. In looking at the questions and issues of diversity facing my new company, the world leader in imaging, I found myself referring to these very pages as well as to information shared with my Motorola team during the GOLD research project.

Today at Kodak we are still a ways from achieving our desired results, but we are clearly headed in the right direction. We have established goals for building and managing a truly diverse corporation. We have assessed our relative strengths and weaknesses in achieving these ends. We have created a new management development process to foster diversity (which, by the way, we call Governance, Organization, and Leadership Development — or GOLD — review). And we are holding managers accountable for delivering a more diverse organization by making diversity an issue in performance appraisals and linking a percentage of compensation to the achievement of diversity goals.

The New Leaders provides us with a process by which to tailor a program to meet our own particular needs — not a cookie-cutter prescription. As Morrison says herself: "Developing diversity is a struggle. . . . As in any change process, this is a long-term effort."

Thankfully there are some pathways for that long journey, and some facts about what works and what does not. We learn from what others have tried how to create opportunities for ourselves. There is also a five-step process for diversity development that gives us a useful template for developing our own efforts, which includes discovering diversity problems, strengthening management commitment, choosing solutions that fit a balanced strategy, demanding results and revisiting goals, and using building blocks to maintain momentum.

In short, Ann Morrison has provided a survival manual for managing *and leading* diverse organizations into the next century. She shares her studied approach for breaking down barriers and quickening the rate of organizational change so that not only more women and individuals of diverse backgrounds succeed, but so that companies like our own succeed as a consequence.

The business case can never be separated from the cause of diversity. Indeed, I would suggest that if one looked more closely at the evolution of business dynamics, the need to not only value diversity but thrive on it becomes readily apparent. For the past decade, business leaders have touted the need to understand the marketplace and to know their customers. Thanks to new technologies we can do that as effectively as the corner store could in the small towns of an earlier era. Mass marketing is being supplanted by segmentation marketing, direct marketing, and even what has been called by some "micromarketing to the market of one." The message is that business is about people and relationships — and we ultimately serve individuals. The better we define their needs and desires, the better able we are to succeed.

The logical corollary of that is that we need people who understand those segmented markets and who can relate to customers' needs and desires on something approximating a one-to-one basis. We also need to use similar marketing techniques in the recruitment and retention of talented and diverse individuals.

As Kodak's own global performance expectation on diversity states: "The connection this has to our business success is clear. If we have a diverse group of highly skilled people in a culture that enables them to apply their collective talents to shared objectives, they will consistently deliver the greatest value to the customer and shareholder. Everybody wins."

You too can win by adapting some of the guidelines set forth in *The New Leaders* to best meet the needs of your own organization.

October 1995   George M. C. Fisher
                                        chairman, president, and CEO
                                        Eastman Kodak Company
                                        Rochester, New York

PREFACE

Usually with high hopes and often with little expertise, many organizations today are attempting to overcome a long legacy of differential treatment based on sex and ethnicity. They are spending millions of dollars trying to solve a complex problem that is often misunderstood and always controversial. Despite the efforts to diversify management, managers whom I call *nontraditional* (those who are female and/or of color) continue to show up more in exit interviews than in succession plans.

People of color and white women are still scarcely represented in the ranks of senior management. The U.S. Federal Glass Ceiling Commission reported in March 1995 that 97 percent of the senior managers of the Fortune 1000 Industrials and the Fortune 500 are white, and at least 95 percent are male. The statistics in this report, titled *Good for Business: Making Full Use of the Nation's Human Capital,* are strikingly similar to those reported five years before. For example, a study conducted jointly by Korn/Ferry International and the University of California, Los Angeles, also documented that people of color and white women held only about 5 percent of senior management positions in major corporations (Dominguez, 1990). Upward mobility for nontraditional managers remains a huge challenge.

The challenge seems overwhelming for many who work to develop diversity in their organizations. They are on their own to develop a workable action plan. This book is meant to help by filling a critical information gap. Despite the proliferation of books and articles on diversity, there is still only limited information available about what to do. Most of the literature currently available about diversity either focuses on raising general awareness about the issue or describes cases in which activities to increase diversity were carried out in a single organization. Also, in many cases, the literature highlights unique barriers for particular groups, such as Hispanic women or black men, without considering the problems shared by all historically underrepresented groups. As a result, some organizations' efforts to diversify management preclude certain groups because it is too costly to create distinct programs or practices for each group. Given such a limited body of information, those who work to achieve diversity are on their own to develop a workable action plan for their organizations.

Why all the turmoil over diversity in the first place? There are several reasons. First is the changing demographics of the workforce itself. The Hudson Institute's 1987 report, *Workforce 2000,* notes that white women, native-born people of color, and immigrants will increasingly dominate the U.S. workforce and that white men will make up less than one-third of the new workforce by the year 2000. Another reason for the increased interest in diversity is the demographics of the marketplace. The predicted decline in the proportion of white men in the overall population will bring about a decrease in the number of white male customers. As companies compete for a share of this increasingly diverse marketplace, diversity within the organization is more likely to be considered a sound business principle. Finally, diversity is a critical issue because it highlights the need to manage more carefully a limited resource — the people of the organization, who provide the goods and services that sustain the business. In the face of such broad demographic change, organizations that do not recognize the need to cultivate and utilize the talents of their entire staff risk losing their competitive edge.

To plan and conduct an effective diversity effort, organizations need a framework that provides a broad perspective and that makes relevant recommendations for all gender and ethnic groups. As readers will see, *The New Leaders* provides such a framework.

Purpose of the Book

The purpose of *The New Leaders* is to help organizations and leaders design and implement practices that will develop diversity within the management ranks. The book provides information and guidelines regarding the practices that have worked in organizations noted for their progress on diversity, particularly at the management level. It clarifies the professional and ethical reasons for developing diversity and provides guidance for identifying nonperformance-related barriers to advancement.

The material in the book is based on research into the experiences of sixteen organizations that have been especially successful in diversifying their leadership. Such a "best practices" method is valuable because the paths for approaching diversity are mazelike and full of potential pitfalls. Readers will benefit from the collective experience of these organizations, which have confronted the hazards inherent in a diversity effort and, in some cases, have recovered from disastrous experiments.

Audience

The New Leaders is intended first and foremost for organizational leaders, since they are in the best position to direct and influence the development of diversity. For them, the book offers a discussion of the key principles of leadership development that need to be a part of any diversity effort. The book is also for human resource managers and others who are responsible for implementing diversity plans and making them a reality. They will find a step-by-step guide to the many trade-offs to be made and obstacles to be avoided in implementing a diversity plan. Finally, the book is for people in organizations who differ in gender or ethnicity from their white male colleagues in management. It is my hope that a better understanding of the issues will help them in their search for acceptance and advancement for themselves and others.

After reading *The New Leaders,* readers will have a solid basis for analyzing and selecting options for developing diversity practices. This benefit is missing in most published work in the diversity arena. In addition, because our research revealed far more agreement concerning barriers to advancement than did other investigations, this book may identify more clearly the nonperformance-related barriers for people who are "different" from those who hold power in organizations. The methods that have proven effective in leveling such barriers have broad application to organizations of various types and sizes.

Overview of the Contents

The book is divided into three main parts. Part One discusses the benefits and challenges of incorporating diversity into a business strategy. Chapter One describes the cumulative benefits that, as our research revealed, an organization can reap by achieving leadership diversity. Among these benefits are stronger marketing potential, increased productivity, and heightened social consciousness. Chapter Two examines the nature and extent of differential treatment based on sex and ethnicity. Getting beyond assumptions about the problem of inequality and developing a deeper understanding of its forms and magnitude are the first steps in developing diversity. Chapter Three shows how three key ingredients for sustained leadership development — challenge, recognition, and support — are critical to promoting the upward mobility of people of color and white women and focuses on how balancing these three ingredients helps promote diversity.

Part Two covers the practices used to foster diversity. This part begins with the presentation of a threefold strategy — education, enforcement, and exposure — designed to open up higher levels of management to nontraditional managers. Each chapter in Part Two supports the development of this strategy by focusing on one of the three main types of practices — accountability, development, and recruitment — used by the organizations in our study to promote diversity. Chapter Four focuses on the use of techniques for increasing accountability for diversity.

It discusses the pros and cons of creating employee-advocacy groups, of linking diversity goals to compensation, and of other techniques used to shape managers' behavior and possibly influence their attitudes. Chapter Five examines the use of management development to foster diversity. Included is a discussion of intensive programs for high-potential managers that involve rotational assignments, mentors, and career-assessment packages. Chapter Six focuses on the use of recruitments to build diversity. Once the sole focus of many diversity efforts, recruitment techniques are now emphasized less. Creative and flexible recruitment tools, however, are still needed in an increasingly competitive labor market to fill the executive pipeline from which future leaders will emerge. Because the incentives and techniques used to recruit promising managers are sometimes controversial, this chapter also considers the risks associated with these practices.

Each chapter in Part Three of the book covers one step in the process of developing a coherent diversity plan that can be tailored to an organization's specific needs. The five steps described in depth in these chapters incorporate basic principles of organizational change that are often ignored because of the history and sensitivity of the issue. Chapter Seven discusses the first step, which is to conduct an internal assessment of the organization's current strengths and weaknesses with respect to diversity. Chapter Eight covers step two, which is to gain or increase the appropriate involvement of top management. It discusses the advantages and disadvantages associated with top-management commitment to diversity. Step three, which is discussed in Chapter Nine, involves carefully selecting a mix of specific actions that fit into a balanced strategy. Step four of the process, discussed in Chapter Ten, concentrates on defining the desired outcomes of the diversity activities that were selected in step three. This chapter also discusses the use of specific goals to both measure and encourage tangible results. Chapter Eleven describes the fifth and final step, which involves deliberately using certain building blocks to maintain momentum and to strengthen diversity activities.

The appendix provides detailed information concerning

the research on which this book is based. It contains brief profiles of the research team members and describes characteristics of the sixteen participating organizations and the 196 managers who were interviewed. The appendix also gives details on the research procedures, including the selection process for organizations and managers, the interview questions, the steps taken to interview managers and convert their responses into quantitative data for analysis, and the precautions used to maintain professional standards in such areas as reducing bias and ensuring confidentiality. Finally, the appendix includes tables that supplement the data in the text concerning our research findings.

Many of the points made and examples used in this book come directly from the statements and experiences of the managers we interviewed. The use of direct quotations throughout the text gives these managers a chance to be heard in their own words. The vignettes that open each chapter are composites of individuals' responses and examples from the organizations in our study.

The GOLD Research Project

Although the appendix describes the research project in detail, the following summary is presented here so that interested readers may acquaint themselves with the background, general approach, and overall philosophy of the project.

The Guidelines on Leadership Diversity (GOLD) Project was originally intended to be a follow-up study of "Breaking the Glass Ceiling," a research project that I directed with Randall White and Ellen Van Velsor at the Center for Creative Leadership (CCL) and that resulted in a book of the same name in 1987. The "Glass Ceiling" project revealed many of the barriers impeding the advancement of white women into senior management ranks of corporate America and described the actions that many exceptional female executives performed to overcome the hurdles they faced.

The GOLD Project was originally intended to complement that study by identifying the corporate policies and practices that would help women advance into higher levels of management. But in the course of researching for an article for

American Psychologist I became convinced that a broader focus on measures to foster diversity overall would be far more helpful to organizations than limiting the investigation to women alone. In effect, the idea was to create a grouping of nontraditional managers. This unusual way of grouping managers is not intended to discount differences within this large group that may be linked to race or ethnicity, class, or sex. Rather, it is an attempt to reveal similarities in the career challenges faced by managers who are not white men.

The GOLD Project was also expanded beyond private corporations to include organizations in the public sector. Managers from government agencies and educational institutions had often questioned us about how our earlier findings related to their situations, and it was frustrating to have no answers for them. Organizations in the public sector employ millions of people and have many of the same problems, needs, and resources as corporations; thus it was important to include several of these organizations in our group. Again, the idea was to look for both similarities and differences that might affect our recommended solutions.

The goal of the GOLD Project was to identify the most promising tools and techniques now being used to foster diversity at the managerial level in organizations and to provide specific guidelines for planning and implementing a diversity effort. The success of the project ultimately rests on the usefulness of these guidelines as they are presented in the book. We believe that four important factors enhance their strength and utility:

1. The guidelines are research-based. Through confidential interviews, we collected information about the experiences and views of nearly two hundred managers of various backgrounds in a broad array of organizations. By conducting personal interviews and asking open-ended questions instead of issuing written surveys, we could allow the managers in our study to define problems and solutions in their own way and in their own words. This approach allowed us to gain critical insight into the subtleties and trade-offs involved in the techniques, such as recruitment incentives or employee advocacy groups, that are used to foster diversity.

2. The guidelines are relevant to a wide range of organizations. Our research involved extensive analyses of data from a variety of organizations, each of which has made advances in unique ways in fostering diversity. We addressed the key factors that allow a given approach to succeed in one organization while a seemingly similar approach fails elsewhere. We were therefore able to explore the interplay between organizational setting and the success or failure of specific techniques.

3. The guidelines are clear but not constraining. They are descriptive and understandable but not so detailed that managers would be encouraged to follow blindly in the footsteps of another organization while ignoring the unique history, priorities, and resources of their own. An essential element in fostering diversity is that an organization's solutions are developed largely by its people for its people.

4. The guidelines are challenging but not overwhelming. Whether a manager or professional is assessing the need for developing diversity, reevaluating a diversity strategy, or measuring progress, these guidelines provide a workable procedure for action. The steps are designed to encourage continued investment and persistence in the face of what may seem to be a discouragingly long road to progress.

The in-depth investigation provided in *The New Leaders* highlights the options available and the process needed to transform the goals of diversity into achievements that benefit organizations. It provides a foundation for the work that must go on within organizations to develop leadership diversity.

October 1995   Ann M. Morrison
La Jolla, California

ACKNOWLEDGMENTS

In a project such as this, there are always more contributors than can be appropriately recognized. Nevertheless, I would like to acknowledge some people who have invested extraordinary effort in this project.

The talent, devotion, and stamina of the GOLD research team are responsible for this project's success. We continually collaborated, argued about the meaning of our data, traveled on short notice, laughed at whatever we could find that was funny, and fortified one another. These twelve people have been my companions and cohorts for the past few years; I cannot thank them enough for keeping the standards of this project exceedingly high while shrugging off the hardships each endured. The people who make up this extraordinary team are Kristen M. Crabtree, Diane Ducat, Carol S. Y. García, Karen M. Grabow, Nur D. Gryskiewicz, Kay Iwata, Edward W. Jones, Jr., Libby C. Keating, Karen McNeil-Miller, Richard A. Morales, Ronald Stratten, and Judy A. Weir.

We were fortunate to have an active advisory committee for this project. The members of the committee generously shared their expertise, their contacts, and their enthusiasm at various stages in the research. The committee includes Ella Bell, a faculty member at the Massachusetts Institute of Technology and an active researcher of women of color, who reviewed early drafts of the interview protocol; Francine Deutsch, who directs the School of Family Studies and Consumer Sciences at San Diego State University and consulted on the initial design and reviewed a later draft of the manuscript; Carole Leland of the CCL-San Diego Staff, who consulted on the initial study design; Ralph Mitchell of the CCL-Greensboro staff, who helped shape the design and interview procedures; and Ruth Shaeffer, a longtime member of the Conference Board and now president of the nonprofit Center for Total Quality Management in Healthcare, Inc., in New York, who advised us on potential sites and reviewed a later draft of the manuscript. Two additional committee members came from CCL's top management: David L. DeVries, the center's executive vice president until the end of 1990; and Walter F. Ulmer, Jr., president of the center since 1985. Both have been diligent collaborators on this work over the years, regularly contributing their ideas and resources.

The Center for Creative Leadership, a nonprofit organization dedicated to bridging the gap between leadership theory and practice, has funded, supported, and sponsored this research project since its inception. The center has provided time, staff, money, and encouragement. Since 1990, most of my time as an employee of the center has been devoted to this project. The research would probably not have been done if it were not for the center's inclination to support complex, time-consuming, unprecedented projects with promising but uncertain outcomes.

The center's top executives, particularly Walter Ulmer and David DeVries, saw the promise of this research in contributing to the development of leadership in organizations, to the improvement of productivity, and to the good of society as a whole. I am grateful to them for the many substantial contributions they have made to this project since 1987.

Many center staff members other than the research team contributed in a number of ways to this research, so many that they cannot all be adequately thanked here. Peggy Cartner, Frank Freeman, Karen Hardie, and Carol Keck in our library did detective work and contributed their expertise over the entire period of the research. Marlene Zagon, who joined the center's San Diego staff in late 1990, worked with the literature

The

base and the manuscript preparation as well as took on other responsibilities as administrator in the later stages of the project. The eagerness of our fellow researchers and the training staff to share in the labor and the fruits of this research has been a tremendous incentive to me to produce meaningful results. I hope that all of the center staff are proud of the GOLD Project and this book.

Two organizations provided funding for the project. The Pillsbury Company Foundation and Michigan Bell Telephone Company each granted a substantial sum to aid this research. Neither organization was promised any reward as a result of the research other than access to the publicly available information that would result. Such nonproprietary investments are critical for projects such as this to survive.

Twelve private sector businesses, two government agencies, and two educational institutions participated in the project as "model" organizations. Their executives agreed to let us interview a number of managers (often including themselves), to give us sensitive information about their organizations' history and employees, and occasionally even to prepare special documents to answer our questions. The contributions of these sixteen organizations and their executives are an essential part of meaningful field research. My research colleagues and I are grateful to the leaders of these organizations for joining this project. We are also grateful to the 196 managers who were actually interviewed and whose insightful and articulate responses were often intertwined with intense emotional reactions to our questions. The energy invested in the interviews was considerable.

In return for their efforts, these organizations have only the possible satisfaction of being included in our analyses and the option of being acknowledged by name in this book. The organizations that chose to be named are American Express Company, Colgate-Palmolive Company, Du Pont Company, Fairfax County (Virginia) Public Schools, Gannett, Kaiser Permanente, Michigan Bell, Motorola, Palo Alto (California) Police Department, U S WEST, and Xerox Corporation.

Three individuals who served as editors of the manuscript of the book deserve mention. Janet Hunter, an independent developmental editor, has worked with me since the early drafts to organize the mounds of research data and materials relevant to the book. Wilfred Drath of the CCL staff worked with me on later drafts to refine the text. William Hicks, editor of the Management Series at Jossey-Bass Publishers, was the one who first saw the promise of the manuscript and encouraged its publication. Many others at Jossey-Bass supported the preparation and production of this book.

The reviewers of the manuscript throughout its evolution also deserve mention. I am grateful to those on the research team and advisory committee, colleagues at the Center for Creative Leadership, and others who contributed their suggestions at various points; to the managers from the participating organizations who reviewed the manuscript in a later stage; and to the anonymous reviewers who offered many thoughtful ideas.

A.M.M.

THE AUTHOR

ANN M. MORRISON is the founder and presiaem of the New Leaders Institute, a consulting and research firm based in southern California. She is a Senior Fellow of the Center for Creative Leadership, where she worked for eighteen years. She serves on the Board of Trustees of Bucknell University, where she received her B.A. degree (1970) and M.A. degree (1977) in psychology. She also holds an M.B.A. degree (1980) from Wake Forest University.

Morrison's main research activities have been in the area of executive development. She has done extensive research on how executives learn to handle the demands of top jobs and what contributes to these executives' success and failure. Her books include *Breaking the Glass Ceiling: Can Women Reach the Top of America's Largest Corporations?* (1987, with R. P. White and E. Van Velsor) and *The Lessons of Experience: How Successful Executives Develop on the Job* (1988, with M. W. McCall and M. M. Lombardo), which received the 1989 Johnson, Smith and Knisely Executive Leadership Award.

Morrison has worked with many corporations and institutions on executive and organization development, research, and training programs. Her articles have appeared in the *New York Times,* the *Los Angeles Time, Psychology Today, Working Woman, Small Business Reports,* and other business publications. She frequently speaks at national professional conventions and executive retreats.

DIVERSITY: THE TURBULENT EVOLUTION OF A SENSITIVE ISSUE

Diversity is a sensitive topic. Consider the reaction of your colleagues and friends, and even your own reaction, to retiring Supreme Court Justice Thurgood Marshall's statement to the press that, as a black in America in 1991, "I'm not free." He likened his experience as one of the highest ranking black men in this country to that of a well-traveled Pullman porter he had known who "had never been in any city in the United States where he had to put his hand up in front of his face to find out he was Negro." Do your associates respond to this statement with cool, reasoned logic, or do they succumb to a swift rush of emotion?

Justice Marshall's simple statement raises an issue that provokes strong emotions from most people. That issue has to do with unequal treatment. Reactions to Marshall's statement undoubtedly run the gamut from a burning rage that our society still separates people of color, according them second-class citizenship, to outrage that a man with such privileged status in our society would make such a preposterous claim; from guilt and shame that so little has changed since the days of the Pullman porter to frustration and anger that the progress against discrimination that has been made in this country is not acknowledged. These and other emotion-packed reactions reflect the range of strong, disparate views on this issue.

1

Diversity is discussed under such labels as civil rights, affirmative action, reverse discrimination, quotas, racism, and sexism. The passion inherent in these matters keeps them alive because it motivates people to take drastic action. For example, the 1963 marches, riots, and sit-ins that preceded President Kennedy's advocacy of what was to become the 1964 Civil Rights Act illustrate the dramatic, often passionate actions that have led to significant changes. That same passion, however, is also a formidable stumbling block to change. The deep emotions with which many people approach the diversity issue interfere with their ability to share the information they have, to influence others with logic and sensitivity, and to win over potential allies. As the debate over the most recent civil rights bill flared, even stating one's position on so-called quotas was seen as politically disastrous. One corporate executive requested anonymity before making the following remark, as reported by Fulwood (1991, p. A1): "The rhetoric is so damn hot. A lot of political jockeying is going on, and there's nothing we could say or do that would be in our best interest. So we're remaining mum until the matter is settled." This message is one that many executives and others across the country have reluctantly accepted: saying and doing nothing about diversity is the best bet because whatever you say or do could be used against you. Avoiding controversy is a basic business principle in many organizations, particularly when it involves the complexity and emotionalism of diversity. It is difficult to solve problems concerning differential treatment of people of color and white women when such problems cannot even be discussed. This reluctance to speak out or stand out on diversity matters has kept many organizations from making progress on diversity.

It is risky to address diversity. The organizations in our study that have tried to foster diversity have witnessed painful if not traumatic confrontations among their managers and other employees. A basic point of polarization relates to responsibility. As discussed by Edsall and Edsall (1991), differences between whites and blacks are attributed by some to blacks themselves and attributed by others to the whites who largely fashioned our society. The controversy over whether people of color deserve or need assistance from whites in improving their living conditions creates a chasm that adds to racial tension. When this kind of controversy is taken up as part of an organization's diversity effort, the process can become very painful. People have suffered through accusations of being racist or sexist, of being lazy or overdependent on others' help, of failing to do enough and care enough over the years to improve the situation, and of being ungrateful for the advances that have been made. It takes a great deal of work to find even small areas of agreement among employees, and outsiders may be even more difficult to please. The only guarantee is that some of the people will be dissatisfied no matter what is done.

Terminology

The controversy surrounding diversity encompasses even the terminology used. There is no lexicon yet to discuss the issues and the players embedded in diversity; many terms acceptable to some come under fire by others. Social scientists have developed theories and terms that cover the many aspects of race and class. Interested readers may want to explore the work of scholars such as Pierre van den Berghe (1967) or William Wilson (1973) for a more comprehensive discussion. Their conceptual thinking contributes to our understanding, for example, of why some differences are more provocative than others and to our appreciation of the central role of power differences in creating tiers of privilege in society that only appear to be caused by sex or ethnic differences. These scientists continue to argue the terminology to convey appropriately the subtle, complex social phenomena that surround diversity.

One hopes that the terms used in this book do not create confusion or controversy in themselves. The terms *black* and *African-American,* for example, are typically used to describe members of this ethnic group, but some people prefer one to the other. The term *black* is used in this book because the majority of black/African American managers in our study used it. Although the term *minority* is still frequently used, it is offensive to many people because it implies a lesser status than that of whites (the *majority*). The term *minority* is also somewhat ambiguous in that it sometimes includes white women; *people of color* is currently a more acceptable term. There is apparently no term that encompasses people of color and white women as a group. Even though they share a common distinction in being different from white men and, as we will see, are generally underrepresented in management, they are usually kept separate from each other through phrases such as "women and minorities." The term *nontraditional* as applied to managers is used throughout this book to encompass white women, women of color, and men of color, understanding that differences among these groups may be as significant as the recognizable difference from white men that they all have in common. The terms *race* and *ethnicity* are also debated. *Ethnicity* is preferred here because it highlights cultural differences as well as physical differences and because it is the more acceptable term in sociology and anthropology. Use of the word *ethnicity* does not imply that skin color or other physical characteristics have a lesser effect on how people are treated than does their cultural background.

Even the term *diversity* is confusing and controversial. The word was not used in human resource circles until a few years ago, but it now pops up regularly in phrases such as "valuing diversity" and "managing diversity." *Diversity* is often viewed as an alternative to *affirmative action,* which has taken on negative connotations because of its association with the government's imposition of "quotas" and failed attempts to integrate the various layers of the American workforce. To make diversity a more innovative and appealing idea, some people are reluctant to define diversity as anything more than an appreciation of differences that may improve an organization's performance. These people are reluctant to include the notion of integration or adequate representation in the definition for fear that diversity will come to be viewed as little more than a new label for affirmative action. Yet any reasonable definition of diversity must include integration itself, not simply an awareness of its value. People with diverse backgrounds and physical characteristics must be integrated into the teams that plan and carry out an organization's activities so that their ideas and skills are used and not merely acknowledged.

How Approaches to Diversity Have Evolved

The meaning of diversity fluctuates partly because the concept is still evolving, and under rather difficult conditions. More people are vying for jobs today than when affirmative action was first introduced. The consequence of making existing jobs available to more people (who may not have been allowed to compete for those jobs without affirmative action) is that jobs are being lost by white men. In previous years, when jobs seemed more plentiful, this loss was not so keenly felt. The current economic situation, however, has made affirmative action a greater sacrifice. Some advocates of diversity have therefore abandoned many aspects of affirmative action to distinguish diversity as a separate concept. Business performance is emphasized as a reason for diversity rather than the moral imperative that permeated the affirmative action movement. Advocates of diversity also emphasize skills and abilities to avoid the problem that affirmative action came to mean hiring or promoting members of covered groups who are less qualified than their white male cohorts. By making diversity seem as different from affirmative action as possible to avoid the problems and mistakes that occurred in the past, this strategy creates its own set of problems, as we shall see later.

The evolution of the concept of diversity can be illustrated by describing a variety of approaches that have been taken over the years, each of which incorporates different assumptions. Five approaches were recently described by Jean Kim (1991) of Stanford University at a conference on diversity. Her model is a more complex version of the three paradigms described by Judith Palmer in 1989. The approaches outlined by Kim and Palmer are the golden rule, assimilation, righting the wrongs, the culture-specific approach, and the multicultural approach.

In the *golden rule approach* to diversity, the idea is to treat each individual with civility, prescribed in the Bible as "Do unto others as you would have them do unto you." According to this approach, the only important differences are individual differences. And since everyone is special and different, everyone should be appreciated and treated the same. Prejudice and systemic oppression are not recognized; individual responsibility and morality make diversity work. While this approach has a great deal of merit, its major flaw is that the golden rule is applied from one's own frame of reference, without regard for the traditions and preferences of the other person. Moreover, the assumption that sex or racial differences are no more important than such individual differences as baldness or extroversion is insulting to those who have encountered discrimination all of their lives. Because of this, the pretension of "color blindness" and ignoring sex differences in this and the next approach weaken both as viable approaches to diversity.

The second approach, *assimilation,* calls for shaping people to the style already dominant in an organization. This approach has created considerable conflict for individuals who feel they must abandon their preferred style, companions, dress, or values while they are working. The conflict of "biculturalism" as described in the research of Ella Bell (1988) and others may be particularly difficult for nontraditional employees such as black women, who are expected to adjust to an environment dominated by white men. Assimilation is now generally regarded as a dysfunctional business strategy in this country because the resulting homogeneity may stifle the creativity and breadth of view that is essential to compete in today's market.

Righting the wrongs is an attempt to address the historical injustices that have systematically put at a disadvantage members of specific groups, such as Native Americans, Hispanics, and women in general. These groups are targeted, often one by one, as they reach a critical mass in an organization, to be hired, promoted, and rewarded more equitably. This approach to diversity is closest to the affirmative action concept, but more attention is given to understanding and taking advantage of the unique characteristics of each group to improve the organization's performance. Because group differences and histories are accentuated, a "we versus they" tension often increases the backlash and infighting that interfere with progress.

The *culture-specific approach* is frequently used to help prepare employees for an international assignment. Employees are taught the norms and practices of another culture so that they can adjust their behavior for that environment; however, little attempt is made to generate an appreciation for the values of that culture. The goal may be to help employees fit in on a superficial level, without any substantive change being involved.

Finally, the *multicultural approach* involves increasing the consciousness and appreciation of differences associated with the heritage, characteristics, and values of many different groups, as well as respecting the uniqueness of each individual. In this approach, diversity has a broad meaning that encompasses sex and ethnic groups along with groups based on such attributes as nationality, professional discipline, or cognitive style. In contrast to the assimilation model, this approach assumes that the organization must change and that the norms must accommodate a wide range of workers. The explicit goal is to strengthen the organization by leveraging a host of significant differences. Polarization is a lesser problem because so many groups and types of differences are recognized and because self-knowledge and interpersonal skills are often emphasized along with education about other groups.

Some may argue that the multicultural approach should be divided into two approaches, one in which valuing diversity is central and one that actually manages diversity. Roosevelt Thomas (1991), for example, distinguishes between the two in *Beyond Race and Gender,* noting that empowerment must be built into an organization's systems in order for those systems to work naturally for everyone; the goal of valuing differences may not go far enough to ensure that the core culture and systems are changed. Thomas and others have attempted to define the elements and goals of a multicultural approach (or approaches), but the definitions remain disturbingly vague. One problem pointed out by Palmer is that this approach is so new that no proven methods or even a common language is uniquely associated with it. Another problem is that many aspects of the multicultural approach are not unique but rather extensions of other approaches. Attempts to distinguish this approach from others instead of acknowledging the overlap seem to add to the ambiguity.

Finding the Best Approach to Diversity

It is tempting to argue that, at least in theory, the multicultural approach is the highest evolutionary stage of and the best approach to diversity. Capturing the unique contributions that everyone has to offer because of his or her background, affiliations, talents, values, or other differences is a worthy goal that is undoubtedly linked to the overall performance of any organization. Other approaches put limits on the types of differences recognized or the means to incorporate them, potentially limiting the positive returns that diversity can yield. In practice, however, the multicultural approach remains largely a mystery. How can we distinguish the extent to which people of color, for example, are advancing because they have been empowered versus because they have benefited from affirmative action? While the theory inherent in the multicultural approach is sound, little guidance is given on how to actually carry it out.

One can argue that the techniques for implementing the multicultural approach can be found in the other approaches. An analysis of how the multicultural approach compares with the other approaches, especially the approach of righting the wrongs, reveals that the differences among them are exaggerated. As noted earlier, the main reason for this exaggeration may well be the perceived need to build distance between a diversity effort and previous affirmative action activities to avoid the stigma attached to the latter. Yet affirmative action is not obsolete because prejudice is not obsolete. Prejudice is still a formidable barrier for nontraditional employees. It would be shortsighted to abandon affirmative action practices in the hope that integration will now occur naturally.

Perhaps the most promising approach to diversity is one that combines the premises and practices of several of the approaches outlined, particularly the goals of the multicultural approach and the affirmative action types of practices in the approach of righting the wrongs. We do group people and assume differences from one group to another. Pervasive stereotypic assumptions about the differences of some groups have a tremendous impact (far greater than assumptions about many individual differences) because they continue to limit opportunities for the millions of individuals in those groups. It would be dysfunctional to discontinue the effort to address large groups of white women and people of color, who have a long history of struggling for equal treatment. An extremely broad definition of diversity is needed for long-term results, but we must avoid spreading too thinly the resources required to ensure progress for some by doing too little for everyone.

The most frightening aspect of moving too hurriedly from affirmative action for targeted groups to promoting the diversity in everyone is that this becomes an excuse for avoiding the continuing problems in achieving equity for people of color and white women. These issues cannot be postponed any longer, even though there are others with differences also worthy of attention. We need to pass through this lengthy, frustrating introductory course in diversity in order to make any meaningful headway in fostering a broader version of diversity. That is why, in our research, we specifically addressed the issues of differential treatment based on sex and ethnicity and the most promising options for solving the problems experienced by people who are different in these respects from white men. While we do not expect that all other differences can be addressed in the same way, we do expect that increasing the acceptance and use of these differences in the upper levels of the workforce is a necessary step in making substantive headway toward diversity in its most encompassing form.

Affirmative action practices should not be limited to recruitment; they should also be used to achieve the goals of multiculturalism that involve developing the potential of all people so that they are able and willing to contribute at the highest possible level. Diversity is needed at the top of organizations just as much as it is needed at the lower levels. One can argue that diversity at the leadership level is necessary to achieve diversity throughout an organization. "Managing diversity" sounds a bit presumptuous, perhaps conveying an image of white men at the top regulating their employees' affairs from afar. Meaningful diversity involves sharing control with people who are "different." Leadership diversity helps ensure that control is indeed shared and that progress is stimulated by pressure from those above and across as well as from those below.

Despite these complex considerations, we must proceed to make diversity a firmer reality at all levels of our organizations. The risks are substantial, including the emotional pain and drain, the political vulnerability, and the personal alienation that accompany many pioneering efforts to encourage continued evolution. We must ask ourselves, "Why?" And then we must figure out how. Part One of this book addresses the question of why the painful process of diversity is needed. The remaining parts focus on how diversity can be achieved, particularly within the leadership ranks of organizations, using as guidelines the lessons from its evolution so far.

LEADERSHIP DIVERSITY AS STRATEGY

Part One examines the rewards that organizations can reap as they take on the difficult and risky challenge of promoting diversity. The substantial benefits of leadership diversity that attract senior executives can be achieved only by overcoming formidable barriers that have accumulated over time.

Readers who are knowledgeable about diversity issues will already be familiar with the potential benefits and the sizable challenges involved in diversity, which are discussed in the first two chapters. Chapter One describes the benefits our research uncovered, often the reasons top management gave for undertaking a diversity effort. Chapter Two discusses the scope and severity of the problems that currently exist in organizations, highlighting the results of our study concerning the barriers that prevent people of color and white women from advancing into senior management posts.

Finally, Chapter Three introduces a model that links the major advancement barriers to key factors in leadership development, a fundamental goal of any leadership diversity effort. This model explains how the barriers deprive many nontraditional managers of the opportunity to develop their leadership capacity in a balanced way.

ONE

ACHIEVING BENEFITS FROM LEADERSHIP DIVERSITY

It is nine o'clock Wednesday morning. On the top floor of corporate headquarters, Jim Clark is being interviewed. Clark is president of AMM Enterprises, Inc., and has fifteen years of service with the company. He is a white man of Irish ancestry, sixty-three years old, married with three children. His office furnishings and view are in the "executive" style. He is dressed in a dark business suit and a muted tie, and he is wearing glasses. His hair is more gray than white, and he looks tired. Jim Clark does not have a charismatic style; he is precise and relaxed, and he seems to be straightforward. I ask him to explain the goals he has for progress on diversity issues in his organization during the next five years. His response is as follows:

> We see a clear advantage in having women and minorities at senior levels. Our management needs to mirror that of our diverse customer base. We have already begun to see the impact on our market share gain. I do believe that our approach is going to help us be out in front in meeting our business goals. I would even go so far as to say that to have a management body that doesn't reflect a spectrum of diversity is, from a business point of view, irresponsible.
>
> There are good business reasons for change, but I personally feel that we are dealing with the issue of fairness. We have to be concerned with the human side of the equation as well. What happens if the demographics suddenly change tomorrow? Are we off the hook to provide equal access to promotions into management?

13

Beyond the Labor Force

Workforce 2000, a report by the Hudson Institute, created quite
a stir in the business community when it was published in 1987,
but it has not been the compelling force for challenge that some
people thought it would be. The report's figures documenting
the demographic shifts taking place in the U.S. workforce, are
certainly dramatic. For anyone not already familiar with them,
the most striking figures relate to the composition of the net new
workforce through the year 2000: only 15 percent will be native white men, while the rest will be native white women (42
percent), native nonwhite women (13 percent) and men (7 percent), and immigrant men (13 percent) and women (9 percent).
In other words, nearly all the growth in the workforce in this
decade will come from people who are not white and male. This
might be shocking news for anyone accustomed to hiring only
white men, and it was touted for some time as the key to con-
verting managers into diversity advocates. In themselves, however, these workforce statistics have prompted more discussion
than action. One possible reason is that many executives, being more interested in the here and now, have little interest in
making changes to deal with upcoming trends for the next century. It is still the 1990s, after all, and many executives may
feel that there are plenty of other, more immediate business problems that deserve priority. Furthermore, many executives now
in their fifties and sixties will retire before the year 2000 and
will not have to face the consequences of labor force changes.
The fact that the workforce has already begun to shift markedly
has not received the attention it deserves, perhaps because the
report's title, *Workforce 2000,* has become so widely associated
with changes in the future.

Yet another reason for the lack of responsiveness to workforce demographics may be that many executives are assuming
that it is possible to incorporate a more diverse workforce rather
easily into the bottom ranks of their organizations. If they are
aware that the figures cited here relate to the net new workforce,
not the total workforce, and that in the year 2000 white men
are still expected to make up nearly a third of the labor force,

many executives may assume that upper-level jobs will still be filled primarily by white men. If these executives assume that white women and people of color will be content to hold only low-level jobs, the need to change the workings of their organizations to accommodate diversity may not be apparent to them.

Other possible reasons for a surprisingly slow response to the reported demographic changes in the workforce include a smugness among some executives concerning their relative standing within their industry or region. Executives whose organizations are already more diverse than others in the same industry may feel little sense of urgency to take action on diversity issues.

For various reasons, reports of the increasing demographic diversity of the workforce have not been an adequate incentive for change. There are, however, additional factors that are beginning to concern a large number of executives. Some of these factors are also reported in *Workforce 2000,* but they have not received as much attention. One factor is that growth in the workforce is shrinking, bringing about a seller's market for labor. According to government projections made in 1988, the U.S. labor force will increase less than 12 percent in the 1990s, compared with 27 percent increases in the 1980s and 1970s. With a preponderance of people of color and white women in the new workforce, this seller's market for labor could mean that employers who do not promote diversity may find it difficult to compete for labor.

Our workforce is not only growing more slowly, but according to many social observers, the new workers are also more demanding of employers. This group of new employees, which is increasingly dominated by people of color and white women, is more and more resistant to "fitting in" at work. Increasingly, these employees want their individual and group needs recognized, and they are less interested in conforming to an organization's already established norms. For example, Hymowitz (1989) points out that both male and female managers want more control over their own destiny, a say in decisions that affect them, and more flexibility in the terms and rewards of employment. Articles in the social science literature, such as Kenneth De

Meuse and Walter Tornow's "The Tie That Binds—Has Become Very, Very Frayed!" (1990), note that loyalty to an employer may increasingly depend upon the extent to which a satisfying work life contributes to a person's overall well-being. More demanding employees, from the lowest to the highest ranks in an organization, are less likely to stay with an employer who does not maintain a leading position in human resource management, which includes an active diversity effort.

Even if there are enough traditional managers (that is, white men) to continue to staff all upper-management positions, attempting to place nontraditional employees in nothing but low-level jobs is not likely to work. Many nontraditional employees have ambitious career goals, and their satisfaction with the organization depends on their advancement and the advancement of others like them. Organizations that continue to reinforce the traditional white male management group will be judged as extremely unfair by men of color and women in general, who expect a fair return on their educational and career investment. Such organizations will also be judged negatively by people of all backgrounds who believe that workforce diversity must be reflected in its supervision and who demand that human potential be recognized regardless of how it is packaged.

These are powerful incentives to change, based as they are on workforce demographics and simple fairness. But there is another powerful incentive: the marketplace. As labor force demographics change, the demographics of the marketplace also change. The consumer market for goods and services is increasingly diverse; formerly small markets are becoming substantial ones that even large corporations want to pursue. According to Lennie Copeland (1988), the spending power of blacks, Asian-Americans, and Hispanics together was estimated at $424 billion in 1990, and it is expected to reach $650 billion by the year 2000.

These figures, while impressive, may simply reflect the fact that these three groups will constitute 25 percent of the U.S. population by the turn of the century. Some states, such as California, are already even more diverse. People of the three ethnic backgrounds just cited already make up 40 percent of California's population, and that figure is expected to rise to

50 percent by the year 2000, according to the *Wall Street Journal* ("Ethnic Mix Gives California Its Youth," 1990). Some consumer groups are becoming more diverse more quickly than others. Experts consulted by *USA Today,* as reported by Carroll and Williams (1990), predict that by the year 2000, 50 percent of all business travelers will be women. Executives whose organizations serve such diversifying markets are likely to find that it pays to build more diversity into their own organizations as one way of responding to changing conditions.

The changing political landscape is also prodding change within organizations with respect to diversity. Blacks, Latinos, other people of color, and women in general now hold many elected and appointed offices. In these positions they have influence over factors that affect how well an organization produces and markets its goods and services, factors such as taxes, advertising options, even the fees that an organization may charge. Some managers have attributed some of the progress made on diversity within their organizations to the growing number of nontraditional politicians in their areas, especially in cities where the political fiber is dominated by people of color. In 1990, black mayors governed twenty-six cities with populations of more than fifty thousand, and the number of Hispanic elected officials more than doubled between 1975 and 1989, with Texas, New Mexico, and California having the highest numbers (Foster, Landes, and Binford, 1990). Women made up more than 30 percent of state legislatures in Arizona, Maine, New Hampshire, Vermont, and Washington (Foster, Siegel, and Jacobs, 1990). This reality, one black vice president told us, creates a sense of urgency inside the organization."

Changes in the consumer market and the political arena seem to capture the attention of executives more than do changes in the labor force per se. Increasing competition from around the world has made even small markets more important to an organization's survival. Because the already brutal competition from both foreign and domestic firms is expected to continue to increase, the competition for growing nontraditional markets will escalate. Whatever advantage an organization can gain to penetrate these markets will be critical.

The Benefits of Diversity

The hard realities of competition and the marketplace are convincing many executives that diversity is a necessary part of their business strategy. They promote diversity for four business reasons: to keep and gain market share, to reduce costs, to increase productivity, and to improve the quality of management in their organizations. Many executives also support diversity for other reasons, not the least of which is a sense that bringing business practices more in line with personal values of fairness is the right thing to do.

The five reasons noted here are similar to the benefits described by researchers Taylor Cox and Stacy Blake (1991), who assert that diversity increases organizational competitiveness. These authors present evidence that sound management of diversity affects cost savings, creativity, problem solving, flexibility, marketing, and resource acquisition, in addition to social responsibility. There is considerable overlap between the benefits cited by Cox and Blake and those reported by the managers in our study.

Keeping and Gaining Market Share

As markets grow increasingly diverse and competition for market share escalates, managers who have an understanding of their customers' preferences become more important. In many organizations, managers are encouraged to learn to think like their customers. While it doesn't necessarily take a woman to understand what female consumers will buy or a Latino to penetrate the rapidly growing Latino market, the experiences and perspectives that nontraditional managers bring to their work can certainly be valuable in building sales. That value is increasingly recognized by executives.

The responsibility to reflect market reality goes beyond creating a representative personnel profile for its own sake. Many managers argue that diversity among the organization's decision makers is the best way to ensure that the organization has the flexibility to capture diverse markets and provide adequate customer service. The understanding and shared experience of marketing managers with other Cuban-Americans or Asian-American women, for example, may motivate them to respond to growing market niches. According to CEO James Preston, Avon was able to turn around its unprofitable inner-city markets, making them its most productive U.S. markets, by handing them over to Hispanic and black sales managers (Dreyfuss, 1990).

In addition to missing out on changes in existing markets, companies that are not aware of market diversity risk losing out on new business. One black manager in charge of production of a widely distributed directory told us how her company lost an important piece of new business. Even though the desired new market was in a southwestern city, the project team failed to tap into the city's predominant Hispanic community. The company lost its bid to a competitor that had an Hispanic manager in charge of the project and had given members of the Hispanic community input into the process.

Managers are increasingly coming to recognize that their ability to represent their organizations' customers and clients is a major issue in marketplace competitiveness. The perception of this ability, by potential customers in particular, can also be a factor in an organization's competitivenss. A manager who is of the same sex or ethnic background as a customer may have greater credibility because that similarity implies shared experiences and, consequently, greater understanding and integrity. Shared experiences such as speaking another person's native language, rearing children, or coping with day-to-day discrimination are sometimes recognized and appreciated by an increasingly diverse customer base in much the same way that membership in certain fraternities or military units has been recognized over the years. These nontraditional kinds of experiences may actually be as valuable in terms of preparing people for senior management roles as any traditionally recognized experiences. In any case, customers may perceive that someone of their own sex or ethnicity is better able to serve their needs, and this can influence them to switch to or stay with one organization rather than another.

Finally, with respect to potential marketing advantages, some executives in our study believe that using diversity to improve their marketing capability within ethnically diverse domestic markets will help them market more effectively internationally. They are looking for ways to apply their experience in the United States to help them enter and build a share in foreign markets. If they can develop responsiveness and an image to improve marketing in our own culturally rich country, then it should be easier for them to gain new markets in foreign cultures. This advantage in a growing global marketplace is yet another important reason for advocating diversity.

Cost Savings

Many executives believe that an effective approach to fostering diversity will save money over the long term and often even in the short run. While the costs associated with specific aspects of doing business are difficult to pinpoint, estimates of cost savings in areas such as personnel are increasingly used to justify investment in diversity. The cost involved in recruiting, training, relocating, and replacing employees, along with providing a competitive compensation package, is a major expense for most organizations. In many cases personnel costs consume at least one-half to two-thirds of an organization's budget; this is especially true for service organizations. Reducing these costs can make a big difference in profitability.

How can fostering diversity contribute to cost cutting? Many managers we interviewed expect diversity efforts to reduce the high turnover rate of nontraditional employees and the costs that go with it. One manufacturing manager in our study was concerned that his company seemed to be training engineers for competing companies, which were luring away some of the most talented employees. He believes that more attention to young engineers, especially women and people of color, will keep this from happening as often. According to Schmidt (1988), women and people of color were resigning from Corning Incorporated at twice the rate of white men, prompting that company to institute some key diversity practices in 1987. The cost of Corning's exodus was estimated at $2 to $4 million a year to recruit, train, and relocate replacements. Other sources estimate the cost of turnover per person to be $5,000 to $10,000 for an hourly worker and anywhere from $75,000 to $211,000 for an executive at around the $100,000 salary level (Auster, 1988; Hinrichs, 1991; Riskind, 1991). The cost to replace more senior executives is probably much higher.

Many managers in our study also believe that replacement costs can be cut by instituting diversity practices that give nontraditional managers more incentive to stay. Being included in a development program, for example, may motivate nontraditional managers to remain with an organization (and to perform to their best ability) because they see further opportunities for themselves. High-performing, nontraditional managers also inspire others to stay and to be more productive. One black woman we interviewed who specializes in career management for her company noted that when a nontraditional manager gets promoted, other nontraditional employees at lower levels feel more committed to the company. That can translate into lower replacements costs. In addition, companies with a reputation for advancing nontraditional managers may more often be sought out by nontraditional recruits, reducing the costs associated with searching for job candidates. Cost savings in recruitment, turnover, and absenteeism are documented by Cox and Blake (1991). Corning's success in reducing costs by substantially reducing the attrition rate of blacks and white women through its diversity activities (described in Chapter Eleven) also provides evidence that a diversity effort can pay off for the organization.

Some replacement costs are especially painful. For example, the cost to replace high-potential, nontraditional managers can be very high because of their influence on others and the substantial investment that has already been made in finding and developing them. Mobil's discovery that its high-potential women were leaving the company at a rate two-and-a-half times greater than comparable men led to changes in how female employees are treated (Trost, 1989). Because the competition for high-performing employees is fierce, organizations are increasingly aware of the need to make changes that will help them keep their high-potential managers in general, and their high-potential nontraditional managers in particular.

Personnel costs are also more painful to executives when the money spent is being wasted. Big settlements to discrimination claimants, for example, frequently represent costs that would not have been necessary had the organization taken action to promote diversity. In 1991, a jury awarded the record sum of $17.65 million in damages to a woman employed by Texaco who claimed she was passed over for management promotions. In a 1988 case, State Farm Insurance was expected to pay $100 to $300 million to women who were allegedly denied hiring or advancement (Nabbefeld, 1988). The allegation that female employees were denied benefits when they were pregnant will cost AT&T an estimated $66 million, according to an article in the *Wall Street Journal* (Keller, 1991). The staggering sums paid in damages and awards are accompanied by costs simply to open a legal case (approximately $25,000) or fees to settle ($50,000) or to take a case through trial ($100,000) (Caudron, 1990).

High legal fees and settlements emphasize that failing to address diversity can be an expensive proposition. According to Ronni Sandroff (1988), nearly 90 percent of all Fortune 500 companies have received complaints of sexual harassment, and more than a third have been sued. The cost per company per year in absenteeism, low morale, and low productivity is estimated at $6.7 million. Job-related stress, which contributes to increased turnover and absenteeism as well as a host of other negative effects (Cummins, 1990), is another expensive problem that diversity efforts can help alleviate, particularly for nontraditional employees.

Although a diversity effort is expensive, it can result in significant savings that will offset the expenses. Short- and longer-term savings in personnel and legal costs can make diversity an attractive business strategy from a fiscal point of view.

Increased Productivity

Although it is difficult to assess the impact of diversity on productivity, many executives in the organizations we studied expect greater productivity from employees who enjoy coming to work, who are relaxed instead of defensive or stressed in their work setting, and who are happy to be working where they feel valued and competent. The cost of changing an organization's climate for nontraditional employees may be high, but the promise of a significant payoff in increased productivity is what keeps the effort alive. For example, according to Chusmir and Durand (1987), if a 12 percent productivity gain could be achieved among female employees by reducing barriers for women, who comprise 44 percent of the workforce, the result would be a 5 percent productivity gain overall.

Despite the complexities of human motivation and ability to perform and the difficulty of measuring human productivity, a compelling case can be made that diversity efforts do have a positive impact. There is strong reason to think, for example, that people are motivated to work harder and more productively when they believe they can be successful. In *Ensuring Minority Success in Corporate Management,* Donna Thompson and Nancy DiTomaso (1988) argue that a multicultural approach has a positive effect on employees' perception of equity, which in turn affects their morale, goal setting, effort, and performance. Organizational productivity is consequently improved. Other research also ties employees' perceptions to elements of productivity. Robert Eisenberger and his colleagues, for example, found a positive relationship between employees' perception of being valued and cared about by their organization and their attendance, dedication, and job performance (Eisenberger, Fasolo, and Davis-LaMastro, 1990).

Innovation, one aspect of productivity that concerns many managers, is apparently affected by diversity. Cox and Blake (1991) present evidence linking diversity to enhanced creativity and innovation. Moreover, in the study led by Robert Eisenberger, employees who felt valued and supported by their organization were more innovative without any direct reward or personal recognition (Eisenberger, Fasolo, and Davis-LaMastro, 1990). Other research on innovation by Philip Birnbaum (1981) and Robert Ziller (1972) showed that heterogeneous groups (in terms of race, age, values, background, training, and so on) are more productive than homogeneous groups. A number of executives we interviewed were convinced that diversity would enhance their organization's ability to find innovative solutions to business problems and to create a wide range of goods and services. A construction manager said, "Any time you broaden the organization with people with different backgrounds, you strengthen the organization.

If diversity does affect organizational performance, then we should be able to point to competitive advantages realized by the organizations in our study, which are among the leaders in fostering diversity. We can do that. *Fortune* magazine ranks the "most admired" corporations each year, using criteria such as quality of management, quality of goods or services, innovativeness, financial soundness, and their ability to attract, develop, and keep talented people (Sprout, 1991). Eleven of the twelve companies in our study were ranked in early 1991 (the twelfth business was not ranked because it is privately held). Of these, 80 percent placed in the top 20 percent. All eleven were ranked in the top half, and more than 70 percent were ranked in the top half within their own industry. These rankings support Rosabeth Moss Kanter's (1983) finding that companies with a reputation for progressive human resource practices had more long-term profitability and financial growth than their counterparts over a twenty-year period. An additional indication that our corporate leaders in diversity are also productivity winners is that three companies in our study have been winners of the Malcolm Baldrige Award for quality.

The impact of diversity on productivity is sometimes obvious to executives. Avon's top sales division for two years was also its most diverse, with a Hispanic woman leading a team of eighteen sales managers that included Asian-Americans, Hispanics, blacks, and whites. According to Schmidt (1988), Avon's chief executive, James Preston, said that the connection didn't surprise him. Other executives are also believers, even though they may not have concrete research data or performance results to back them up. They believe because the connection makes sense. In an interview with *Financier* magazine, Colgate-Palmolive's chief executive Reuben Mark commented: "The first semester of any psychology course is going to tell you about the effect of a person's problems on their productivity. By definition, if we can reduce external pressures, improve the way the people think about themselves, their family life and the company, productivity is going to increase" (Lee and Mark, 1990, p. 29).

To the extent that diversity efforts can alleviate the problems and improve the perceptions of employees — both the nontraditional employees who have borne the brunt of discriminatory treatment in many organizations and their white male counterparts, who must also be prepared and motivated to perform — productivity will be improved.

Better Quality of Management

Simply including nontraditional employees in fair competition for advancement can improve the quality of management by enlarging the pool of talent from which to choose. In our study, one Native American woman, who is in charge of a technical area, noted that in her company, "There is a tremendous pool of people we haven't utilized. We have clerical people with Ph.D.'s and M.B.A.'s. We can start tapping those people."

Diversity activities may unblock some highly qualified and able nontraditional employees who are stuck in clerical and other low-level jobs. For example, in one company we studied, a diversity program was designed to help identify and advance high-potential employees. The program identified a woman who had been a clerk in the company for the preceding twelve years and had never been considered for a management position. The director of an engineering unit in the company estimated that now that the woman was unblocked, she would reach at least the fifth level of management within five years.

A number of managers we interviewed maintain that including nontraditional managers in fair competition will strengthen the cadre of all managers, including those who are white men. A diversity program, with its enhanced competition for jobs, can encourage the more competent white men to perform even better, while the less competent ones are weeded out. The senior vice president of a health care organization, a white man, pointed out that a diversity program stands to benefit all strong-performing individuals, including white men.

Responding to the management challenge posed by greater workforce diversity also gives managers an opportunity to learn and grow, to become more competent in areas vital to their organization's success. Managers we interviewed pointed to the usefulness of diversity in prodding managers to learn fresh approaches to business problems, to see issues from new perspectives, and to add new contacts to their business networks. One black woman, commenting on her experience in supervising the participants of a developmental program for high-potential women, told us, "Managing one of these women really sharpens my skills. It makes me a better manager and a better employee, and it makes us a better corporation."

Exposure to diverse colleagues can help managers develop breadth and openness. In fact, Donald Campbell Pelz's classic 1956 study revealed that scientists who had frequent contact with colleagues different from them in terms of values and background were the highest performers. Because of these potential benefits, some executives in our study view the ability of managers to handle diversity as a criterion for their continued success. The ability to be part of an effective diversity strategy is something an increasing number of these executives are looking for in high-potential managers of any ethnic background.

The quality of management can also be improved by building more effective personnel policies and practices that may eventually benefit all of an organization's employees. Diversity efforts typically target personnel practices for reform, and the changes made in them often benefit traditional employees along with the nontraditional. Programs to develop high-potential managers, for example, are often changed or intensified to meet the needs of some underrepresented groups. However, changes such as adding training for mentors or building in a personal assessment component make the program more effective for all the participants, including white men.

Even when programs are initially restricted to nontraditional managers, some spillover effects can spread the benefits to many other employees. What an organization learns in trying out a "special" program may later be broadly applied to all employees. For example, our study found that some techniques for developing managers and more objective procedures for evaluating promotion candidates were originally developed for nontraditional managers and later adopted for wider use.

New personnel practices, especially those tied to a diversity effort, are likely to be closely scrutinized by cost-conscious managers who need to be convinced that they are warranted. Some diversity-related practices, therefore, are more carefully thought out than the practices already in place. This often comes about through the use of task forces and employee groups that are part of a diversity effort. Such groups help design, review, or endorse personnel practices to ensure that they are thorough and fair. One manager praised the role of an employee group in assuring that new practices are as good as they can be: "You try stuff out on this group regarding decisions you're considering, and they speak for employees. Better decisions are made sometimes because of their input. For example, there was a new compensation plan in the works. The compensation people were going to make a change, and I brought them into this group. The group worked through not only the impact on women and minorities but also the general administrative details for all managers that made it a better plan." Often, simply asking, "Is this fair and appropriate for women and for people of color?" can help an organization strengthen its human resources in general, its human resource practices, and its broader business practices.

Other Benefits of Diversity

A significant benefit of diversity, simply put, is increased fairness. This is both a business and an ethical issue. On the one hand, as the connections between fairness and better business performance become clearer, it is easier to invoke fairness as a goal of diversity. On the other hand, many managers we interviewed expressed a strong belief that their organizations should act with fairness for its own sake regardless of whether it made better business sense. One chief executive of a high-technology company put it this way: "There is a philosophical difference now, which comes from the heart. It is a sense of fairness in methods and practices. We care about what people think and feel. That is progress."

Other managers we interviewed described their pride in creating a more open, flexible, responsive, and responsible work environment where people can be happier, not just more efficient or productive. Such an organizational climate is one of the less publicized benefits of successful diversity efforts.

Finally, the managers we interviewed pointed to the benefits of diversity beyond their organizations. Some managers want their organizations to be agents for change, to make the world a better place. One black administrator, for example, told us that more black men in her state go to prison than to college because, she said, the school system is failing that group. The diversity effort in her institution is aimed at getting more blacks and other underrepresented groups into educational leadership positions. The effect of this on children, she feels, will be to help them overcome their feelings of inferiority created by stereotyping and get greater benefit from the educational system.

Although some managers may argue that business has few if any obligations to the larger community, other managers insist that being a good community citizen eventually benefits their business. One white male business executive in our study expressed a very strong view about the role of business in the community and how diversity efforts can benefit both. He said, "The bigger picture we have to deal with is the minority situation in this country. [In this area] the situation is so desperate and so in need of role models, that if we in corporations can't advance minorities so they can turn around and do what needs to be done in their communities, I don't see any of us surviving."

Diversity efforts have the potential to play a significant role in solving the problems that plague organizations and society at large. Although support for diversity is increasingly tied to business issues, social responsibility is still an incentive for many executives. However, much remains to be done before diversity is fully realized and the benefits noted here can be reaped. Chapter Two reveals the extent of the gap between where we are today and where we could be tomorrow.

TWO

CHALLENGING THE BARRIERS TO OPPORTUNITY

It is 2:30 P.M. on Friday at the regional office of AMM Enterprises. I am talking with Dee Bodine, director of marketing for the northwest region. Bodine is a fifty-two-year-old black woman who has remarried and has two grown children. Her office is tastefully furnished and includes a small conversation area with a couch. She is wearing a tailored dress and large gold earrings. She is warm and gracious and seems very down to earth. Dee Bodine has been with the company for a long time, steadily moving up the ranks. I ask her whether she thinks women or people of color face barriers or special problems in advancing to senior management. She answers:

> You know, I didn't feel old before we started talking, but now you've reminded me of how long I've been around here, and I'm beginning to feel old [laughter].
>   Yes, absolutely, there are barriers to moving into senior management. It starts at the one-on-one level. People see us as weaker, less qualified, and a bigger risk. Therefore, we don't get picked for key assignments that would give us visibility and credibility. The few of us who do get chosen live in a very nonsupportive, lonely, pressure cooker kind of environment. The personal perceptions translate into both formal and informal practices that exclude us.

Demographic shifts in the labor force, the marketplace, and the population in general, along with increasing competition, have

29

made issues of diversity a more immediate challenge for executives. As discussed in Chapter One, there are tremendous benefits to be had by fostering diversity in an organization, but they must be earned by successfully countering a host of stumbling blocks. The challenge of developing diversity should not be underestimated. Some of the problems have been with us for decades, while others are relatively new and unfamiliar. To find the best solutions to these problems, we need to understand.

There has been a significant reduction of some forms of racism, sexism, and other discrimination in this country. The Civil Rights Act of 1964, among other key pieces of legislation, helped reduce some of the most blatant forms of discrimination that put men of color and women in general at a disadvantage. There is evidence, however, that the force of these changes has essentially been checked in recent years, particularly with regard to the upward mobility of nontraditional managers.

In 1986, Korn/Ferry found that of 1,362 senior executives only 29 were women and 13 were people of color, a total of 3 percent at a time when women and people of color made up 51.4 percent of the workforce. According to one survey reported by Braham (1987), in 1979, blacks occupied 0.2 percent of the senior executive positions and that figure had increased to only 0.3 percent by 1985. Another survey reported by Braham (1987) showed a decrease in blacks at senior levels during the same period: from 0.4 percent to 0.2 percent. In addition, blacks have lost momentum in management overall. Blacks made up only 4.9 percent of the management ranks in 1987 compared with 4 percent in 1980 ("Debate — Affirmative Action Is Doing the Right Thing," 1990, p. 10A).

Hispanics, too, apparently lost advancement momentum in the 1980s. In California, for example, despite an increase in the Hispanic population from 19 percent of the total state population in 1980 to 30 percent in 1989, Hispanics still made up only 7 percent of the state's executives. Dan Cook (1989) notes that the list of only seven Hispanic presidents or chairmen of large corporations nationwide is "rivetingly short."

Fortune magazine's 1990 survey of 799 companies turned up only 19 women among the 4,012 directors and highest paid executives. Not much had changed since 1978, when the same survey located 10 women among 6,400 executives.

These statistics indicate that moving into middle management is still a problem for some traditionally underrepresented groups. Moving beyond middle management is an even greater problem for most nontraditional managers who confront a "glass ceiling" that limits their advancement. Although the U.S. government reports that 30 percent of corporate middle management is made up of women, blacks, and Hispanics, these groups make up less than 1 percent of chief executives and those who report directly to them ("Bias in Promotions at the Very Top Targeted," 1990). Even if it takes fifteen or twenty years to develop a general manager, as some executive development specialists have concluded, if time were the only factor, we should have seen more advancement than this in the twenty-eight years since the passage of the 1964 Civil Rights Act, and we should have seen continued improvement throughout the period. Clearly, a lack of enough time is not the only force preventing upward mobility for nontraditional managers.

We can learn some lessons from what has been accomplished since the 1960s in reducing barriers for women and people of color. We can also learn something from the subsequent loss of some of this momentum as we confront the current situation. The problems of diversity that challenge us today are not entirely the same as the problems that confronted us as recently as the late 1980s. Our understanding of differential treatment and its consequences must continue to grow if we are to solve the problems facing us today.

A Historical Overview

In the past, a number of publicly accepted practices excluded people of color and white women from many institutions and positions of influence. Jobs were advertised separately by male or female, white or "colored," allowing organizations to exclude people they viewed as undesirable. People of color and white women were confined largely to low-paying jobs. As recently as 1983, white men, who made up about half of the labor force, held 96 percent of all the positions in this country that paid more than $18,000 a year ("Blacks in Management," 1983). In addition to job discrimination, prestigious schools denied admission to many women and people of color. Universities such as Yale and Princeton, among the schools typically considered feeder institutions for management jobs, explicitly refused to admit women as undergraduates until as recently as 1969.

In the past, racial and sexual discrimination also existed at levels of blatancy that may be hard for those who did not experience them to appreciate fully. It was socially and legally acceptable to treat blacks, Latinos, Asian-Americans, Native Americans, and other people of color as being inferior to whites and to give white men more career opportunities and preferential treatment than others. As antidiscrimination laws were passed, the resulting access to educational institutions and occupations helped people of color and white women compete more effectively. However, the university degrees and professional credentials that served as criteria for many jobs were still held largely by white men. "Lack of education" became a widely accepted explanation for the slow movement of nontraditional employees into and through management; this argument is still used today despite educational achievements that sometimes favor women over men and people of color over whites, as we will see later.

When affirmative action legislation started to take hold, it did little to address the underlying assumptions and stereotypes that plagued nontraditional managers and created the barriers to advancement that persist today. Many white male managers viewed people of color and white women as inferior in intellect, training, and motivation. When the law forced them to hire and promote nontraditional employees, some responded with what one manager we interviewed termed "malicious compliance"—deliberately appointing nontraditional candidates who were weak or ill-suited to the jobs available so that they would have little chance of succeeding. Some managers delayed taking action until the last minute, and then they had to find people to hire or promote as a "quick fix" to meet the required quotas. When these hurriedly chosen people couldn't handle the job or couldn't get the resources they needed to carry out their new responsibilities, some managers' stereotype-based prejudice became even stronger. They pointed to these specific and inevitable failures as evidence that nontraditional managers in general couldn't do the work. Many employers have since become very cautious about hiring or promoting any nontraditional managers because of such early, ill-fated attempts. The lack of enforcement of affirmative action guidelines under the Reagan administration reinforced these employers' reluctance to keep trying, and the movement toward diversity slowed considerably.

Today the legal incentives operate in a different context. There is much more diversity in the workplace and in society overall. Managers are searching intensively for competitive advantage and often turn to their human resource practices to gain an edge. Employers now have compelling business reasons to follow and even exceed the legal requirements to comply with affirmative action guidelines. Many people have become aware of cultural differences, the value and the inevitability of diversity. But prejudice continues to permeate organizations in subtle, nearly invisible forms because stereotypic assumptions have been built into their organizational norms and everyday practices. For example, in our study we found that the recruitment process may continue to screen out people of color who do not have the same background as the whites who were recruited in the past. We learned that managers routinely pass over women for special assignments because they don't want to strain the family. And we discovered that nontraditional managers don't take outside classes because they don't know about them or don't believe they will ever pay off. These systemic barriers often predetermine the choice against nontraditional managers, and even well-meaning people perpetuate unfair treatment simply by using the organization's conventional processes. This not only restrains diversity, but it also powerfully restrains individuals from contributing in meaningful ways to the organization's goals.

The Most Critical Barriers to Advancement

The most significant barriers today are the policies and practices that systematically restrict the opportunities and rewards

available to women and people of color. This is a fundamental
finding of our study. We discovered twenty-one distinct barriers, which we categorized into thirteen types. These barriers
are listed in Table A.8 in the appendix.

There is a remarkable consensus among the 196 managers
in our study on the most critical barriers to advancement. Across
industries, sectors, level and function, sex, and ethnic backgrounds, managers agree that the following six barriers are the
most important.

1. Prejudice: treating differences as weaknesses
2. Poor career planning
3. A lonely, hostile, unsupportive working environment for
    nontraditional managers
4. Lack of organizational savvy on the part of nontraditional
    managers
5. Greater comfort in dealing with one's own kind
6. Difficulty in balancing career and family

These six barriers account for more than half of all the barriers
mentioned by the managers in our study. They are also repeat-
edly revealed in various forms and combinations in other studies
that focus on career development and advancement. These include a study commissioned by the Executive Leadership Council on driving and restraining forces for black senior executives
(Baskerville and Tucker, 1991); a study conducted by Catalyst
(1990) on career barriers for women in management; and research by the U.S. Department of Labor (1991) for the "glass
ceiling initiative."

Prejudice: Still the Number One Barrier

The single most frequently mentioned barrier is prejudice. More
than 12 percent of all managers' responses described how the
perception of differences as weaknesses limited advancement opportunities for white women and people of color. Prejudice is
defined here as the tendency to view people who are different
from some reference group in terms of sex, ethnic background,

or racial characteristics such as skin color as being deficient. In other words, prejudice is the assumption (without evidence) that nontraditional managers are less competent or less suitable than white male managers; it is the refusal to accept nontraditional managers as equals. Ethnic and sex differences are sometimes used, consciously or not, to define "inferior groups" in a kind of caste system.

A survey by the University of Chicago's National Opinion Research Center (Smith, 1990), along with other research findings, shows that stereotypes are still prevalent. This survey revealed that whites believe that people of other ethnic backgrounds are less intelligent, less hard working, less likely to be self-supporting, more violence prone, and less patriotic than whites. The Executive Leadership Council's study (Baskerville and Tucker, 1991) found racism to be the most serious career hurdle for black executives, and Catalyst's (1990) findings showed stereotypic preconceptions, or prejudice, to be the biggest advancement barrier women face today. Stereotypes about people of color and women in general are common among managers, and the managers we interviewed described a variety of them.

Some stereotypes apply to certain groups in particular. In our study, for example, we learned that Asian-Americans are said to be so research oriented and technically focused that they are not able to supervise people or communicate well in general. Hispanics are said to be unassertive; they "sit back" in meetings while others hurl and debate ideas. Some managers consider Asian-Americans and Hispanics "too polite" (and consequently, as lacking conviction), perhaps because of their concern for showing respect or maintaining cooperative teamwork. One white executive noted that there is also a trust barrier for Asian-Americans and Latinos, who are sometimes perceived as dishonest and corrupt. The prevailing stereotypes of blacks, we discovered, are that they are lazy, uneducated, and incompetent. Women are often assumed to be indecisive and unable to be analytical.

One Hispanic manager we interviewed pointed out how stereotypes affect business decisions. In contrast to blacks, who are more outspoken, he said, Hispanics are quiet and shy, and they don't disagree as much because they respect authority. Because of this, he continued, "If I had four subordinates, and I had to lay off one, I'd choose the Hispanic. The black woman would scream the loudest. The black man would meet me in the parking lot. The white man, well, maybe I'd lay him off, but I'd probably pick the Hispanic because he wouldn't say anything."

Stereotypes apply more generally to nontraditional managers. One example is the assumption that differences in accent or the grammar used by members of different ethnic groups mean that people in those groups are inarticulate or unconvincing in speech. Many managers perceive such speech differences as a career liability. One black director in our study who worked in a company with extensive international operations commented on the so-called language barrier that many Asians confront because of their accent. He found it incongruous that an accent was a handicap for Asians when other accents—French, British, or Australian, for example—were no handicap at all for white foreigners working in the United States. We interviewed one black administrator who worked in an educational institution and described how the stereotyping of differences serves to reinforce prejudicial beliefs. According to this administrator,

> Oral language is a disadvantage for blacks. Any ghetto language is a trigger for whites—it's associated only with black people, and it's threatening to the general population. There is an almost visceral reaction to it. They discount what you're saying. This is the biggest problem black people have, but not because white people have good oral language. Many don't. They use poor grammar, they have regional accents, they make up words. . . . It's acceptable, even endearing, for whites, but not for blacks. Blacks are seen as uninformed, threatening, at a lower level.

In some cases, it seems that no matter what nontraditional managers do, it is open to a negative interpretation. Women, for example, may be faced with contradictory expectations. The stereotypes of women include being hesitant and indecisive on the one hand and too pushy or "butch" on the other hand. A research study by Linda Carli (1990) found that women who speak tentatively and uncertainly, using such phrases as "I don't know much about it, but . . . ," are better able to influence men. However, that approach is not acceptable in most management groups. Researchers Carol Hymowitz and Timothy Schellhardt (1986) conclude, "Top executives are quick to feel the woman who is tough isn't being womanly, while the woman who isn't tough isn't worth having around." In a study published in the *Harvard Business Review* (Sutton and Moore, 1985), nearly half of the male executives surveyed said they would not feel comfortable working for a woman.

Stereotypes make it acceptable among some traditional managers to ignore, disparage, or discount the qualities and contributions of nontraditional managers. As we learned in our study, people of color and white women are systematically screened out as candidates for more senior management posts when prejudice, as defined here, operates, that is, when a point of difference is highlighted as a flaw. Under such conditions, a nontraditional candidate's accent or hair style may be viewed as a flaw, and that may be enough for rejection. As one Hispanic manager who told us he faced "real animosities" at a previous workplace said, "The fact that I graduated first in my engineering class didn't make as much difference as the fact that I looked different."

Clearly, however, all differences are not based on stereotypes. Nontraditional managers, like everyone else, often have very real limitations that must be considered in hiring or promotion decisions. Nevertheless, the limitations of a nontraditional manager may be a greater liability than the limitations of a white male manager. A black manager in the employee relations field gave an example of how managers tend to isolate and emphasize the limitations of a person of color without giving appropriate attention to his or her strengths. This manager was invited to sit in on a meeting to select a manager for a department in turmoil. The black candidate had proved his skill in handling a troubled environment but not his administrative ability. A white candidate had demonstrated administrative skills. Others already in the department also had good administrative skills and could handle many of the administrative responsibilities. Yet the selection panel focused on the administrative aspects of the job and chose the white manager. In effect, the black manager was compared to the white manager on the basis of his area of relative weakness, even though that may have been less relevant to the job than was his area of strength.

Prejudice prevents many managers from seeing others without the filters that turn differences into liabilities. When prejudice operates this way, flaws are imagined, weaknesses are exaggerated, and failures are attributed to the nontraditional manager's sex or ethnicity rather than to individual differences. Managers we interviewed told us that expecting less from women and people of color is a notion so pervasive that it sometimes affects nontraditional managers' perceptions of themselves.

This effect was demonstrated when the human resource staff of a large corporation in our study decided to conduct a version of an experiment that had been done in other settings to test for prejudicial attitudes toward women and people of color. The staff put together several identical versions of a generic résumé of a job candidate but attached different pictures to each copy: a white man, a black man, a Hispanic man, a black woman, and a Hispanic woman. They asked executives in the corporation to write a job description of each résumé. The manager we interviewed continues the story: "They read over the résumé and described how they would use the person described on the résumé. They assigned the two women of color to the "administrative tasks." The men of color were perceived as suitable for "real" [line] tasks. We did the same study with a group of women of color writing the job descriptions, and we got the same result. This was a sad revelation of perceptions and expectations."

This example shows how prejudice, a barrier in itself, can increase and create other barriers to advancement, such as contributing to the waning confidence and motivation that some nontraditional managers experience. In fact, prejudice is probably a contributing factor in most of the barriers we identified. By permeating policies and practices in very subtle ways, prejudice continues to deprive nontraditional managers of advocates, resources, and power. That is why, we believe, prejudice is the most often mentioned and most powerful barrier.

Poor Career Planning

The next most often mentioned barrier in our study was poor career planning and development. This is largely associated with the lack of opportunities for white women and people of color to get a series of varied work experiences that will qualify them for senior management posts. One Hispanic manager who joined a company after completing an engineering degree described the difficulty he had building a well-rounded track record. In his words, "When I signed on, I said I didn't want to be an engineer. I asked for a line assignment. I was put in engineering. I had a special assignment in a line function for a while, and I was told I did well. I asked to stay in the line. I was put back into engineering. When I got my M.B.A., I asked for a line job. I was put into engineering. They were looking out for me."

We also learned from our interviews that white male decision makers are often reluctant to assign nontraditional managers to the challenging, high-profile jobs that have rich learning potential and add credibility to a manager's track record. One manager described the problem in his organization this way: "The problem here is the syndrome of not wanting people to fail. The attitude of senior management is that we don't make bad people decisions and that we live with our decisions forever. The company wants to look good, and it won't move nontraditional managers into nontraditional positions, including higher-level jobs."

Some executives, as we have seen, have fallen into the trap of making prejudiced assessments of nontraditional managers' capability. Some executives have become reluctant to promote another nontraditional manager once an earlier nontraditional manager's promotion has been a failure. Some executives, when handing out key assignments, simply think first of the other white men with whom they have become better acquainted. In all these cases, the assignments such executives choose for nontraditional managers from the start are likely to be less visible and less central to the core business operations than the assignments given to white men. One manager in our study concluded that as these limiting assignments accumulate, the odds grow that the nontraditional managers will be limited in terms of future promotion because they do not have the required depth and range of job experience to be considered for senior-level jobs.

Studies conducted at the Center for Creative Leadership (CCL) and elsewhere by researchers such as John Kotter (1990) of Harvard University have identified a range of assignments that appear to be important in the development of white male executives. These assignments include major start-ups and troubleshooting, sometimes overseas, as well as serving on important task forces, taking on a headquarters staff job, and receiving promotions that significantly increase a manager's responsibility. Such assignments involve autonomy, visibility, access to senior management, and control over considerable resources. They are often used as tests and rewards for the people judged to have high potential; they constitute the "fast track" in many organizations.

Other studies conducted at CCL and elsewhere have also shown that the types of assignments just described do not appear nearly as often in the track records of female executives. Reports by Patricia Ohlott, Marian Ruderman, and Cynthia McCauley (1991); Ellen Van Velsor and Martha Hughes (1990); and Ann Morrison, Randall White, Ellen Van Velsor, and the CCL (1987) have shown that women's job experience included few if any start-ups and troubleshooting assignments, domestically or overseas, and far fewer line management jobs. Whether these kinds of assignments are as important for developing nontraditional managers as they appear to have been for developing white male managers is still being addressed. In either case, however, such assignments are still being used as criteria for higher-level jobs. Therefore, the lack of experience in these kinds of assignments is a serious barrier to advancement. Reinforcing the findings of our study, Catalyst's 1990 survey of corporate CEOs shows that the lack of career planning and planned job assignments for women is a serious barrier to their advancement. Moreover, a U.S. Department of Labor (1991) report states that "credential building experiences" and "career enhancing assignments" are often unavailable to people of color and white women.

Surveys of people of color in management confirm that the lack of prime job assignments constitutes a major barrier to their advancement as well. A survey led by Nancy DiTomaso (DiTomaso, Thompson, and Blake, 1988), for example, identified factors that hinder success for people of color. The lack of promotion opportunities and the preponderance of staff assignments were high on the list (p. 135). Managers in our study also pointed out the tendency for nontraditional managers to be in staff positions rather than in line management. Most feel that the choice was not their own to make, but a few believe that nontraditional managers are making those choices themselves, gravitating toward the human resource area and other staff functions.

In this study on people of color and white women and in our earlier study on women confronting the glass ceiling, we learned that deciding whether to accept a staff position or waiting to be offered a line job is one of the dilemmas many nontraditional managers face. They choose to accept a staff job for various reasons. In some cases, they believe they have no choice, that they will not be offered a different job if they refuse a staff job. In other cases, the immediate prestige of being the highest-ranking or highest-paid Hispanic manager in the organization, for example, may attract them. Also, promotions may be faster through a staff function than they would be in the line. Although some nontraditional managers may be perfectly satisfied with a staff role throughout their careers, those who believe that a temporary assignment in a staff function will eventually lead to a career in line management and rich prospects for advancement are often disillusioned when their careers are stalled. Without the kind of career guidance often provided by mentors or a systematic career planning program, it is easy to choose a staff job for the wrong reasons.

Most organizations have few career planning tools available to any managers. As we discovered, however, the recognized lack of mentoring for nontraditional managers makes them particularly vulnerable to poor career decisions. A reliable mentor can help a manager determine the value of a certain job offer in relation to his or her present job, help the manager negotiate the acceptance of a staff job on the condition that the next move is into line management, help the manager know when and how to lobby for a promotion that doesn't require relocation, and so forth. Not having a mentor who is trustworthy and knowledgeable about career mobility is a factor that further contributes to the problem of poor career development.

The relative inexperience of nontraditional managers in working toward upper-management levels within corporate settings makes career guidance even more critical. From our interviews, we learned that a lack of organizational savvy about how to get along and get ahead in the corporate world is another barrier related to career development. Many nontraditional managers, for example, do not have a good sense of what to expect on the fast track, or how to know whether they are still on or off the track, or what rate of advancement is reasonable. These and other aspects of career development may be more easily mastered by white men with more experience and a better developed network. The ability of nontraditional managers to negotiate and make decisions is hampered by their relative lack of information about how the system works and how to make it work for them.

Taking account of all these strands of evidence, we conclude that poor career development is cumulative because as a career progresses, it becomes increasingly difficult to overcome low-profile or ill-conceived assignments. Without the kinds of assignments that are considered prerequisites for senior management posts, nontraditional managers are likely to be overlooked. Thus it appears that early and continuing problems in career development are partly responsible for the discouraging situation today, a situation in which executives grumble that they can't find enough qualified nontraditional candidates for senior-level jobs.

Poor Working Environment

The working environment for many nontraditional managers is lonely, unfriendly, and pressure packed. At the higher levels, they are still dramatically outnumbered by white men, many of whom, deliberately or not, regularly treat them differently from the way they treat their white male colleagues. Our interviews revealed that nontraditional managers are excluded from luncheons, social events, and even the friendly camaraderie that occurs in most offices. They are often a curiosity to their colleagues, who watch them closely and sometimes scrutinize their work and behavior for possible mistakes. Some people of color and women have even commented that other people withhold information from them and sabotage their work in order to undermine them. Because they are still the exception in many groups and because prejudice shapes others' perceptions of them, many nontraditional managers find the working environment a frustrating, draining advancement barrier.

A black personnel director told us that in her corporation, "The climate is not there yet to just walk in, to be like one of the other people. Women and minorities have to be better. There's always someone raising the bar while you're in the air. . . . I'm tired." This personnel director and others noted that the pressure and isolation are not only exhausting, but they also combine to create another problem that represents a catch-22 for nontraditional managers. On the one hand, when they do need help, they can't admit it and ask for help for fear of being written off as incompetent. On the other hand, because of the pressure to be consistently outstanding and the need to avoid serious mistakes, their not asking for help can be suicide. Although white male managers may be subject to this dynamic to some extent, they do not face it in an atmosphere of prejudice. An Asian-American manager who doesn't know what to do after receiving a key customer's threat to sue, for example, or a black female manager who needs to take time off during a busy season to care for an ill parent runs the risk of reinforcing stereotyped attitudes in asking for help or support.

Another factor we learned about that contributes to a poor working environment for nontraditional managers is that there are few if any other nontraditional managers to be role models and mentors for those rising beyond middle management. Many managers in our study pointed out that they were dependent on white men to advise and promote them, which was often ineffective. Ruby Keele (1986) describes the "credit theory of mentoring" that makes it difficult for nontraditional managers to get the support of higher-level executives. The theory is that to get credit and support, nontraditional managers must first demonstrate that they really do not need credit and support and that other people, skills, and contacts are available to them. Often they are not. When they are, they can be a powerful force in shaping a career. A black woman who had been in the personnel function of her company told us how she intervened to save another black employee from what she described as a racist manager. When she learned that the subordinate had been labeled a poor performer by her manager, she went to talk to the subordinate, who threatened to leave, saying she wanted to work with more blacks. "Do you want to be around blacks, or do you want to have access to blacks?" the intervener asked. "If you have money, you can go away on weekends or whatever and have access to other blacks. But as a poor performer, you can't do that. Do you want to leave this company with the reputation of being a poor performer? Fix your performance, and then you can leave." The woman we interviewed then went to the other black employee's boss and insisted that he put his subordinate in the remedial action program usually reserved for designated high-potential employees. They both did their part, and the subordinate was eventually promoted.

According to managers we interviewed, white men are not usually eager to support someone with a different perspective or different values, and many find it difficult even to communicate with such an individual. One Mexican-American manager had discovered that senior managers feel they need some sort of special language to relate to him. They ask him, "What college did your father go to?" He responds, "My father is a laborer." They feel that they can't understand him because his experience is so different, and they use that as an excuse for not mentoring or assisting him and people like him.

We also learned that nontraditional managers often have no one to talk to about their fears, their mistakes, and the rage they feel over being treated differently from others. There is often no one to help them objectively assess their abilities and their behavior or to help them cope with the uncertainty they may feel about their role in the organization and the expectations others have of them. There is often no one to help them feel comfortable. One manager commented, "My first ten years were spent in areas where I was the only black. I had no one to talk to." If they do seek comfort by spending time with other blacks or Mexican-American employees, for example, they may be perceived as "segregationists" who have little loyalty to the organization. Even when blacks eat together in the cafeteria, one human resource executive remarked, it is perceived as a revolution. Yet if they remain isolated, they may be seen as arrogant or resentful, and being isolated, they may not be able to perform well. Finally, as we have seen, if they try to "integrate" with white men, they are often met with stereotyping and even outright rejection.

The loneliness and unfriendliness of an organization is often magnified when nontraditional managers relocate from urban centers to smaller, less diverse towns. They can be subject to harassment. Making friends is difficult, and finding services such as hair styling may be impossible. According to our interviews, this helps explain why some nontraditional managers are very cautious about moving away from an occupation or location in which they have built a support system. If they are unsure about the level of commitment they have from their organization, some nontraditional managers are likely to reject relocations because they involve additional barriers to their advancement.

Lack of Organizational Savvy

The managers we interviewed told us that people of color and white women often fail to advance because they don't know "how to play the game" of getting along and getting ahead in business. They appear to lack the preparation and knowledge that would allow them to put their experiences and their expectations in the context of their organization's culture. Nontraditional managers don't seem to pay adequate attention to organizational politics and the agenda of their colleagues and bosses, and they don't seem to be strategic about their own career development. In some ways, all nontraditional managers share the problem of being newcomers who have been placed in management roles without any real expectation that they will advance to senior levels. Therefore, little if any effort has been made to prepare them for such advancement. In other ways, the problems seem to be distinctively different for Hispanics, for Asian-Americans, for blacks, for white women, and for other groups because of particular aspects of each group's organizational experience.

One of the problem areas mentioned for Hispanics, Asian-Americans, Native Americans, and sometimes women in general is an inability to assert themselves and their views. Some members of these groups feel that their upbringing makes it more difficult for them to behave competitively in many business settings. A Native American manager told us about how cultural traditions get in the way of effective corporate communication. For example, we learned that when Asian-Americans, Hispanics, and Native Americans show respect by not initiating conversation with older people or when they foster teamwork by not continuing to argue with a senior manager who doesn't accept their idea, they are seen as subservient yes-people not willing to take a stand. Women with these ethnic backgrounds have an especially hard time communicating this way because they have been reared to support men and seek their approval. More than one Asian-American employee group has asked for courses in assertiveness to help them combat this problem.

The opposite problem seems to plague many black managers, who are frequently seen as too aggressive. A black woman told us about attending a conference and getting uncomfortable with the only other black attendee who, she felt, was too vocal, too confrontational, and didn't have a need to fit in. He made others uncomfortable with him, she believed. Another black woman mentioned the defensiveness that may prompt some blacks to keep pushing for recognition and to exaggerate differences through their style, dress, and language. She said that many blacks, especially at the entry level, come into her organization assuming that the managers won't like them. So they invest their energy in fighting their fear of the white men instead of putting it in their job or in learning more about the industry. White men and others in our study believe that some blacks are unrealistic in expecting too much too soon and don't accept the idea of working their way up step-by-step.

Women are perceived as unwilling to take the risks necessary in business and naive about how to look out for themselves, partly because of their socialization. Managers in our study commented that women don't know how to negotiate titles (often assuming instead that they will get the title they deserve) or how to get credit for their ideas and talents. One black woman explained that women need more of a "kamikaze attitude" to move ahead — taking risks but knowing that if you're too vocal or confrontational, no one will want to be your manager. Blacks, she said, had made more progress in her organization than women because they had approached senior management more forcefully. "The blacks said, We are a viable people and we deserve opportunity. Here are the names of black people who have potential. The women said, We'd like you to consider us for jobs, as if they were saying, Take my life and figure it out."

One disadvantage that seems to be common to all nontraditional groups is an inability to create and manage networks. Because their networks are not as strong as those of many white men, they don't get as much information about industry trends and where the company is headed. Without strong networks and mentors, it is difficult to gain expertise in corporate politics; yet naïveté in this domain can easily derail a career. Managers in our study pointed to deficits in these "soft" skills related to understanding the organizational culture and context as a barrier much more often than they mentioned a lack of formal education. The fact that the managers rated such organizational savvy as more important than formal education may indicate that courses and degrees are now less relevant to success in the executive suite than they once were.

Ironically, this may be happening just as many nontraditional employees have caught up with or surpassed their white male colleagues in terms of formal education. Even in technical areas, which were most often cited as an educational deficit, the number of people of color and women who have earned degrees is impressive. In 1989, for example, more people of color than whites graduated with a doctorate in engineering (Carter and Wilson, 1991). The number of women with technical degrees has also been steadily increasing. Women earned 27.9 percent of science and engineering doctorates in 1989, up from 20.9 percent in 1979 (Mooney, 1990). Other disciplines also provide important preparation for executive posts, particularly business administration. In this area, some nontraditional groups have made strong gains over the years. In 1990, for example, 30 percent of the students at the top twenty business schools were women (Roman, 1990).

Yet according to the managers we talked to, education is still considered a problem for some ethnic groups, particularly for many blacks and Hispanics. Economic hardship and other access problems have kept some nontraditional managers from achieving educational credentials. However, managers in our study pointed out that education is simply not valued in some cultures. One black manager in corporate employee relations said that blacks and Puerto Ricans have traditionally not gone into science and math because there are no role models for them in these areas and so they don't see opportunities for themselves in these fields.

There is also the question of whether a formal education will pay off for people of color to the same extent that it does for white men. A recent study found that white, college-educated men earn a third more than black men with equal education ("White College Graduates Make a Third More Than Blacks," 1991). Obviously, then, education does not equalize the earning power of blacks with that of whites. If young people continue to shun education for the kinds of reasons we have been talking about, the lack of formal education may remain a barrier for members of some ethnic groups.

Greater Comfort in Dealing with One's Own Kind

Consciously and unconsciously, managers, like people in general, tend to feel more comfortable around people who are like themselves. As a result, they often choose to associate with those who are like them rather than with those who are different. In the case of white male managers, this natural tendency would appear to be amplified by some of the institutionalized forms of prejudice discussed earlier. The president of a West Coast company, a white man, described the problem this way: "Cultural differences are tough for white males to deal with. We hire those who are like us; we perpetuate ourselves in the belief that it's easier to relate to someone with the same values, the same looks, the same perceptions. If anyone thinks about it, that's what they think."

Even without prejudice, then, many white male managers may be reluctant to embrace diversity. They may not intend to hire and promote candidates who are like them, but they may often favor white men because, through familiarity and comfort, white men seem to be the best people for the job.

On the other hand, discomfort with nontraditional managers, which can and often does come from prejudice, may also arise out of a simple lack of familiarity. Ethnic groups still do not mingle socially with others in many communities, so white male executives have little interaction with people of color outside the office. This social distance can create discomfort at work, perhaps because of a class issue. One white human resource executive in our study had detected a hierarchy of comfort based on class distinctions: at the top, below whites, were Asians; at the bottom were blacks and Puerto Ricans; in between were Cubans and other Hispanics. A young, black operations executive remarked at the end of her interview, "In every job I've ever had, I've had to make people comfortable with the fact that I am black. 'It's okay,' I say. 'Yeah, I am black.'" While some ethnic groups are more socially distant from white men than others because of perceived class or other issues, interaction with any different ethnic group is likely to cause many white male executives some discomfort. White men, as the dominant business group, have had less need than others to reach out to different groups by learning their language and traditions. These executives' relative insulation over the years makes it more difficult for them to relate to members of other ethnic groups.

Of course, white male executives have had considerable interaction with white women, but not as peers in business. As many managers in our study pointed out, this leads to a tendency for them to treat female managers as they treat their wives, daughters, or secretaries, in short, in what they see as familiar and accustomed roles for women. As a result, many white men still resist the idea of women being their equals as managers, and they consequently don't often support women's advancement. Many white men will probably direct most of their extra effort to help someone else's career toward those with whom they have had more experience and feel more comfort.

The natural tendency to relate more easily to people who are similar to oneself applies to everyone. This is one reason why ethnically based employee groups are active and valued. The exclusion of women and people of color from upper-management positions, however, is increasingly regarded as a significant problem because it interferes with the effective use of human potential. As population demographics shift and competition escalates, this problem is likely to get more attention from executives.

Difficulty in Balancing Career and Family

According to the managers we interviewed, the struggle to reconcile home and work is still largely a woman's problem, and the decisions that women must make often postpone and even preclude their advancement into senior management. Bearing and rearing children conflict with full-time dedication to a career. We learned that maternity leave is undefined or unavailable in many organizations, so women often put their jobs in jeopardy when they become pregnant. It is impossible for many women to continue to work evenings and weekends or to travel frequently once they have children, and many women don't want to. Many women wait until their thirties to have children, a time when they are expected to be proving themselves on the corporate fast track or on the tenure track in academia. Once this period is over, it is very difficult to be reconsidered as a high-potential executive candidate.

Organizations have historically provided little support for women who confront the dilemma of meeting both their career and their family needs, and we were told that there is still some reluctance to address this issue. A number of managers commented that many executives have little understanding of or sympathy for the work/family conflicts that typically fall to women to solve. One operations manager explained that as a woman with children, "You can put in sixty to eighty hours a week as a working mother, but your employees don't understand and your boss doesn't understand." As a result, personnel policies geared to a man with a wife at home are slow to change, and many women are dismissed because of their family responsibilities. Women are reluctant to speak up for what are still considered "women's issues" (maternity leave, dependent care, flexible working hours, and job sharing) for fear they will be seen as agitators or even as being ambivalent about their own career. Some women actually do become ambivalent, more interested for a while in rearing a child than in pursuing a promotion.

Competing demands represent a career advancement barrier for many women and, increasingly, for men as well. Even for women without children, the responsibility for maintaining a marriage or a significant relationship sometimes seems to interfere with work, perhaps because of societal expectations about the role of women in relationships. A human resource executive in one of our model companies told us that one woman about to get a promotion instead opted for a demotion because her husband was complaining about the amount of traveling she was doing. The executive emphasized that this kind of conflict affects women more than men even though both travel. As she put it, "We haven't had a man do that [take a demotion] in the last five years." Relocation is an even greater problem for many women in a relationship because their husbands or partners (who may be paid more than they) are not likely to accompany them on a move.

Many women's outside responsibilities make it harder for them to meet the high expectations for performance that their bosses may have for them. Household chores alone take more of a woman's time than a man's time, even when no children

are involved. Data compiled by Daniel Evan Weiss (1991) reveal that women who work full time spend another twenty-five
hours a week doing housework, while men spend only thirteen
hours. When young children are involved, mothers spend seventeen hours a week on child care, while fathers spend only five
hours. Often women also carry out many of the social obligations involved in a relationship. Societal norms may be more
to blame than rigid personnel practices in organizations, but
the squeeze being put on many talented women continues to
drive some away and to limit the contributions of many who stay.

Other Barriers to Advancement

As Table A.8 in the appendix shows, we learned about a number of other barriers standing in the way of advancement for
nontraditional managers, including economic restrictions and
the lack of accountability for diversity. Many of these other barriers are discussed in later sections dealing with the tools and
the process to foster diversity. For now, we will examine just
two of these — backlash and infighting — because managers have
only recently recognized them as significant problems.

"Cultural shifts bring anxiety for white men" was the head-
line of an article in the *Washington Post* (Duke, 1991, p. A1).
The article documented the reactions of some white male managers to the changing composition of the management ranks in
their organizations, particularly their feeling of being a minority
in the presence of more Asian-Americans, Hispanics, blacks,
other people of color, and white women. Marking historical
events may also prompt backlash. The fiftieth anniversary of
Japan's attack on Pearl Harbor, for example, was anticipated
with dread by many Japanese-Americans, according to Sonni
Efron (1991). Japanese-Americans expected a backlash of anti-
Asian animosity and hate attacks, fueled in part by resentment
of Japan's growing economic clout at a time when the U.S. econ-
omy was faltering. Susan Faludi's 1991 book, *Backlash,* explains
that backlash against women has consistently been triggered by
the perception that women are making progress toward equality.

Backlash was found to be one of the ten most significant
restraining forces in the advancement of black senior executives,

according to an Executive Leadership Council's study (Baskerville and Tucker, 1990), perhaps because of resentment or fear. Such feelings have prompted some white men to rebel against their organizations' affirmative action and diversity efforts by undermining diversity practices. Some have even charged reverse discrimination. According to managers in our study, backlash has become so prevalent that it now represents the primary weakness in diversity efforts.

One view holds that backlash by white men is a natural, expected consequence of diversity. In the *Washington Post* article by Duke (1991) cited earlier, Professor William Keller of Columbia University's school of business is quoted as saying, "The white males who have always been in a privileged class now find themselves, in effect, not receiving the kind of undivided attention that they have in the past, and that's a real tension point" (p. A14). Author and researcher John Fernandez (1991) further explains this tension by noting that white men used to have to compete for promotions with only 33 percent of the population — other white men. After the 1964 Civil Rights Act, white men had to compete, at least by law, with the other 67 percent of the population as well. The increased competition with people of color and white women, whom many white men believe to be inferior or deficient in some way, has led to what Fernandez calls "severe psychological dislocation, and cries of unfair treatment and reverse discrimination" (p. 209). He concludes: "Corporations should recognize [backlash] as a normal reaction of people who are at risk of being displaced from a privileged power position. This is especially painful because white males, always a minority of the population, have perceived themselves to be a majority" (p. 209).

Backlash is a barrier to fostering diversity, and it is sometimes provoked by the very practices used in some diversity efforts, such as laying off white men even when they are not the "last in" employees in order to maintain the proportion of nontraditional employees. Resentment against ethnic employee groups appears to be increasing in several organizations in our study because downsizing has cut job opportunities and the "unrepresented" white men feel that employee groups have unduly influenced personnel policies. Backlash is also prompted when

nontraditional managers are given opportunities that their white
male bosses or colleagues were not given, such as faster promotions or invitations to special meetings or social events. Breaking tradition by accommodating nontraditional managers in any
way upsets some traditional managers.

Educational attempts have been aimed at reducing backlash by helping white male employees understand that strict fairness has seldom if ever been the sole criterion for promotion.
Nevertheless, some managers in our study believe that it is unrealistic to expect to eliminate backlash because white men have
lost some of their privilege and they do face more competition
today; they cannot be expected to like that or even to accept
it without a fight. The challenge of diversity efforts includes keeping backlash under control to hold its disruptive impact to a
minimum.

Infighting occurs when one underrepresented group vies
with another for power, status, and privileges. Blacks, for example, sometimes fear that other nontraditional groups will
receive the best promotions or the biggest pay increases. White
women are sometimes resentful that black men are given the
opportunity for accelerated career development instead of them.
In a kind of sibling rivalry, women and other nontraditional
groups in all combinations express hostility toward others when
they feel their own slice of the pie is not big enough.

At the National Urban League's 1991 convention, president John Jacob targeted infighting as the topic of his keynote
address (Kennedy, 1990). He urged blacks to ally with other people of color or risk having whites pick and choose among minority
groups in granting social and economic gains. Jacob, like others,
believes that whites sometimes use divide-and-conquer tactics
to increase friction among ethnic groups. He fears that infighting is particularly damaging to American-born blacks, who will
remain at the bottom while other ethnic groups, more acceptable
to whites, leap ahead economically. Other groups are growing
rapidly, and some will soon outnumber blacks in the United
States. The 1990 census figures show that the number of Hispanics is almost equal to the number of blacks (22.3 million
Hispanics, compared with 29.9 million blacks) and that the fast-
growing group, Asian-Americans, already numbers 7.2 million.

The dramatic increase in hate crimes to record levels indicates that backlash and infighting are problems in society in general, not just in organizations. Fairchild and Fairchild (1991) and others have noted that the growing diversity in the population has increased interethnic tension to the point of violence. The Los Angeles area, as most of us know from watching the violence that ensued from the Rodney King verdict, has been a hotbed of this tension. Before this much-publicized event occurred, however, other racially motivated hate crimes plagued the area: a black schoolgirl was killed by a Korean merchant, blacks and Latinos went at each other at a local high school, urban warfare broke out in Long Beach between Latinos and Cambodians, and white supremacists continued to come out of the closet. The fear of losing whatever gains have been made to another group is a powerful force that alienates people from one another. Backlash and infighting have become serious problems as recent demographic shifts have occurred in the population.

Overall, a variety of barriers keep nontraditional managers from advancing in organizations. The majority of these barriers fall into two categories. The first is historical exclusion, the fact that white men have dominated the executive ranks of most organizations for many years. Because of their socialization, their reluctance to share their power and privilege with others, and their natural proclivity to associate with people like themselves, white men keep people of color and white women from moving into their circle. The second category involves deficits in various kinds of qualifications; this makes it difficult to find and accept nontraditional candidates for executive posts. Finding women and people of color with traditionally accepted credentials (such as an M.B.A. or an engineering degree) or experiences (such as military duty or line jobs) remains elusive to many managers; yet many managers are also reluctant to accept a different set of qualifications or to provide alternatives for those who cannot follow a traditional career path. These two themes amplify each other and create imposing barriers to the advancement of nontraditional managers.

The barriers to advancement have changed to some extent over time, and each level of progress has brought a new set of issues to be resolved. Until nontraditional managers began to be advanced into upper management, for example, the white male executives already in place did not feel so threatened by them. Until blatant discrimination became illegal and "politically incorrect," the subtly disguised versions of racism and sexism did not have to be confronted. Until diversity began to cover a greater variety of ethnic groups, the fewer nontraditional groups in a given organization received more attention and had greater solidarity. Therefore, within any organization, the specific problems that now exist may reflect the level of progress that has already been achieved. Discovering which concerns and barriers are the most critical to employees now is an essential part of moving ahead, and it is the first step in any effective diversity effort.

Although the specific barriers to advancement differ from one organization to another, their effect is the same. Barriers to nontraditional managers prevent any organization from preparing a full cadre of potential leaders to take over in the future. That cadre must be more diverse than it has ever been, and the techniques used to develop leadership talent must also be more diverse and creative than ever before. Chapter Three addresses the need to change current models of leadership development and presents a framework for developing leadership in the context of diversity.

THREE

SETTING GOALS FOR SUSTAINED LEADERSHIP DEVELOPMENT

Susan Woodly, a division finance manager, is being interviewed on a Tuesday morning during her visit to headquarters. Woodly is a white, thirty-five-year-old woman of German and Swiss ancestry. She is married and has one three-year-old child. The conference room on the fourth floor of the headquarters building, where she arranged for us to meet, is somewhat bare but not uncomfortable. Susan Woodly is neatly dressed in a gray suit, but she appears to be a bit nervous and rushed. As we get into the interview, she relaxes. My question to her is, "You are unusual in that you have reached a level in management that many of your counterparts have not. What is there about your characteristics or circumstances that makes you different in this regard?" She responds:

> It has been very difficult for me. When I began to move up, three areas of "trial and tribulation" surfaced. The first I remember as clear as a bell, when I got a promotion in my department. In the lunchroom I overheard my colleagues, whom I considered to be friendly and supportive, complaining that I had gotten that promotion because I was a woman. That was very painful.
>
> Next, I began feeling that I could never say no to requests for what I call "volunteer PR work." At one point I was representing AMM Enterprises on a total of five community boards. I also felt that I couldn't afford a failure, that the burden of my being a woman put me under microscopic scrutiny. I was afraid my job perfor-

mance would slip and I would fall behind my white male
colleagues, who didn't seem to have the same demands
on their time. With all of this, I also had the tug-of-war
of trying to balance family and career.

What has really helped me survive is the recognition of my situation by people I report to and the support
they have shown. We've also started a support network
to help ourselves keep from derailing.

Our research has identified a variety of benefits that can accrue
to organizations that effectively pursue diversity, along with a
variety of barriers that interfere with developing diversity. Within
all this variety, however, is a theme that unites some of these
important benefits and barriers. That theme is leadership development.

One goal of many diversity efforts is to find and develop
the organization's future leaders, those talented managers who
will help the organization prosper now and in the future. This
goal involves enlarging the pool of candidates from which leaders
of the future will be selected by including more nontraditional
managers. The premise is that a larger pool of talented candidates will eventually improve the quality of leadership. Diversity efforts also focus on improving traditional methods of preparing people for leadership. Better, more effective methods of
leadership development applied to a larger pool of candidates,
it is argued, can enhance organizational productivity, profitability, and responsiveness to business conditions.

This chapter examines three components of leadership
development — challenge, recognition, and support — as they influence and are influenced by the barriers discussed in Chapter
Two. The purpose here is to show how the prospects for effective development are affected by the condition of being a nontraditional manager. The challenge-recognition-support model
of development is the result of our research findings as well as
common practices in management. The model's three elements
appear to work together over time to provoke and sustain development. The *challenge* of new situations and difficult goals

prompts managers to learn the lessons that will help them perform well at higher levels. *Recognition* includes acknowledgment and rewards for achievement and the resources to continue achieving in the form of promotions, salary increases, and awards. *Support* entails acceptance and understanding, along with the benefits that help a manager incorporate his or her career into a full and fulfilling life.

Our model assumes that to sustain development, all three elements must be present in the same relative proportions over time. Figure 3.1 shows the three elements in balance. What seems to happen in practice, however, is that imbalances regularly occur, particularly for nontraditional managers, because the element of challenge overwhelms the other two elements. Our research indicates that some aspects of challenge may be overlooked, recognition may be slow, and traditional support systems may be inadequate. The barriers to advancement that were identified in our study contribute significantly to this imbalance, as Figure 3.2 shows. The consequences for women and people of color, and sometimes for white men as well, can be exhaustion, repeated failures, or opting out of a debilitating work situation.

Challenge

One of the most important methods used to prepare people for executive jobs is to plan a sequence of assignments that provide individuals with continual challenge. The practice of changing or rotating jobs every year or two is commonly used as a "fast track" for aspiring executives. Ideally, job rotation not only

**Figure 3.1. A Balance of Three Components
for Sustained Leadership Development.**

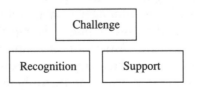

Figure 3.2. Imbalance Created by Barriers to Advancement.

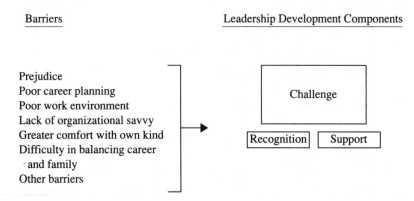

Barriers   Leadership Development Components

Prejudice
Poor career planning
Poor work environment
Lack of organizational savvy
Greater comfort with own kind
Difficulty in balancing career
  and family
Other barriers

Challenge

Recognition   Support

exposes managers to the workings of an organization, but it also puts managers in situations that require new or better skills than the previous assignment demanded. Research done at the Center for Creative Leadership and reported in *The Lessons of Experience* (McCall, Lombardo, and Morrison, 1988) identified developmental assignments that have figured in the success of the sample of managers in that study, which was composed almost exclusively of white men. These assignments include promotions with dramatically increased responsibilities, transfers into staff functions at corporate headquarters, participation in task forces, troubleshooting stints, and start-up experiences that often involve time overseas. These assignments partly overlap with those CCL found to be important for white female executives, described in the book *Breaking the Glass Ceiling* (Morrison, White, and Van Velsor, 1987).

These assignments are important because they force managers to broaden their perspectives and learn a range of skills that will presumably help them be effective in executive-level posts. Often the assignments are also used as examinations: if the job is well done, the manager may go on to a higher-level assignment; if not, then the manager is wiped off the slate of high potentials, given a respectable if stagnant job, or eased out of the organization. Such assignments are valuable because they demand a great deal from the incumbents. They provide the challenge for people to learn, to grow, to develop to their fullest potential. The challenge provided by demanding assignments has become recognized as a key ingredient in leadership development.

Eight Sources of Challenge

As McCall, Lombardo, and Morrison (1988) note, assignments that provide challenge appear to share the following eight common characteristics. These characteristics may represent the key ingredients of challenge for traditional white male managers.

1. *Dealing with the boss.* Challenge arises when the boss is inexperienced or indifferent. The boss may also have a difficult style or even serious managerial flaws.
2. *Dealing with staff members.* Challenge also arises when the staff is inexperienced, recalcitrant, or incompetent. Some staff members may hold a grudge against the manager for being promoted over them.
3. *Other significant relationships.* Advising senior executives, negotiating with outsiders, and collaborating with people from different backgrounds and functions or regions of the organization all create challenge.
4. *High stakes.* Challenge is created by the extreme visibility of certain assignments, especially with top management. Tight deadlines and financial risk add to the challenge.
5. *Adverse business conditions.* Often seen in overseas assignments, the challenge here includes the physical hardships of harsh climate or lack of adequate living facilities, hostile officials, or conflicts with local business practices and values.
6. *Scope and scale of the job.* Managing a large number of subordinates, including subordinates who are geographically separated, and including subordinates who are experts in their own right all provide challenge.
7. *Missing trumps.* The lack of traditionally required credentials or background characteristics, which requires a manager to establish credibility while learning the new job, also provides challenge.

8. *Starkness of transition.* Challenge is created by the suddenness or the extent of change involved in a transition, sometimes including personal life changes as job changes occur.

These eight sources of challenge in developmental assignments might be considered traditional elements of challenge for white male managers. Many organizations recognize them, and some organizations have incorporated them into their developmental programs and practices. Although the same elements of challenge may also figure in the development and success of nontraditional managers, they may not adequately capture the types and extent of challenge experienced by nontraditional managers whose job situations do not conform to the traditional patterns. The additional or exaggerated sources of challenge that nontraditional managers regularly encounter may not be factored into their preparation and assessment, which may consequently interfere with their progress.

Additional Challenges for Nontraditional Managers

The barriers to advancement described in Chapter Two create additional sources of challenge for many white women and people of color in management. Such barriers include prejudice, isolation, and conflicts between one's career and personal life. It is not difficult to imagine, for example, the increased difficulty of dealing with a boss who not only lacks certain skills and has a difficult style but who is also prejudiced. Similarly, there may be added difficulty in dealing with prejudiced subordinates, peers, and outsiders. The addition of prejudice to the first three sources of challenge listed above complicates and deepens the challenge in ways not often encountered by white men. Therefore, the challenge of dealing with prejudiced colleagues may go unnoticed by them.

Perhaps because of prejudice, the standards for performance may be higher for nontraditional managers than for their white male counterparts. In this study and in our earlier research on women in management, we discovered that women and people of color in management are often expected to perform at a higher level than white men who hold or who have held the same jobs. Doing a job better than anyone else has done it is likely to add to the challenge nontraditional managers experience.

Coping with adverse conditions is another ingredient that may increase the level of challenge for nontraditional managers. In describing the challenge of troubleshooting assignments, for example, white male managers sometimes mentioned the hostility of their co-workers who resented their advice, their attempted interventions, and even their very presence. Moreover, their limited assignments in foreign countries sometimes entailed coping with capricious or unfriendly government officials. Although such hardships are typically confined to certain types of assignments or locations in the reports of these white male managers, the same hardships appear to constitute the daily life of many nontraditional managers, even those in the progressive organizations included in our study.

Our findings indicate that there is still a great deal of resentment and hostility from subordinates who dislike reporting to anyone not white and male and from co-workers who feel threatened working side by side with a nontraditional manager. Some colleagues may not be hostile but merely skeptical. They may not be directly opposed to an integrated workforce, but they suspect that nontraditional managers are simply not up to the task, and they are consequently cautious in the way they relate to, delegate to, and rely on a white woman or a person of color. Like some of those who are outrightly hostile, these co-workers, consultants, suppliers, and customers may rationalize the presence of nontraditional managers as the outcome of a quota system. A Chinese manager in our study said that her boss had told her to "be as un-Asian as possible" and to have her Asian subordinates "be un-Asian" as well because the department "looks like an Asian connection." She had to be constantly concerned about looking, acting, and seeming like an Asian as she performed her job.

The adversity that surrounds nontraditional managers regardless of their assignment adds to the challenge of the work they are doing. Not everyone is hostile toward or suspicious of nontraditional managers, and not all white men are immune from being resented; however, these responses appear to be considerably more frequent for people of color and white women. Adverse conditions that many white men report as a temporary hardship are a constant part of nontraditional managers' work environment, following them from assignment to assignment, from place to place, throughout their careers.

There is also some evidence from this study and other research that the pressure and visibility associated with their performance may also be greater for nontraditional managers, adding even more challenge to their work. All conscientious managers are likely to feel pressure to perform their jobs well, but our research indicates that a nontraditional manager is noticed more, watched more, and judged more than a white man, if only because so few nontraditional managers appear in the management ranks of many organizations. Managers in this study and in our earlier study of the glass ceiling for women in management noted that for many nontraditional managers, the added pressure of working "under a microscope" is frustrating and draining. As one Hispanic manager explained, "Those minorities who are going up get excess scrutiny. They are put under a microscope, and there is pressure not to screw up." Being the sole Asian-American marketing manager or the first black executive in an organization puts nontraditional managers in a spotlight that relentlessly publicizes their actions. Their observers include not only their bosses and their colleagues who are curious, if not doubtful, about their competence but also the other women and ethnically diverse colleagues who desperately want them to succeed so that they, too, may be given a chance some day to show their worth.

The burden carried by many nontraditional managers to represent their demographic group while performing their job is one that can raise the level of challenge beyond that of white male managers in whatever assignment they have. Because nontraditional managers represent not only their organization but also their ethnic group or gender (and sometimes also the concept of diversity in general), they are constantly called upon to promote the cause. The media want them for stories and profiles.

Social scientists want them for research projects. Other men of color or women, with ambitions of their own, want them as role models and regularly call them for advice or favors. Nonprofit organizations ask them to speak at conventions. Their bosses sometimes nudge them to serve on committees and task forces as the ranking woman or person of color to represent that point of view. Employee groups beckon them to mentor others of the same sex or ethnicity. Top management may want their help in recruiting other nontraditional employees. The amount of necessary "volunteerism" within and outside the organization escalates for nontraditional managers, who must also continue to do their jobs in a consistently outstanding fashion to stay in good stead with their bosses.

While some nontraditional managers shun volunteerism and some white male managers elect to contribute considerable time to both traditional and nontraditional causes, the reality seems to be that women and people of color are under considerable pressure to choose more and do more. Those who do not support traditional activities run the risk of alienating their white male colleagues. Those who do not support their demographic colleagues risk being ostracized by them as a "queen bee" or the like. Their visibility permits them no refuge from multiple, sometimes conflicting obligations.

An additional challenge for many nontraditional managers is balancing career demands with outside demands. The managers in our study generally agreed that women experience this challenge more than men because the responsibilities of bearing and rearing children, maintaining a household, and managing social relationships are still disproportionately borne by women. Women with the financial means to hire help are typically freed from handling these duties personally, but this does not reduce their degree of responsibility. They still must hire and manage people to perform such jobs, intervene when sickness or problems occur, and account for the results. The continuous challenge of juggling home and family demands with job demands creates conflict and stress that women in particular are expected to manage. Some men are also strained in seeking a balance between the two; Hispanic men may be especially vulnerable, as some managers noted, because their culture puts a high value on family life. However, the day-to-day responsibilities of child care or elder care, cooking and cleaning, entertaining, and so forth are those that further increase the challenge for many women as they pursue their career goals.

Overall, it would not be surprising to find that the level of challenge in a given assignment for nontraditional managers is considerably greater than that experienced by white men. Combining the demands of meeting higher performance standards, regularly confronting adversity such as hostility or harassment, working in a spotlight and contending with the expectations of both nontraditional and traditional groups, and struggling day after day with care-giving and social duties significantly affects the degree of difficulty of a particular assignment. Some executives may have concluded that if nontraditional managers have more difficulty performing in an assignment, it must be because they are not as capable as their white male counterparts. But this conclusion can be countered with the argument that greater difficulty comes from the extra demands that are both within the assignment and surrounding it. The "same" assignment given to a white male manager and a nontraditional manager is hardly the same at all.

The Danger of Limiting Challenge

Because of the extraordinary challenge nontraditional managers face, some executives may be tempted to provide some relief by assigning nontraditional managers to less consequential jobs. Yet this is likely to perpetuate a vicious cycle that blocks their advancement. Because of prejudice and other barriers, there is already a tendency to deselect women and people of color from strategic, central assignments. Nontraditional managers are already more likely to be put into peripheral or staff positions that are considered to be less important to the organization's performance. Then, when a higher-level opening comes up, they are not likely to get the job because they lack experience in strategic, central positions. The cycle feeds on itself to limit nontraditional managers' advancement potential. These managers will probably be increasingly frustrated over not getting opportunities to prove their worth to the organization in ways that are likely to be recognized and rewarded. And because their credibility as potential executives hinges on a solid track record of important jobs, gaps in their record may cause them to plateau later. They may lose opportunities to learn some of the lessons that could help them become effective in higher-level posts. They may feel that the level of challenge is too low rather than too high if they are not experiencing the same elements of challenge that have characterized the careers of managers who preceded them.

Instead of reducing the level of challenge by limiting nontraditional managers to assignments perceived to be less critical (and less demanding), one alternative is to reduce the demands from other sources: use the same performance standards for all managers, traditional and nontraditional; reduce the impact of prejudice; promote a larger cadre of nontraditional managers so that the demands on any of these individuals to represent their sex or ethnic group are lessened; provide benefit packages that allow managers to fulfill outside obligations while pursuing their careers. Alternatives such as these can provide relief from some of the additional elements of challenge without interfering with nontraditional managers' advancement potential. These options not only reduce some of the extraneous challenge that distracts many nontraditional managers from the work at hand, but they also increase the recognition and support that nontraditional managers need to keep going.

Perhaps one of the biggest mistakes organizations make in attempting to increase diversity in management is misusing challenge. Challenge is either heaped upon nontraditional managers until they burn out, or they are protected from overwhelming challenge, which often contributes to their derailment. Relying on challenge alone to develop the leadership potential of nontraditional managers is a dangerous trap. The elements of recognition and support need to be factored in to balance the level of challenge for the leadership development process to be most effective.

Recognition

It is difficult for many white male managers to appreciate the demands that people of color and women in most organizations face. A policy of equal treatment is often administered from the vantage point of white men. These white men may not recognize the challenge of "fitting in" and countering co-workers' stereotypes; they may not encounter acts of discrimination and therefore cannot fathom the difficulty of managing the rage caused by such acts; they may not have been deprived of counsel or colleagueship as they made their way up the ladder. Yet it is important that white men and others recognize demands and hardships such as these when assessing the promise and the performance of nontraditional managers.

Some managers in our study commented that women and people of color seem to be ambivalent about taking key jobs in their organizations. One reason may be that the expected rewards fall far short of the additional demands and sacrifices required. A CEO interviewed for a previous research project told us that women were expected to perform at a level at least as high as men but that no woman would be promoted into one of the top ten positions in the company no matter how well she performed. Without the rewards to compensate for their investment, many nontraditional managers opt out, adjust their input to match the likely output from their employer, or scale down expectations of themselves to fit their career prospects.

Recognition comes in many different forms. Some of the most common are listed here:

Pay: salary and total cash compensation

Promotion: advancement to positions of greater responsibility

Perquisites: company car, club memberships, financial incentives and advice, and so forth

Participation: inclusion in decision making

Autonomy: freedom to act on one's own without supervision

Resources: staff, budget, and time to do the job

Respect and credibility: having one's priorities and opinions considered and valued

Faith: the expectation that one's productivity will continue in increasingly responsible positions

There is still strong reluctance to give nontraditional managers the same authority and rewards that go to their white male counterparts. Unequal pay, for example, is documented even in staff jobs generally believed to be appropriate for women. In the human resource field, a 1990 salary survey reported by Thompson (1990) shows that men make 37 percent more than women in comparable jobs. Only in one of the lower job grades does the average salary for women come close to that for men. At upper-management levels, the salary gap may be even greater. A salary study published in 1987 by the U.S. Chamber of Commerce reported that women at the vice president level and higher in corporations make 42 percent less than men. At one organization in our study, an indicator of success was that female engineers are now making more than 90 percent as much money as men in the same position.

Lower salaries, fewer perks and benefits, and slower promotions are certainly not the exception for nontraditional managers, according to many managers we interviewed and as documented elsewhere by Ann Morrison and Mary Ann Von Glinow (1990), Claudia Goldin (1990), Barry Gerhart and Sarah Rynes (1991), Kathleen Cannings and Claude Montmarquette (1991), and others. A black manager in our study described what she called the "build a better black syndrome." That is, people of color and white women always need to be better, to be developed further, to be promotable. The tendency in some organizations is to develop nontraditional managers until they are virtually guaranteed success in a position; this sometimes means that they must do the job before they get the job (without the salary increase and privileges). Some managers who have seen the negative impact of promoting a woman or a person of color and watching her or him founder in the new job are now reluctant to promote another until they are absolutely certain that she or he will succeed. They prefer to give a woman or person of color responsibility for a while before they dispense the commensurate authority. In cases such as these, discrepancies in recognition and rewards reinforce the notion that women and people of color are not as good as white men, which in turn perpetuates prejudice.

The advancement barriers identified in our study surely create at least some of the discrepancies in recognition. Prejudice, for example, may contribute to an unwillingness to pay higher salaries or grant perks to nontraditional managers or to give them freedom to do their jobs without constant monitoring. Researchers Amado Cabezas and Gary Kawaguchi (1988) state that for Asian-American men and women, "Low returns on their human capital investment rather than deficiencies in their investments accounted for about two-thirds of the income gap relative to U.S.-born white men." Continuing discrimination, they conclude, plays an important part in the lower payoff that Asian-Americans receive for their education and experience in comparison to white men. A lack of career planning and organizational savvy may also be responsible for the loss of promotional opportunities that would better prepare nontraditional managers for senior-level posts. Discomfort may cause traditional executives to exclude people of color and white women from participating in the decision-making process. These and other barriers we discovered limit the recognition available to nontraditional managers.

Recognition plays a significant role in giving women and people of color appropriately challenging assignments and in rewarding their performance in them. One manager in our study mused that white men are "brought along in baby steps" throughout their career, but many nontraditional managers have much more traumatic transitions thrust upon them. Giving women and people of color more credit for their experiences and achievements, even if they have been somewhat different from those of white men, and giving women and people of color the resources to make steady, incremental changes in their knowledge and skills are difficult tasks made even more difficult by the need to make up for lost time. Nonetheless, recognition is a necessary component in developing leaders for the future.

Support

Along with challenge and recognition for their skills and achievements, men of color and women in general also need support systems to help them cope with the additional demands they face. Challenge, even with commensurate rewards, can prove to be an overwhelming burden for managers if there is no relief from some of the demands that conflict with their job responsibilities. The following are among the most common forms of support:

> *Collegiality:* friendly association with co-workers
> *Acceptance:* acknowledgment and approval
> *Advocacy:* backing and endorsement
> *Permission to fail:* leeway to make mistakes and learn from them
> *Information:* news about the business and the organization
> *Feedback:* data about one's abilities, prospects, and reputation
> *Flexibility:* the option to tailor a job to one's own strengths or circumstances
> *Stress relief:* reducing anxiety and tension by accommodating family and other outside demands and by preventing on-the-job hostilities

A lack of colleagueship and acceptance contributes to the isolation and discouragement many nontraditional managers feel. Organized employee groups often try to fill that void by helping women and people of color feel more comfortable and more confident in their organization, providing camaraderie and encouragement if not training as well. One black manager we interviewed found that his black colleagues helped him reconcile mixed feelings about his work environment.

> There's a schizophrenia about the behavior of blacks
> in corporations. On the one hand, I want to know
> why all the decision makers are white. That's how
> I feel at home, with my friends. Somehow when

I go to work, I don't ask that. The employee group
brought the internal me and the external me closer
together, more in focus. I'm not as offended, and
I don't show the offense at the little subtleties I see.
I want to make my point, but I don't want to be
branded so my points are discounted.

Advocacy from more senior managers can be difficult for
many nontraditional managers to obtain; some traditional senior
managers are simply not comfortable with them or perceive them
to be less competent than white men. When nontraditional managers are recommended for a position, they may find that they
have no leeway to define or enlarge the job and no possibility
of taking actions that are not guaranteed to pay off. Playing it
safe may be a condition for continued advocacy, and this rules
out many opportunities to learn and grow. One executive in
our study thought that his company ought to put someone of
color or a white woman in charge of a start-up venture, giving
the person five years to make it work and, if it does, 15 percent
of the profits. "That's what they do for white males," he said.
But many managers avoid the possibility of failure and the potential rewards and learning that go with it because they still often
attribute failure to a nontraditional manager's ethnicity or sex.
A human resource executive described the "undercover racism
and sexism" in her company. "If a male makes a mistake," she
said, "they attribute it to the individual, not to the sex. But if
a black manager makes a mistake, they might say, 'We should
try a white manager next time.'"

Information and feedback are also important components
of a support system. Networks and mentors, when they are available, perform a valuable service by including women and people of color in the informal information channels and by giving
them feedback about their abilities, their performance, their
career options, and how others perceive them. A number of nontraditional managers in our study felt a need to develop their
organizational savvy, but the sources of that savvy are often
scarce. White men in higher-level positions often don't mingle
socially with nontraditional managers, so there are few oppor-

tunities to get information through the grapevine. Furthermore, white male executives are sometimes uncomfortable giving constructive criticism on the job to people of color or to women. A human resource manager in our study commented that the lack of feedback available to female managers limits their ability to make the right impression: "Male managers here are hesitant to identify the soft points of women. We need a vehicle to give them feedback. Women don't know what they are not doing. They need more awareness of the image they present, when they give the perception of Are they tough enough?"

Employee groups and networks of nontraditional employees sometimes provide a supportive forum in which criticism is exchanged and valued. Other avenues and sources of information are also needed, however. A number of nontraditional managers in our study have relied on one or two mentors to give them honest, performance-related feedback as well as information about business plans and problems. For those who don't receive regular or structured feedback from a mentor, outside training programs that emphasize assessment and feedback may fill some gaps.

An important form of support for managers who are increasingly part of a two-career family and who are building leisure and family activities more deliberately into their lives is the leeway to develop their careers in different ways from those used in the past. The relocation requirements for advancement in some organizations, for example, have created serious problems for women and for some men who fear the separation from a spouse, dysfunctional effects on their children, or upheaval of their preferred life-style. Some senior managers are beginning to realize that mobility may not be as important for development as other, less expensive alternatives that also broaden the perspective and network of managers. The average cost of relocating a manager is nearly $40,000 (Scovel, 1990). If the main benefit is a change of scenery, which sometimes happens with unplanned moves, then alternatives make sense.

At least one high-potential manager in a large organization in our study protested about the organization's extensive mobility requirements. The traditional requirement of moving among all seven regions was recently modified; an individual now needs experience in only three of the regions to qualify for a senior management position. Modifications such as this may help organizations streamline their development practices as much as they help managers who, for personal reasons, do not want to relocate.

A number of the organizations in our study are also doing more to help managers find an acceptable middle ground between career demands and family demands by providing resources for dependent care, maternity leave, and alternative work schedules. Such support makes it possible for women in particular to devote more concentrated time to their work while still fulfilling family obligations.

Finding a Balance

Various types of imbalance are common in the development process, particularly where women and people of color are concerned. The most typical problem is a surplus of challenge that is not compensated by appropriate levels of recognition or support. When this happens, the dropout or burnout rate is likely to escalate. Nontraditional managers who may appear to be incompetent, overwhelmed, or unappreciative may actually be victims of a dysfunctional development strategy. The extraordinary level of challenge that women and people of color often face, combined with the lack of recognition and support in comparison with that given to white men, helps explain why some nontraditional managers gladly leave their employers.

Other types of imbalance also occur. When the level of recognition exceeds the level of challenge, for example, complacency or guilt may result. A fancy executive title and a fat paycheck do not fit well with a job with a vague purpose, little clout, and few resources. Such a combination may have a debilitating effect not only on the individual's development but also on how supervisors and decision makers view that person's prospects for advancement.

Support systems that exceed challenge or recognition may impair the development process as well. Collegial interaction without much skill building or increased productivity, for example, can make a company seem more like a social club than a performance-oriented organization. As support systems improve for nontraditional managers, some of their contextual hardships will be reduced, and there will be less need to recognize these kinds of challenges in their performance. Better child care, for instance, helps parents concentrate on their job performance without distraction or guilt; the hardship of conflicting demands is less of a factor to consider in planning or evaluating job performance. It is still appropriate, however, to acknowledge the skills and stamina parents develop in having and rearing children.

In general, the need to balance challenge, recognition, and support has been recognized for some time. What has not been considered, however, is the impact of the "hidden" additional demands that primarily affect women and people of color in management. As the challenge escalates, the recognition and support systems needed to sustain and replenish even the most ambitious people must also increase. Over time, that balance is likely to be a more effective development strategy for the nontraditional managers who represent a key part of the talent pool available for leadership positions of the future.

PART TWO

LEADERSHIP DIVERSITY AS PROCEDURE

This part of the book describes an assortment of tools, or practices, for fostering leadership's diversity within organizations. The practices emphasized here are those mentioned most frequently by managers in our study as being part of their organizations' diversity effort. These tools therefore represent the most promising methods for increasing the participation of people of color and white women at key levels of the organization.

Each organization in our study uses a different combination of practices, but there is also considerable overlap. Some are clearly more central than others to the diversity effort, according to the managers we interviewed. The centrality, or importance, of the practices was factored into the rank ordering of our list, as explained in the appendix. The seven practices ranked highest are as follows:

1. Top management's personal intervention and influence to promote diversity, including affirmative action, and accountability for diversity (used in all sixteen organizations)
2. Targeted recruitment of women and people of color for entry-level, nonmanagerial positions (thirteen organizations)
3. Internal advocacy groups or task forces (ten organizations)
4. Emphasis on equal employment opportunity statistics or personnel profiles (nine organizations)

5. Incorporation of diversity into performance evaluation goals or ratings or the review process (twelve organizations)
6. Targeting of female employees and employees of color in the management succession process or in replacement planning for management posts (ten organizations)
7. Revision of promotion criteria and the decision-making process to reflect diversity goals and to help counter institutionalized barriers to advancement (eleven organizations)

The full variety of diversity practices is impressive. We discovered no less than fifty-two different practices. Further, more than half of the organizations in our study used at least twenty different practices as part of their diversity efforts. A complete list of the fifty-two diversity practices mentioned by managers in our study, in rank order of importance, appears in Table A.9 in the appendix.

The purpose of Part Two is to describe several diversity practices and begin to sort them so that managers can select and combine them into a powerful, coherent diversity effort. There are three main types: accountability, development, and recruitment practices. Each of the three chapters in this section is devoted to one of these three types.

The following figure shows that the diversity practices are the means by which a threefold strategy of education, enforcement, and exposure is implemented. The goal of the threefold strategy is a balance in challenge, recognition, and support to achieve sustained leadership development, as discussed in Chapter Three. Ideally, the practices should support a balanced approach to diversity by contributing to all three strategic components. The education component of the strategy has two thrusts; one is to prepare nontraditional managers for increasingly responsible posts, and the other is to help traditional managers overcome their prejudice in thinking about and interacting with people who are of a different sex or ethnicity. The second component of the strategy, enforcement, puts teeth in diversity goals and encourages behavior change. The third component, exposure to people with different backgrounds and characteristics, adds a more personal approach to diversity by helping managers get to know and respect others who are different.

Diversity Practices for Supporting a Threefold Diversity Strategy.

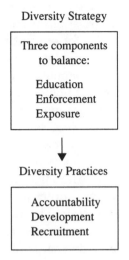

Diversity Strategy

> Three components
> to balance:
>
> Education
> Enforcement
> Exposure

Diversity Practices

> Accountability
> Development
> Recruitment

Chapter Four describes practices that increase accountability for diversity. Twenty-three of the fifty-two practices uncovered in our study are of this type. Many of them are geared toward the enforcement component of the strategy. As a group, these practices address all three elements of sustained leadership development, helping to provide a balance of challenge, recognition, and support to nontraditional managers.

Chapter Five describes development practices, which include both formal programs and informal techniques to help nontraditional managers prepare for greater responsibility and higher-level jobs. This type also includes programs aimed at increasing traditional managers' awareness of and responsiveness to diversity. Eighteen of the fifty-two practices are of this type. Development practices are largely educational efforts, although exposure is often an explicit goal as well. Enforcement provisions are sometimes also built into development practices.

Chapter Six examines recruitment practices. Finding and attracting talented nontraditional managers are still an important component of many diversity efforts, although perhaps less emphasized today than in the past. Eleven of the fifty-two practices are of this type. They include tools and techniques for gaining public visibility for organizations that want to establish themselves as leaders in the diversity arena. Some organizations have very effectively used public relations techniques to promote themselves as employers of choice for nontraditional employees. The visibility that they enjoy as a result often gives them a recruitment edge. Although other benefits also accrue from having a progressive public image, the vehicles for achieving these benefits are included in the recruitment group. Recruitment practices, like development practices sometimes have built-in enforcement provisions to ensure that affirmative action steps are taken, but they generally support the education and exposure components of the strategy. Although the main thrust of recruitment practices may be to offer nontraditional managers challenging opportunities, such practices also increasingly rely on support systems and forms of recognition to make them effective.

Our categorization of diversity practices into three types — accountability, development, and recruitment — is similar to the findings of Donna Thompson and Nancy DiTomaso in their 1988 study of eight large organizations. Thompson and DiTomaso grouped organizational policies and practices into five categories: top management support and involvement, management accountability, recruiting, training and other human resource management programs, and external relations (p. 236). In addition, the three practices they found to be most important for ensuring the success of people of color in the companies they studied are the firm commitment of top management, affirmative action, and more formalized management development programs (p. 313). The similarity of these researchers' findings with ours suggests that these practices are critical to the diversity efforts of a wide range of organizations.

FOUR

ESTABLISHING ACCOUNTABILITY FOR DIVERSITY

It is 8:30 in the morning on the second day of the GOLD research team meeting. The entire team of ten interviewers and two data analysts met all day yesterday in this same conference room at the La Jolla Marriott. Today, the final day of the meeting, the researchers will discuss their perceptions of the interview responses. The walls are awash in flip charts, the results of the first day's briefings on the major findings from each of the sixteen organizations participating in the study. I open the meeting with a brief review.

> When we ended the session yesterday, we had identified a list of accountability practices that we agreed to discuss today: succession planning procedures, employee groups, pay incentives, and promotion systems. We identified these practices as key accountability tools for achieving diversity. To quickly review what we already said about accountability, we noted that different people see accountability very differently. Even those of us who interviewed people at the same company got very different impressions from different managers about the types and effectiveness of accountability practices in the company. Maybe that says something in and of itself. Despite that, here's what we know about the who, what, and how of accountability:
>
> > Who? There is definitely a pattern of viewing diversity as a shared responsibility between line and staff.

One organization even gives a cash bonus to line managers who bring in people of color who have not been identified by the human resource department.

What? Many organizations measure progress "by the numbers," and there is no apology for doing that. One company, for example, takes no personnel action without first examining the potential impact on targeted groups.

How? There are many different tools. One organization has constructed an evaluation system to "remove personal judgments" from selection decisions. A number of organizations have specific goals for managers to recruit and develop nontraditional employees. Succession plans at several organizations require identification of high-potential white women and people of color. And we were a bit surprised that employee groups in some organizations seem to have a great deal of bargaining power. At one organization, managers in an employee group felt they had the power to "force the agenda and cut out the BS."

We definitely need to spend some more time today analyzing these practices.

The importance of accountability in diversity efforts is difficult to overemphasize. Six of the seven most frequently mentioned diversity practices noted in the introduction to Part Two are related to accountability. Another sixteen of the fifty-two total practices are concerned mainly with giving managers accountability for meeting diversity goals. It is clear from our study that executives in many of the more progressive organizations rely heavily on accountability tools as a core part of their diversity efforts.

A complete list of the twenty-three accountability practices identified in our study, in rank order, is shown in Table A.10 in the appendix. (The procedure used for rank ordering is also described in the appendix.) This list is headed by top management's intervention and influence, and it contains an array of practices, including the use of employee groups and special monitoring committees of the board of directors, methods to tie performance evaluation and compensation to managers' diversity efforts, and policies that encourage flexible work arrangements and benefit packages. Two of these practices involve allocating resources to diversity efforts, such as assigning skilled personnel specialists to help facilitate meetings of employee groups and providing child-care resources to attract and retain employees. These resources, along with policies and procedures, help reinforce diversity objectives.

The use of accountability practices appears to be much more common in business than in the public sector. Two of the top six accountability practices were reportedly used *only* in the private sector: interventions in the succession planning process (ten of our twelve businesses) and the practice of tying diversity goals to managers' compensation (six businesses). The practice of linking performance appraisal goals and ratings to diversity was also reported more frequently in the private sector (ten businesses compared with two of the four public organizations in our study). Two other tools not in the top six that appear to be used only in the private sector are internal audits that address diversity issues and the practice of inspecting lists of vendors to be sure that firms run by people of color or white women are adequately represented.

Accountability tools typically pertain to managers' rseponsibility to treat nontraditional employees fairly. Many, however, are meant to ensure that managers' evaluations of subordinates and other outcomes are based on performance, which includes standards other than those pertaining to diversity. A number of managers in our study were adamant that both traditional and nontraditional managers must be accountable for their own performance level and that these tools can incorporate more objectivity into the assessment of the overall performance of all managers. The need for these tools and for greater accountability for equal treatment on the part of executives is stressed in the U.S. Department of Labor's (1991) report on the "glass ceiling initiative."

Accountability practices as a group clearly support the enforcement component of the diversity strategy. They provide the means to shape managers' behavior in ways that more actively foster diversity. Although the desired behavior includes providing more challenging opportunities to nontraditional employees, for example, in the form of rotational assignments, the emphasis of enforcement is on providing appropriate recognition for the achievements that many nontraditional managers have already accrued and on building the support systems that are often lacking for people of color and women in general at upper levels of management. Reducing pay gaps, information gaps, promotion oversights, and the impact of conflicting work and family demands are some of the goals of these enforcement tools.

How to Distribute Accountability

The allocation of accountability is a complex and delicate process. Certainly, responsibility must be distributed throughout the organization if diversity goals are to be achieved, but who should bear the burden of setting and meeting these goals? In some respects, the buck stops only at the top. All enforcement techniques require top management's direction and support. Nevertheless, hoarding responsibility for diversity is not an effective strategy for top-level executives. In Chapter Eight on the role of top management, we see how long-term efforts can be crippled by the failure of senior executives to distribute accountability for diversity throughout their organizations. The challenge to senior executives is not whether to share the burden but how to share it.

Staff Support or Line Accountability?

As more executives identify diversity goals as business objectives, accountability for diversity spreads more widely throughout the management ranks. Top executives must decide whether to rely on a staff group for some diversity activities or to expect the line management to handle diversity on its own. In the past, when affirmative action was regarded more as a government requirement than a business mandate, organizations typically set up small staff offices to see that the affirmative action guidelines were followed. These offices, whether they are separate affirmative action departments or have been blended into larger human resource functions, are still active in many organizations, relieving line managers of some responsibility for setting diversity goals, for identifying and tracking high-potential nontraditional managers, or for establishing links with schools and other sources for locating talented people of color and white women.

Having a staff group dedicated to diversity goals has certain advantages. Affirmative action or diversity offices have typically been staffed with women and people of color who are deeply committed to achieving progress. Their employment in this function improves the organization's diversity profile in itself. In some cases, the affirmative action activities have influenced the work of surrounding human resource professionals, making diversity a legitimate issue for the entire function. Allowing the somewhat specialized work of diversity to take place in a protected corner of the organization recognizes the expertise and perseverance required.

The advantages, however, may no longer justify the separation of diversity activities from mainstream business operations. While some managers we interviewed had high praise for the achievements and credibility of their affirmative action or diversity staff, others were discouraged that the staff members had not been equal to the task in terms of their competence or clout. The critics argue that because this function is still not regarded as contributing to central business objectives, the staffing process may lack rigor and there may be few avenues for this group to influence operations managers.

The challenge today seems to be to take diversity issues out of the human resource bailiwick and place the responsibility for diversity squarely on the shoulders of operations managers. One approach being considered in a few organizations is to abandon special staff groups and instead build diversity into the ongoing responsibilities of all managers. Advocates of this approach argue that diversity should be discussed and monitored as part of managers' normal work routines, just as other business objectives such as sales or customer service are often handled.

Shifting responsibility from a staff function to the line need not be an all-or-nothing proposition, however. A strong, well-defined staff may be retained to help refine diversity goals, to provide expertise and encouragement to line managers, and to compile the results of diversity activities. This kind of support does not have to interfere with integrating diversity goals and activities into the day-to-day business management; as a result, managers throughout the organization can be involved and invested in fostering diversity throughout the parts of the organization over which they have some control.

Some managers worry that without attention from a dedicated staff group, line managers may relegate diversity issues to the back burner in deference to other, more traditional business objectives. If diversity is truly to be developed, the enforcement component of the diversity strategy, as described in the following pages, must be used to keep diversity a top-of-mind issue for busy managers. Employee advocacy groups, for example, sometimes serve the same functions as internal affirmative action officers. Such employee groups may be more effective than a staff group because members are more dispersed and more familiar with various aspects of the business and because they may encourage other managers and individual contributors to share responsibility for achieving diversity goals throughout the organization.

Clearly, decisions must be made concerning which individuals and groups are accountable for planning and carrying out diversity goals. Some senior executives who have been involved in diversity efforts over the years have come to believe that wide dispersal of accountability is the key to success. The more they are able to share responsibility, they report, the more progress they make.

Two Factors in Distributing Accountability

The allocation of accountability takes many forms, but two conditions must be met to get the best results. First, it is worth saying again that top management should remain involved in the diversity process. Sharing responsibility is not the same as shirking responsibility; there is always an important role for senior executives no matter how many others are also accountable. The president of a $4 billion West Coast company explained that his managers are being evaluated on their ability to recruit, retain, train, and advance people of color and white women. These criteria are a condition throughout the corporation, from the CEO whose bonus is affected by performance in these areas down through the ranks. In short, he noted, any manager who doesn't care about diversity as a value will lose.

Many senior executives in our study want their managers to value and initiate diversity goals, but they also insist that their managers work toward diversity whether they like it or not. Top management often provides the incentive managers need to add diversity goals to their already busy work schedules. Colgate-Palmolive CEO Reuben Mark (Lee and Mark, 1990, p. 30), describes how he and other executives get managers to do more than give lip service to diversity activities through what he calls mild coercion:

> When that manager who is giving lip service knows that he or she is getting paid on three aspects — volume, profit, and individual objectives — and when those individual objectives for this particular year have to do with women in management and minority promotion, and at the end of the year he or she is going to be evaluated specifically on that, and that the money that he or she gets in March is going to reflect that, it certainly has a bit of clout. So I think you have to use those kinds of tools and use them hard.

The second condition to be met in allocating accountability effectively is to set numerical goals, although these should not be used to the exclusion of other indicators of progress in diversity. An emphasis on equal employment opportunity (EEO) statistics and workforce profiles characterize many of the diversity strategies used in the progressive organizations we studied.

Monitoring numerical measures is a critical motivator for managers. As one director of a human resource function put it, "People do whatever they think they'll be measured on. If it counts, they'll do it. If you have them set goals on things no one will ever measure, they'll never do it."

There are sensible, meaningful ways to use statistics as enforcement mechanisms. Past mistakes in enforcing statistical goals often led managers to take short-sighted, dysfunctional actions, and in some cases led to considerable white male backlash. Many executives learned the hard way that it is not enough to hire by the numbers when no provision is made either to improve the recruitment procedures or to follow through to develop and advance the new employees. Since then, some executives have broadened their statistical measures to encourage behavior leading to long-term integration of white women and people of color into management.

Statistical measures have also been adjusted to match more closely managers' control over outcomes. Instead of simply counting the number of nontraditional managers who are promoted each year, for example, promotions have been tied to the number of openings that were available in each department or subsidiary. Managers' expectations have been more closely linked to the resources and opportunities at their disposal. Even so, some executives are still unconvinced that individual managers should be accountable for what they consider to be an organizational problem. For example, Sheryl Hilliard Tucker and Kevin D. Thompson (1990) note that Xerox discontinued the practice of tying affirmative action goals to managers' compensation because some recruitment and retention problems were considered to be problems within the corporate culture, beyond individual managers' control. A couple of the organizations in our study have retreated from tying some numerical measures of diversity to managers' bonuses or merit increases for the same reason or because executives were unhappy with the short-sighted behavior that resulted. These organizations may return to linking diversity goals with managers' pay once the statistical measures are improved or once there is more widespread acceptance of diversity as a legitimate business goal toward which, like volume or profit, each manager is expected to contribute.

Many of the practices used to spread accountability for diversity among managers incorporate the two important conditions just outlined: the commitment of top management and the use of reasonable statistical measures. The effectiveness of any accountability practice may depend on how well these two conditions are met.

Accountability Tools

The specific tools used to create accountability for diversity efforts are quite varied. Those described in this section are the accountability tools most often used in the organizations we studied and among the most significant tools in their entire diversity strategy.

Internal Advocacy Groups

Groups of employees acting as lobbyists within their organizations were active in increasing accountability for diversity in more than half of the sixteen model organizations in our study. These internal advocacy groups are usually comprised of women or members of an ethnic group such as blacks, Hispanics, or Asian-Americans, and they are sometimes limited to those at a certain management level. Depending on the membership criteria, these groups range in size from only a few dozen members to thousands of members in large corporations where employees at all levels may join.

Most advocacy groups are based on the demographic characteristics of ethnicity or sex. Therefore, it is fairly common to find black managers' groups or Hispanic employees' groups, for example, which may be called networks, caucuses, or panels. Other advocacy groups have formed around other characteristics that employees share, such as those with a gay or lesbian sexual preference or those who are veterans of the Vietnam War. The number of employee groups in different organizations varies. Generally, larger organizations have more groups.

The roles and power of advocacy groups also vary dramatically from one organization to another. In some cases, these groups began as internal networks or support groups and evolved into groups that lobby and negotiate for better treatment. Most of the groups described to us as central to an organization's diversity effort have regular, direct access to the chief executive officer or chief operating officer, typically through a group's president or a small number of its officers.

Some of the negotiating power of such groups comes from the information they receive about personnel administration, although their access to information varies considerably from organization to organization. Some groups get advance notice of every major development in the organization, along with information about every opening and promotion throughout the organization. Some groups have access to even the most sensitive records concerning pay, benefits, and other employment data, and they use this information to get action. Some groups periodically review the organization's personnel profiles and recommend changes to hasten progress in diversifying management. An officer of one advocacy group described the power of his group this way: "Some white men feel serious pressure. One vice president almost got fired by the black group. He had no black distribution managers in the South. We sent a letter to [a more senior executive], and this vice president got a phone call—his job was on the line."

Why do some top executives give advocacy groups so much information? Some executives view sharing information as sharing responsibility for diversity problems and their necessary solutions. Some pointed out to us that when groups are used as a sounding board for proposed policies or actions, their early input sometimes saves the company considerable money and embarrassment. Advocacy groups represent a resource for top management; they can help top management deal with the sticky issues inherent in increasing diversity. These groups sometimes take on the difficult task of prioritizing a plethora of issues and making appropriate recommendations to senior management.

As strong as advocacy groups can be, they are not without liabilities. According to one female personnel executive, "One weakness is that we have to have it. Another is that it's becoming institutionalized. . . . We need a way to keep issues on the table, but I don't like the idea that people expect these groups to keep going. Another weakness is that it excludes 50 percent of our business — white males."

Because of these and other liabilities of advocacy groups, some executives limit how they may operate. In one case, a human resource manager was required to attend the initial organizing meeting of a group. In another case, a group was forbidden to meet until a task force had presented its recommendations for diversity activities. In some cases, a facilitator approved by top management is expected to participate in every meeting. (In these cases, the organization usually pays an outside consultant a facilitation fee.) Moreover, some groups are instructed to tie their recommendations to the organization's business plan or mission statement.

Few top managers in our study spoke in favor of the formation of advocacy groups within their organizations, and some admitted feeling anxious when such groups were created. Nevertheless, the advocacy groups that have evolved and that appear to be effective in promoting diversity for their organizations have the confidence of senior management to give considered, helpful advice. Therefore, these groups get attention and the resources to continue their advocacy. A white male vice president who witnessed the evolution of advocacy groups in his company during his thirty-year tenure explained the relationship between these groups and the company's officers this way: "Other companies don't think of an advocacy group as a crucial, high-level change agent in the company. They think of it as a group they "permit." If officers don't spend significant time with them, advocacy groups won't be any good. Our groups continue because of their positive impact, their inviting collaboration by the company's leadership, and the value they bring. They are not adversarial; if they were, they wouldn't exist anymore."

Groups that refrain from being advocates for individuals have the most credibility throughout the organization, according to several managers we interviewed. Although it is difficult for group members to ignore an individual's plea for help, they find it is necessary to limit their advocacy to the policy level in order to fulfill their mandate. Some group leaders who made the mistake of arguing individual cases were described in our interviews as failures.

One concern about advocacy groups and those employee networks in general that are open only to members of one ethnic group is that they will contribute to the fragmentation and infighting that are divisive to nontraditional employees as a whole. Some managers would rather have a task force or committee representing members of both sexes and various ethnic groups, which may build cohesion and keep efforts from being duplicated from one group to another. The closest thing we saw to this concept was a task force formed in one company by representatives of various advocacy groups to decide on the immediate priorities for the diversity effort. For employees who are not ready to be represented by a demographically mixed group, a combination such as this may be a way to capture the advantages of each type of group.

Some managers in our study were anxious that advocacy groups might become the unions of the future, with the potential to strangle organizations in lengthy negotiations over all sorts of employment conditions. Any employee group needs to be managed with care and consideration, sharing responsibility with senior management for both the process and the outcome of diversity efforts. When that is done, the group's strength in distributing accountability throughout an organization can be very impressive.

Administrative Practices

Progressive organizations commonly revise the procedures used in personnel administration to increase accountability and thus foster diversity. Although this practice is somewhat less drastic than forming advocacy groups, it is typically recommended by the advocacy groups that operate. All but one of the organizations in our study have modified existing administrative procedures to give managers more incentive to accept and include nontraditional managers. Three types of administrative procedures are most commonly revised: performance evaluations and consequent financial rewards, succession planning, and promotion systems. The first two, as pointed out earlier, are more common in the private sector than in the public sector.

Many managers in our study believe that changes in these administrative procedures are both symbolic and operationally necessary to convince employees that diversity is both desirable and possible. Such reinforcement is essential because of the time and effort managers must expend, in addition to their other duties, to find, prepare, and advance women and people of color. It isn't easy to combat the advancement barriers that have thwarted nontraditional managers for so long. That is why so many organizations have revised their accountability practices in recent years to include more emphasis on and more consequences for managing nontraditional managers, as well as people in general.

Most organizations begin with the performance appraisal process. Twelve of the sixteen organizations in our study have revised their appraisal procedures, supplementing traditional performance standards with specific expectations about hiring and developing nontraditional employees. Increasingly, appraisals include the effective use of human resources along with goals related to other business factors; diversity goals are typically included in the human resource area. Numerical goals are often included to measure progress against expectations and these goals tend to be broken down by department or division so that unit managers have specific goals for their own area.

One organization in our study with revenues exceeding $25 billion includes diversity goals along with profitability, commitment to co-workers, and customer service as one of four standard factors in managers' performance appraisals. Measurement of all these goals is expected as part of the evaluation process. Another large company in our study that includes affirmative action goals as part of the "people management" in managers' performance appraisals includes specific measurement standards for performance. Performance expectations are in the form of specific numbers and percentages of nontraditional employees in several professional and managerial job categories as well as in a manager's total unit. Each manager who has responsibility for hiring or promoting at these levels is expected to outline an action plan for meeting the numerical expectations. Other diversity goals are also encouraged as part of this management-by-objectives (MBO) appraisal system.

Some organizations have bolstered their evaluation systems with additional performance data from sources other than the managers themselves and their bosses. Responses from attitude surveys, for example, are occasionally used as part of managers' formal evaluations. Subordinates' responses to items about how fairly they are treated and the opportunities available to them are not only given to managers but are also used in calculating an overall evaluation rating. In at least one organization, the responses are carefully screened to include in the evaluation only those factors over which a manager has control. The representation of nontraditional managers above a certain level, for example, would not be considered for a manager who has no say in hiring or promoting at those levels.

In some organizations, unfavorable survey responses require a manager to prepare an action plan for improvement, whereas very favorable responses require no additional work. Unfavorable results may be determined by a particular cutoff point on the scale used (anything less than a 3.5 on a scale of 1 to 5, for example), or they may be deemed unfavorable strictly in relation to the results of other managers surveyed within the organization. In a company not in our study, the managers whose results fall into the bottom quartile of all those surveyed are required to be resurveyed eighteen months later rather than proceeding through the normal three-year cycle, and they are expected to show improvement. The extra work involved in explaining responses that are less than stellar and in correcting the conditions that prompted those responses serves as an additional incentive to managers to meet diversity goals.

After including diversity goals in the performance evaluation, the next step and one that organizations often take is to attach consequences to managers' evaluations in the form of merit pay or bonuses that correspond to their performance ratings. In the earlier MBO example, a manager's bonus is determined by the performance level documented on the appraisal form. In this case, profitability goals account for less than half of the overall performance rating. People management, including diversity management, and the quality of the company's products account for the majority of managers' performance goals and, consequently, are the principal bases for the annual bonuses. Theoretically, when such performance data is fed into a financial calculation, there is more incentive for managers to do a good job in managing their people and building a good working environment for them. However, the financial impact of performance on diversity issues must be significant to effect a change in managers' behavior, and some organizations still fall short in this regard.

Bonus calculations are usually made by matching the proportion of the performance goals to the proportion of the bonus. If, for example, 10 percent of a manager's goals deal with diversity, then 10 percent of her or his bonus is affected by performance in that area. What this means for most managers is that only a very small part of their compensation is affected by the progress they make on diversity. Managers who meet only 50 percent of their diversity goals, in this example, would receive half of the 10 percent portion related to diversity, and their overall bonuses would be cut by only 5 percent. The question they must ask themselves is "Will all the extra work to find and develop nontraditional employees pay off for me?" All too often, the financial reward is not enough to change what managers have been doing for most of their lives. Carla O'Dell and Jerry McAdams (1986) suggest that any cash incentive to change behavior must be at least 5 to 8 percent of an employee's salary.

A stronger way to link diversity progress to compensation is being tried in at least one organization in our study. The requirement is to reach a minimum level of goal achievement in each performance area to receive any bonus. That is, a manager has to meet 80 percent of his or her goals in the human resource or diversity area and in each of the other performance areas to be eligible for any bonus. Even if the manager achieves 80 percent of the goals in all other performance areas but only

50 percent of the diversity goals, then the manager receives no bonus at all. This type of calculation, in which one performance area is contingent upon others, prevents any one area from being neglected.

Two premises lie behind such a contingency technique for determining pay or other administrative consequences. One is that people development is at least as important as other performance criteria. The second premise is that managers have as much control over the development of people as they have over the other business indicators that are measured. If these two premises are accepted, then such a contingency technique makes a good deal of sense.

Putting more punch into individual performance appraisals is a practice reported in three-quarters of the organizations we studied. Six of the sixteen organizations tied diversity goals to financial rewards such as merit increases or bonuses. It is difficult, however, to break traditions about what a manager's job entails, even when explicit standards are used. The idea of holding managers accountable for development of people is still an uncomfortable one for many executives, and the revised administrative systems are not always carried out as they were intended. One black woman reporting to the president of her company noted that the consequences of poor performance on diversity goals are often waived. "We still forgive too much regarding our affirmative action programs," she told us. "We should have kept the targets and worked harder to reach them. When we fall behind, we shouldn't postpone the deadlines. If a woman is a high-potential corporate resource and her manager hasn't done anything to develop her, we should hold that manager accountable."

It is commonly accepted that hiring, developing, and promoting people depend on a number of other factors and business conditions. Managers who don't meet their goals in this area often get a sympathetic ear from their superiors, and compromises are struck. When business conditions change or when other business events upstage diversity activities, these goals are often dismissed as impossible. For example, according to one employee, "A ton of legitimate reasons are given for the lack of upward mobility. The latest reason for not promoting [minorities] is that there is a surplus of directors and officers since we just consolidated one big piece of the company."

Other problems also complicate the process of making managers accountable for diversity. Performance appraisals are notorious for being inexact and infrequent. Merit pay and bonus systems are susceptible to blandness, if not manipulation; many managers, for example, would rather pay all employees the same average merit increase to avoid having to explain to them why some got bigger raises than others. To fortify their efforts to hold managers accountable for diversity, it is no surprise that six of the twelve organizations in our study that use performance evaluation as a diversity tool also use pay incentives, and all twelve rely on revisions in their succession planning or the promotion/selection process to bolster the influence of managers' evaluations on diversity. These packages of programs may help them enforce diversity more effectively.

In the area of management succession planning procedures, many organizations have not been substantially changed to accommodate diversity goals. Instead, nontraditional managers and employees have been explicitly included as high-potential candidates for future openings in the organization's key management positions. Through the urging or demands of top management and with the aid of detective work by the human resource staff to identify nontraditional candidates, managers are required to include people of color and white women on their annual list of replacement candidates. Alternately, in some cases, managers are instead expected to create a separate list of women and people of color who are their top candidates for promotion. Senior managers in particular are sometimes told to come to a key personnel meeting with lists of the top ten women in their unit, the top ten people of color, and the top ten white men they consider to be the best candidates for their own and other key managers' positions. Naturally, it does little good to have nontraditional managers on replacement charts if they are never selected, so in some of the more progressive organizations, the process of building more diversity into succession planning doesn't stop with lists. At the insistence of the

CEO and president of one company, for example, all of the people who report directly to them are expected to meet and get acquainted with everyone on the "top ten" lists of people of color, women, and white men presented at the annual replacement planning meeting. This kind of intervention ensures that nontraditional candidates will not be overlooked by executives who may be more inclined to stick with the managers they have known over the years.

Such forced familiarization may seem to be an artificial way to create opportunities for nontraditional managers, but it can be an effective way to save some talented people from obscurity. Those identified on replacement charts are expected to be nurtured, tested, and noticed by managers in positions to advance them. Specific development plans are sometimes created for each person on the list to move each of them along the fast track; operations managers share responsibility for carrying out these plans. Thus, accountability for managing these few corporate human resources is spread across an influential group of managers.

Interventions in succession planning are generally not visible to most managers because of the extreme secrecy normally accorded the process itself and the resulting lists of high-potential candidates. In contrast, intervening in promotions can be a very visible signal to a large cadre of managers that things are changing and that the expectations of top management now include advancement of nontraditional managers. For this reason, promotion policies and procedures are receiving considerable attention in some organizations.

Management promotions often represent the culmination of years of development and preparation, yet the subjectivity of promotion practices often cuts nontraditional managers off from serious consideration. According to our study, discomfort with someone who is "different" and the use of higher standards to assess people of color and women in general are among the key reasons for differential treatment of nontraditional candidates, and these are being recognized and corrected in some organizations. One white male executive we interviewed explained how different the promotion standards are in his organization. Managers are so afraid that a person of color might fail in a higher-level job that they delay the promotion, he explained. Because of this, when people of color are eventually promoted, they rarely fail. White men who are promoted, in contrast, have much more leeway and a higher failure rate. His judgment was that for every white man who is successfully promoted, three fail in the new job.

While other organizations might not tolerate such a high failure rate, many of them do use a "high risk, high reward" promotion strategy to stretch high-potential traditional managers. Failure to do the same for people of color and white women is a signal that they are not considered to have high potential. Building more objective criteria into promotion decisions is one approach being used to give equal opportunity to nontraditional managers. The track record of nontraditional managers, which includes quantifiable results such as sales increases or quality improvements, is used whenever possible to dispel doubts about their competence or appropriateness for higher-level posts. Including job analysis data in selection decisions and using more sophisticated selection techniques such as assessment center exercises are other methods that can help control the subjectivity of the process.

In the 1950s, AT&T developed assessment centers to identify high-potential managers. Since they were required as part of the 1973 AT&T consent decree to identify promotable women within the company, assessment centers have played an important role over the years in creating equal opportunity for nontraditional managers. Some organizations have begun to rely on assessment center techniques to assess the potential of both traditional and nontraditional managers. Some managers may believe that using assessment center technology is a foolproof way to ensure fair treatment, but that is not the case. Researchers Richard J. Klimonski and William J. Strickland (1977) caution that the assessment center raters may be accurate in their predictions not because they are objectively assessing managers' skills but because they can anticipate how other managers in the organization, their colleagues, will react to them. Assessment center operations, like any other selection method, require rigor.

One approach to promotion that may help avoid problems is to build diversity into the decision-making bodies. In some of the organizations in our study, women and people of color are regularly included on panels that evaluate, select, and promote managers. The problem of assessing promotion candidates who are "different" can be reduced if some of the decision makers are nontraditional managers themselves. Such representation also helps assure that seemingly objective criteria will be interpreted fairly across lines of sex and ethnicity. Having the perspective of nontraditional evaluators along with that of white men, even when the criteria are clearly specified such as in an assessment center, may be instrumental in controlling subjectivity in the promotion process.

Making the promotion process more responsive to the need for diversity may mean simply sweeping aside traditional excuses for not promoting people of color or women. When promotion panels are diverse, according to a white female manager in our study, those excuses are easier to dismiss. In her experience on promotion panels, she has encountered and countered a lot of excuses that her fellow panel members would have used to rule out nontraditional candidates had she not intervened. Among the excuses she cited were the following:

> She looks so young.
> I'm not sure a black man would make it in that city.
> If he just had one more degree . . .
> She's pregnant.
> She's just had a baby.
> She'll never move.

Accountability means having to adequately justify situations in which women and people of color are not considered or not selected for promotions, whether a policy to that effect exists or not.

Direct intervention by top-level executives in the selection and promotion process is sometimes necessary to ensure that diversity goals are not overlooked. Procedures to include and even to fairly assess nontraditional candidates may be in place, but they may not be extensive enough to counter the subtle, informal deterrents that prevent people of color and white women from advancing. We found that executives who did some digging on their own to find the underlying reasons for differential promotion rates got some unpleasant surprises. For example, one executive promoted to head a regional office was disturbed to find that there were no female field representatives in that region. When he was told there were no female applicants, he decided to check it out. "When I talked to the women there," he told us, "I discovered they had refused field jobs because, they said, 'They'll get us.' The men told them they'd be assaulted and raped in the field." He took direct, unprecedented action to begin to remedy the situation. He went to one of his managers and told him to promote a qualified woman from his group to field representative immediately. And he cautioned the manager, "If she fails, you fail."

In another case, a major public incident involving black managers at a large company prompted top management to begin an investigation. A key manager was assigned to investigate the incident and the issue of racism within the company. He discovered that the formal administrative procedures to assess promotability were not adequate to ensure that people of color would in fact be promoted. According to this manager, "One issue that blacks brought up was, We keep getting developed to get developed to get developed. . . . For example, one black man with two degrees was told he was qualified for a job as branch manager. He was rated "ready now" on the form. But he was never interviewed when the job opened. Instead, they brought in a white manager who was failing in his current job." This key manager also took immediate, unprecedented action to fix at least part of the problem. On the spot, he got another branch manager promoted so that the black candidate could move into his job.

The potential impact of changes in administrative procedures such as performance evaluation and allocation of pay, succession planning, and selection and promotion procedures can be enormous. These and other administrative tools help distribute accountability for diversity throughout the organization. They don't automatically guarantee that barriers will be broken down, but they can be extremely effective when energy and attention are devoted to them, including the relentless support of senior executives. Other types of reinforcement may also be needed to support these administrative procedures, such as general policies against racism and sexism. Such policies set the tone for how procedures will be carried out, and they give people who feel unfairly treated a way to address problems. Many organizations, for example, have policies or mission statements that emphasize humane and fair treatment of all employees; such instruments can provide a basis for taking action against differential treatment. One Native American manager, for example, described the outcome when senior management began punishing managers who violated the company's policies on diversity:

> Middle managers have been fired. There have been three cases, two within the last two years. One involved verbal abuse of homosexuals — they took their cases to the EEO group, and the manager was given a warning. Then it happened again, so they fired the manager. Another middle manager was fired for sexual harassment of a secretary, and another was abusive. This sends a powerful message that first comes through the grapevine and then comes down from vice presidents to their managers: inappropriate behavior will not be accepted.

Clear standards and values that rule out racism and sexism as acceptable behaviors under any circumstances reinforce the practices that affect one individual after another. An organization's mission statement and key policies have the potential to influence all the major accountability practices mentioned here. They may also influence other accountability tools some organizations use, such as a grievance procedure or a complaint resolution process for customers. While these particular tools may be less directly linked with upward mobility at senior levels, they can be important in building the pipeline and reputation that will keep talented nontraditional managers from leaving an organization.

The effective use of modified procedures for evaluation, promotion, and the allocation of financial rewards to foster diversity is also dependent on the availability of qualified nontraditional candidates. Candidates must not only be recruited, but they must be adequately prepared to take on demanding managerial assignments. Chapter Five examines a number of development techniques.

FIVE

CREATING MEANINGFUL DEVELOPMENT OPPORTUNITIES

It is late Tuesday afternoon, several weeks after the research team meeting. Two of the team members are sitting with me around a table in my office at the Center for Creative Leadership. We are trying to identify core elements of the development programs used in the model organizations. Interview notes from one of the organizations have been pulled from the file to illustrate a thorough, well-designed program. We are looking through the interviews held with managers who participated in that development program to get their point of view. What did these participants say about the program? One researcher offers this information:

> Here's something from a line manager who participated in that development program. She is a black woman, thirty years old, single, with a master's degree in international business. The notes from her interview read: "First there was an intense evaluation, the basis for realistic five-year goals. Career planning modules were required, including interviewing senior officers to address the question "Do I want to be part of their organization?" A self-evaluation helped us identify our own deficiencies, and we got intense feedback from the HR manager and our coaches. The plan we submitted was either blessed or revised, and then we had to do all the legwork ourselves. We had to find our own mentor in the part of the organization we wanted to go into, someone above the fourth level, where there were mostly white men."

The other researcher adds the following information from another interview:

> This manager, who has an M.B.A., also went through that program. He is now a staff assistant to the senior vice president. He is a twenty-seven-year-old Hispanic man, married, with no children. He said in the interview, "I've been real lucky. I have an excellent mentor. We wrote a contract that includes what I expect from him, like training and visits. He flies in once a month to meet with me. My plan states time frames and exact jobs. This job is my first promotion, which will last six to nine months. Next will be a promotion to managing in the field, for six to nine months. Then back into this organization to manage my current peers. Then I move into the director level in a field facility. My mentor is to keep me informed of these openings as they come up. He's been very active. Others aren't."

We find notes from another interview with a manager who was accepted into the same program. This manager has a director-level staff position at corporate headquarters. She's white, forty-three years old, married with two stepchildren, and she has a bachelor's degree in psychology. Her comments are mostly about the feedback she has received in the program:

> We are evaluated. We get lengthy appraisals quarterly, with a numerical rating. We know how we are impacting the business unit that has picked us up. How am I different? I'm much more enlightened, more aware of my deficiencies and strengths I never knew I had. I'm more aware of verbal communication, and the underlying meaning of what is said. I'm more aware of strategies for controlling situations. For example, when I was at a meeting and I gave a good idea and others didn't agree, my first reaction was to get angry. I learned to network before the meeting, even weeks ahead, to get supporters. I control the outcome. And I'm more aware of how to turn things around in my favor. This job, for example. They flatly refused to train me because they knew I was on the fast track. I got no support. My manager wouldn't

meet with me. I called my mentor, and he let me vent and kept me from complaining to my manager's boss. He told me to send a memo to my manager to set up a meeting.

On the basis of this information and earlier discussions, the researchers and I conclude that the developmental program we have been examining includes the following core elements: abundant feedback, rigorous appraisal, mentoring, proactive career planning by participants and the company, and fast track promotions. In other words, this development program appears to be strong because it has several components and the active participation of outside managers as well as the participants themselves.

Development has been the missing link in the diversity efforts of many organizations. Some executives have assumed that building a critical mass of nontraditional workers at lower levels would ensure that "the cream would rise to the top." Some executives who have brought a white woman or a person of color into the management ranks have assumed that integration and growth would occur. In many cases, the anticipated results failed to occur.

The CEO of one organization commissioned a task force to improve recruiting of nontraditional employees in the organization. After investigating the situation, the task force members informed the CEO that the organization's diversity problems were due more to a lack of development of the recruits than to recruitment problems per se.

Development that is assumed rather than managed continues to be the Achilles' heel of many otherwise strong diversity efforts. Education of both nontraditional and traditional managers is needed to make enforcement a realistic process and to encourage constructive interaction among white men, white women, and women and men of color. Development practices inform traditional managers about the need and the means to foster diversity, and this may increase their willingness and ability to take some initiative toward diversity or at least to comply with basic expectations about their behavior toward nontraditional managers. Most development tools, however, concentrate on preparing nontraditional employees for greater responsibility and advancement.

Development practices are needed to address the advancement barriers identified in our study, including the number two barrier, poor career planning and development that holds many nontraditional managers back. Development practices address all three aspects of the goal of sustained leadership development: they can provide challenge to aspiring executives, accelerating the depth and richness of the learning that will enable them to handle top jobs; they can provide recognition (simply being selected for an accelerated program, for example, is one form of recognition); and they can also provide support, for example, through collegial gatherings with other nontraditional and traditional managers outside their department or normal reporting relationships.

Emphasis on the use of development tools to help achieve diversity is relatively new compared with the use of recruitment tools and some accountability practice. Even in our model organizations, adding or tailoring development practices to aid diversity objectives is still somewhat new and in some cases represents the weakest part of their diversity efforts. Perhaps because development tools are relatively new in the diversity arsenal, they are a subject of argument. Some arguments center on the best way to prepare and integrate nontraditional managers, and other arguments are concerned with developing traditional managers to improve their ability to value and manage diversity.

As with other types of practices, there is a vast array of development programs and activities. Table A.11 in the appendix shows eighteen kinds of formal and informal practices that are used in the organizations we studied. The rest of this chapter describes various types of development programs and techniques, along with some of the benefits and pitfalls of each. The following eight developmental tools ranked highest in our study:

1. Diversity training programs (used in ten organizations)
2. Networks or support groups within the organization (nine organizations)

3. "Fast track" development programs for employees desig-
    nated as high potential (seven organizations)
4. Informal internal networking activities (eight organizations)
5. Job rotation (seven organizations)
6. Formal mentoring programs (seven organizations)
7. Informal mentoring programs (seven organizations)
8. Entry development programs for newly hired employees
    designated as high potential (four organizations).

Most of the organizations we studied use several types of
development tools. In fact, six of the organizations reported using
at least eight different development practices. Some of these appear to be used more frequently in the public sector than in business, while the reverse is true for only one tool. Of the top eight
tools listed above, job rotation and formal mentoring programs
were reported more often in public institutions. All four public
organizations but only three of the twelve businesses in our study
used job rotation. Three of the four public organizations had
formal mentoring programs, whereas only four of the twelve businesses had such programs. Another development tool—programs
to interest employees in management or administrative jobs—was
also used in more public organizations (two, compared with only
one business). We found no apparent reasons for these differences. The one development tool reported more frequently in
the private sector is a high-potential development program limited
to women or to people of color (used in five businesses but no
public sector organizations). It is possible that executives in
government and education have had less freedom to restrict activities to members of certain demographic groups.

In the following discussion, development practices are
categorized according to four main types that represent the array of possible technique: diversity training programs, development programs, mentors and networks, and assessment and
feedback.

Diversity Training Programs

Diversity training programs, typically labeled "Valuing Diversity" or "Managing Diversity," aim to make people more aware

of the issues and the opportunities that exist in reducing differential treatment, including awareness of the attitudes, behaviors, and biases that make advancement more difficult for nontraditional managers. Such programs attempt to change people's attitudes about those who are different from them. In most cases, the programs are designed to help white male managers recognize the prejudice they may have toward women and people of different ethnic backgrounds. This is an important goal because our research shows that prejudice is the number one barrier to advancement for nontraditional managers.

The idea that traditional managers need some kind of special training to help them participate in achieving diversity goals is becoming more widely accepted. The results of a survey by John Fernandez (1981) showed that of all the potential candidates for some sort of special training, white men were seen as most needy by virtually all groups of managers, including white men themselves. Nearly half (47 percent) of the managers surveyed said that white men have special training needs; only about 35 percent said that women or people of color need special training.

Potential Benefits of Training

A manager in our study described diversity training programs as "good background music" to the policies and practices that shape people's behavior. In contrast to some managers who believe that employees' attitudes and biases are irrelevant to employers (so long as employees' behavior isn't discriminatory), this manager feels an obligation to shape employees' attitudes so that they are more in line with the behavior expected of them; thus employees are moved toward upholding the "spirit of the law" instead of simply complying with rules. The education diversity training programs offer can be an important supplement to the education most managers normally receive.

A well-designed diversity training program is an eye-opening experience that can provoke managers to change their behavior toward nontraditional employees. Until they participate in such a training program, many white managers are unaware of how women and people of color view them. Through diversity training, some white men (and others as well) face the intellectual and emotional struggle to recognize their own racism or sexism, though as we will see, this must be done in a way that respects their feelings. One academic, Peggy McIntosh (1988), has tried to capture that struggle in her writing, as she herself comes to terms with the unearned privilege she has accepted and enjoyed all her life: "I began to count the ways in which I enjoy unearned skin privilege and have been conditioned into oblivion about its existence, unable to see that it put me ahead in any way, or put my people ahead, overrewarding us and yet also paradoxically damaging us, or that it could or should be changed" (p. 4).

Educating managers about how they inadvertently contribute to differential treatment may help them change their behavior. Diversity training may also help people understand the roots of prejudice. Many people, for example, don't know that Anglos' negative attitudes toward Mexicans grew out of the strong feelings of the English against Catholics and Spaniards while they were settling in North America. Education about historical events and superstitious fears may prompt people to reconsider their assumptions about other groups. Understanding how prejudice hurts co-workers may also lead to change. Some men who attended a meeting of their organization's women's employee group, for example, were horrified to learn about the cruel and dangerous hazing stunts that their female colleagues had been subjected to in their own organization. The personal pain revealed to them as these women recounted their experience gave the men some insight into the toll prejudice takes.

One controversial aspect of diversity training programs is how the issue of group identity versus individual differences is handled. Alerting managers to group differences based on culture and socialization is an important step toward valuing diversity, but relying too much on sex or ethnic group identity to explain individuals' feelings or behavior does a disservice to diversity education. For example, emphasizing Hispanics' reluctance to disagree with co-workers without also pointing out variations among the various ethnic groups typically included under the umbrella term *Hispanics* (people with roots in Mexico versus Cuba, for instance, or those who live in Los Angeles versus Tucson or Miami) and without noting the variations from one individual to another can reinforce thinking about people as stereotypes rather than as individuals.

One technique used to debunk stereotypes is to highlight the positive aspects of various nontraditional groups, increasing the likelihood that traditional managers will see nontraditional managers in a more positive light. A middle-aged black woman, for example, told us that some traits historically seen as black traits are now seen as desirable managerial characteristics. Her company is one of many that used to follow a rigid business plan in a regulated environment with direction from the parent organization. In the current environment of competition and uncertainty, company executives value managers' flexibility, their ability to react quickly to changing situations. In this woman's training program, the seminar leader commented that blacks do that better than anyone else, citing as evidence the so-called black style of "hot dogging" in playing basketball or running a football. The woman noted that the reaction of the whites in the class was to counter, "Blacks aren't the only ones who do that."

The mark of a good diversity training program, according to a number of managers we interviewed, is that it helps break down stereotypic thinking. Many factors contribute to the way people are: race, sex, and cultural background are certainly important. However, other factors, including living and working conditions, education, and individual personality characteristics, are also important. Education that allows managers to untangle their stereotypic attitudes toward others is an important vehicle for adding meaning to the policies and procedures used to change managers' behavior.

Types of Diversity Training Programs

Diversity training comes in many different forms. The classroom education format is the most common; in it, small groups of perhaps twelve to thirty managers meet for up to three days in the company's training facility or at a local hotel. Instead of assuming a lecture format, however, the training may consist mainly of experiential exercises and discussions that help participants examine their own assumptions about people who are "different." Videotapes that illustrate situations in which white women or people of color are discounted may be used to prompt discussion. Theater groups from universities have also been used to act out situations and then take questions from the audience. Because prejudice goes unchecked and unchallenged when it is kept under wraps and there are few if any other legitimate forums in which to discuss prejudice, getting employees to talk openly about their feelings and opinions is the goal that many facilitators of these programs set.

The results of training programs that foster open disclosure, however, are mixed. On the positive side, graduates of these programs may find it easier and more acceptable to give on-the-spot feedback to co-workers than to let resentment build up within them. A Native American woman in a technical field pointed out that people in her company are now more willing to express their feelings when something is said that hurts or offends them. She commented that the education programs have "empowered people to say, 'I'm worthy of not being talked to that way.'" Such immediate, focused confrontations may keep anger from building up over time and give people a greater sense of control over their working conditions, perhaps contributing to the decrease in union grievances that she also mentioned.

On the other hand, programs that encourage open disclosure can also exacerbate problems if they focus on confrontation without providing adequate education. Some programs have become thinly disguised reprimands to white men about their prejudicial ways. For example, one pluralism class that was meant to help people understand the perceptions and feelings of others turned into a one-sided faultfinding exercise. According to one manager, a white man was put in the center of the class and harassed, upsetting others in the class and making the intergroup situation worse than it was before. Short-term programs may be especially prone to increasing tension by opening wounds related to prejudice and then running out of time to treat them adequately. As a result, participants, angry that they have been exposed, may become even more glued to their preexisting stereotypic beliefs.

Management of the education process and the confrontations that normally result from disclosure is clearly an issue in training. Training that includes any taste of vengeance can easily backfire. The ability of the facilitators to turn a tension-ridden process into a constructive learning experience is a key factor in effective programs, as is making sure that adequate resources are available to participants during and after the training. A woman of color who had participated in a five-day training program with more than twenty others felt that more than two trainers should have been involved in the program to help participants deal with the sensitive, emotional issues that were raised. Furthermore, she concluded, trainers should have been available for consultation after the training because the other participants, however supportive, are not prepared to deal with the major issues. Such a shortage of resources, in her view, has a destructive result: "Some people leave training with more biases or more emotional problems than they had when they came in."

Alternative training forms that will perhaps better integrate constructive confrontations into an ongoing search for solutions are currently being tested. A few organizations have formed small groups of employees, sometimes called core groups, that meet regularly every few weeks to explore diversity issues. A major advantage of this type of training is that it allows group members to develop a relationship over time, sometimes with people of the opposite sex or those from different ethnic backgrounds, so that they can build a supportive climate and learn from one another. While some managers have high praise for this form of training, others believe that the structure—or lack of it—is a liability. The often unsupervised process, they fear, inadequately protects members from psychological beatings and other dangers of intensive, interpersonal training. The dangers may be minimized if time is devoted in the early stages to building familiarity and camaraderie or if a group is more homogeneous. One black woman speaking at a conference, for example, commented that her experience in a black female core group had been very positive and that core groups seem to work best when diversity is limited to the same sex or race. If this is the case, then managers might question the educational impact that such homogeneous groups have.

Training to increase awareness of stereotypes and prejudice is sometimes supplemented by specific instruction concerning the organization's affirmative action policies and procedures. Managers are often unclear about the purposes of affirmative action, and their misunderstandings lead to problems in implementation. Training programs that combine these two goals communicate the rationale behind increasing diversity in the management ranks and the expectations senior management has for all managers in meeting diversity goals.

In sum, on the plus side, training programs clearly have a role in extending a commitment to diversity from a few top managers to those who have day-to-day responsibilities for hiring, developing, promoting, and supporting people of color and white women. Education and discussion forums can help managers move beyond mere compliance and take the initiative in making diversity a reality. Training that is pinpointed to a particular group or goal may be helpful, even necessary, in a diversity plan. Diversity training for a mixed group of high-potential managers, for example, may be an extremely effective supplement to the exposure they get to people unlike themselves through other activities. Training programs that focus on the organization's diversity policies and practices — why they were put into place, how they work, and progress made and expected — also appear to have enormous potential in supporting change efforts.

On the minus side, however, the usefulness of many diversity training programs is questionable. A stand-alone "quick fix" training program may give the illusion that diversity is a priority, but it is unrealistic to expect much from it. A black executive in our study who was responsible for diversity issues in his company referred to one short-term, sensitivity-group type of program as "a crock" because "it is ludicrous to expect that you could change the attitudes of white male managers in half a day." It may also be overly optimistic to expect that a two-day or even a five-day training program, by itself, can counter the forty or fifty years of socialization that many managers have experienced.

At their worst, diversity training programs can be an expensive and risky distraction from other developmental activities. Besides the potential downsides already mentioned, legal issues may also be involved. According to Stevens (1991), notes from a training program at Lucky Stores may be used as evidence of discriminatory attitudes of company officials. Such legal liabilities add to the risk of training programs that encourage disclosure. In short, diversity training, particularly in one-shot doses, may be a waste of resources that could be better invested in other development activities, such as those described in the next section.

Development Programs

While diversity training programs focus on diversity as a management issue, development programs relate to a variety of management skills and issues. Some development programs are aimed at increasing the representation of nontraditional managers in senior management by selectively providing preparation and career opportunities. Such programs offer assistance in the form of training, assessment and feedback, coaching and guidance, and broadening job experiences, factors generally recognized as important for anyone's advancement into senior management.

The development program described in the vignette at the beginning of this chapter is such a program, one of the more structured and comprehensive ones we encountered in our study. One participating manager recalled some of the program's history and described how carefully participants were screened and selected.

> Two previous programs didn't last. One was a program to put women in nontraditional jobs. It just got you in the door, then you were stuck. The other was a one-week assessment program that was going along, but then senior management would change, and new criteria were needed or used by them.

This program is the only one I know of that has survived. A representative from each employee group (blacks, Hispanics, and so on) was involved in the planning, and several people spent every weekend for two years developing this program. We targeted top management as our audience, and we went to each ahead of time and then made a presentation. We asked for three things: a fast-track program for minorities, that each growing business unit create its own action plan for diversity because the most opportunities would be at those units, and that top management sponsor a one-day meeting for seventy-five handpicked key managers to explain the issues to them and ask them to be change agents.

The limited fast-track program was a one-time only proposition. After that, we would have a mix of people in an ongoing fast-track program. Applications for the new program were very extensive — six pages, which took three or four days to fill out. Then there was an audiotaped interview with an HR manager, which lasted three to four hours. They also interviewed candidates' managers, for about the same amount of time. There were 6,000 eligible minorities; 1,800 applied. Fifty were chosen by a committee. It was all done on a point system, with points for education, foreign language, outside activities such as community or church work and fundraisers, and so on. Since many candidates were in very structured jobs, we needed to look outside the job for indicators of leadership potential.

Most development programs are not as formal and comprehensive as the one just described, either by intent or because of limited resources. Certainly the expense of development provides a compelling impetus to limit what is included in a program, but saving money isn't the only important guideline in designing a program. We found, for example, that even terminoloy is an issue in some organizations. Some managers feel that the idea of a "program" contradicts the somewhat free-flowing, ongoing learning process that they see as the ideal developmental thrust, and they hesitate to construct a separate set of activities for development.

The designers of a development program must address at least three basic questions:

1. What kinds of training components will be included, and how structured will the training be?
2. Who is eligible for the program?
3. How "public" will the program and the participants be?

Training Components and Frequency

Some development programs focus on training as a way to prepare candidates for higher management posts. The training provided as part of a development program is usually not focused on diversity issues per se but rather on management skills and aspects of leadership development such as communication and networking. The perceived lack of organizational savvy that keeps many nontraditional managers disadvantaged is something that formal education alone is unlikely to correct. The content of training components supplements what is typically covered in formal education, and the "schmoozing" participants do with the presenters and with one another may be at least as important as the training content. Being able to associate faces with names and getting acquainted with individuals whom they will later feel comfortable calling often benefit both the participants and the presenters.

An annual development program in one educational institution involves semimonthly seminars with key insiders and well-known outside professionals, who inform participants about current issues in education and what is going on in their own institution. These meetings, at which speakers are expected to express themselves openly about issues important to them, give participants not only factual information but also an understanding of why people feel and behave the way they do in their jobs. The network built through such a program can be an aspiring executive's chief asset.

The reason that the practice of sponsoring regular monthly seminars is commonly used as part of development programs in organizations may be that this has become the preferred format for well-known community leadership development programs. In these programs, leaders of a city or metropolitan area (such as the mayor, officers of local corporations, and county commissioners) and sometimes their antagonists (third-party political candidates, officers of environmental groups, and so forth) present their views on local issues to a small group of selected citizens interested in becoming more involved in community activities. The interaction with local movers and shakers gives citizens better preparation to take active roles in managing their community. In an organization, a monthly seminar series might involve department heads or division presidents explaining the work of their units along with their goals, achievements, and frustrations.

Monthly classroom sessions incorporated into a larger development program can help nontraditional managers build their knowledge of and exposure to influential people. However, some nontraditional managers feel that they also need a more flexible type of training to advance. What some call "existence training" focuses on how to survive in the organization, how to politic, and other kinds of inside information that typically, according to one Hispanic woman, "has been given on the golf course or whatever by white men to white men." This kind of training can be difficult to incorporate into a formal training curriculum because it may require a great deal of interaction with company officials and in-house specialists.

To help high-potential managers acquire "existence" skills, some organizations build into their development programs components that require independent action or consultation with individuals who are not closely affiliated with a structured program. Self-initiated contacts and experiences with mentors or colleagues outside the group help focus development on each participant's individual characteristics. A career planning exercise, for example, revealed a window of opportunity for one woman identified as a high-potential manager in her organization. She explained, "I sat down with my mentor, assigned to me as part of the program, and the advice I got was, 'Don't look at level or salary but at what you want and like to do.' So I listed activities like marketing and community relations, and I found jobs that encompass those. In the interviewing process, I found someone who was creating a job to do all those things. He was writing a job description when I called him. So then I talked to the directors who could choose someone for that job. That's the job I have now."

Although this story is more positive than most we heard, it shows what is possible. Development programs aim to give participants tools to engineer their own advancement, including those that help them personalize the information they receive. Assigned mentors or coaches, assignments such as formulating a career plan, or additional outside training are all possible supplements to a core program providing formal group training. These additions make programs much more flexible and can help motivated, creative individuals strike out on their own to learn what is most important to them and to take charge of their own career development.

Rotational job assignments are often a key part of formal development programs. Job rotation allows participants to experience a variety of challenges that stretch their skills and help them identify their career interests. As explained in Chapter Three, these challenging assignments broaden managers' development and also embellish their track records. Job rotation has been used in various forms for many years, sometimes within development programs and sometimes as a stand-alone development practice. In some organizations, job rotation or "cross-training" is so common and accepted that some managers don't associate it with a program, perhaps because assignments are made on an individual or ad hoc basis. However job rotation is used, it is an essential part of management development. Four of the organizations in our study use job rotation in conjunction with formal development programs. Managers in another three organizations indicated that job rotation is used instead of a formal development program. In two other organizations, targeted assignments for women and people of color are being used as a development tool in addition to formal development programs.

   Flexibility and informality allow development activities
to be tailored to individuals and adjusted as business conditions
change. However, excessive flexibility can be a disadvantage.
A program that is too loose may be hardly a program at all,
and without a structure to support intended individualized activities, little may actually be accomplished. We found, for example, that some development practices touted by key executives
and staff managers are unknown to nontraditional managers
in the organization, and the programs are carelessly administered
(strong candidates are overlooked, and there is no follow-up after
the program.) One manager in our study with ten years of experience in the personnel function of her educational institution noted that a development program that has been a considerable help to some people of color remains out of reach to
many others because it is handled so informally. The program
allows teachers or administrators to take an administrative job
(as openings occur) on a trial basis for up to two years without
taking a salary cut or risking their present job. She believes that
this program relies so heavily on existing networks that it is unfair to women and people of color. As she told us, "Who is chosen
for these positions is not well publicized and may be prearranged.
I think the program is misused and unfair to women and minorities who aren't informed and so are excluded from consideration."
   Other research confirms that managers are not well informed about the career development systems in their organizations and that the grapevine is the primary information source
for career opportunities. John Fernandez's (1981) survey results
reveal that managers are confused about career development
systems in their organizations. This suggests that too much informality in career development activities may put them out of
reach of managers, especially nontraditional ones. Because informal activities are less systematically communicated than formal ones are, information is less likely to reach managers who
have a less developed network. Fernandez (p. 251) notes, "The
fact that, except for Asians, men are by far better informed in
these areas than women are suggests that not only is career-
planning information poorly disseminated for most managers
in general but also that women are at a greater disadvantage

than men are in obtaining career information. In addition, out of all male groups, black men are least informed."

Development practices should have enough flexibility to be responsive to individuals' needs and to take advantage of the opportunities available in different parts of the organization. But development practices also need enough structure to permit systematic communication and to help guarantee that they will receive enough attention and resources to be conducted effectively.

Eligibility for Development Programs

Once the question of components and structure has been addressed, the next question to be answered in designing a development program is how exclusive or how open the program should be.

Some executives argue that it is necessary to segregate at least some development programs to remedy the underrepresentation of blacks, Hispanics, Asian-Americans, Native Americans, and white women in senior management. In fact, five of the sixteen organizations in our study conduct development programs that are exclusively for nontraditional managers. Managers sometimes justify limited-eligibility programs as a necessary consequence of past differential treatment that has left many nontraditional managers with special disadvantages unique to their sex or ethnicity.

Many managers accept the idea that women or people of color need special training to compete effectively for senior management posts. According to one education executive in our study, for example, "Training programs should be geared to women, not to the general population. They need to know, for example, what barriers face women and how to handle them, like what is 'aggressive' versus 'assertive' behavior."

Other managers in our study recommended special training in communication for nontraditional managers to lessen an accent or to make more forceful presentations, for example. Other research (Morrison and Von Glinow, 1990) indicates that blacks may need special training in managing conflict or controlling their own rage (because of the extraordinary hostility many blacks face) and that women may need special training in soliciting performance feedback during performance evaluations. John Fernandez (1981) has identified several areas of training that managers most often recommend for women or people of color; technical skills and overcoming lack of previous work experience, dealing with white/male subordinates and peers, understanding political aspects of management, and learning how to be successful or accepted in a white male organization. Fernandez's analyses also reveal, however, that managers who believe that women or people of color need special training are those who also have the most stereotypic views of nontraditional employees and rate themselves low in their ability to accept women and people of color in the workplace. Therefore, Fernandez questions the objectivity of managers who recommend special training for nontraditional managers, even when they simply mean supplemental training in areas traditionally recognized as important for managers.

If prejudice is behind the notion that nontraditional managers need special training, as Fernandez suggests, then restricting training programs may not be justified. On the other hand, limiting training to women or to members of certain ethnic groups may be beneficial because of the opportunity for participants to interact with others like themselves. Training that a black employee group provides for its members, for example, may be valuable primarily because it gives blacks a chance to get to know other blacks in the organization, to learn from their successes and failures, and to get their advice on both career and personal issues. The opportunity to network through a structured program may be one reason why managers advocate programs limited to nontraditional managers.

Another potential advantage of restricting programs to nontraditional managers is that this approach may represent the best use of scarce development resources. In one of the five organizations in our study that have a restricted program, for example, the original program proposal called for an equal number of white male and nontraditional participants, but the slots for white men were not approved by senior management. These executives may have made that decision in the hope of using limited resources of money, time, and available rotational positions to make the greatest impact on diversity.

Using resources with a visible purpose—in this case to reinforce a stated commitment to diversity—may be another reason behind executives' decisions to limit participation. It is important to some executives to be seen as taking a strong stand to counter historical discrimination. Reserving certain opportunities for nontraditional managers, who have been denied opportunities in the past, is one visible way for executives to "walk their talk."

Advantages such as these have influenced many executives to sponsor segregated training programs. However, there are also disadvantages, which have probably played a role in persuading executives in eleven of the organizations in our study to keep development programs open to traditional managers. One danger of limiting development programs to nontraditional candidates is that such programs lose prestige; they are discounted as second rate, catering to a less qualified cadre of employees. As pointed out earlier, segregated programs may reinforce the stereotypic perception that nontraditional managers need remedial help because they can't qualify for the "normal" development activities that have been provided for white male managers over the years. Moreover, participants in segregated programs may encounter resentment from their peers and bosses for being given special treatment. Such programs sometimes become corporate "ghettos" that get distanced from an organization's mainstream activities, and resources to continue their operation may evaporate after an initial start-up flurry.

The potential for backlash, then, seems to have made some executives reluctant to create development programs exclusively for nontraditional managers. This reluctance is felt even though these same executives may sanction other programs limited to other special groups of employees, such as high-potential candidates or newly hired managers. And even though employees excluded from such programs regularly question why a few managers are singled out and given opportunities not available to other, more senior and above-average employees and why newcomers get benefits that longtime employees cannot get, such criticism and resentment have not stopped these exclusive practices in many organizations. Yet the resentment and potential backlash tied to ethnicity and sex issues because of their emotional charge may prompt some executives to prohibit or abandon this kind of special program. Resentment may even increase once some progress in advancing nontraditional managers has been achieved. One black female executive in our study commented that her male colleagues don't want any systems to help women advance because they claim women are already well represented in the twenty-three-member management team. "What more do you want?" she told us men ask her, "There are already four of you."

Some executives prefer to integrate development programs on the theory that open programs foster more interaction and acceptance across sex and ethnic lines. A few top executives have announced that their organizations do not restrict any developmental program to or from female and ethnically diverse employees, and many managers favor open access to any training important to any candidate for advancement. While this philosophy can be commended on some grounds, the reality all too often is that (1) the precious few resources for development must be focused on a few of the most promising individuals, and (2) the factors that have traditionally excluded women and people of color from developmental opportunities persist today.

An illustration of what may be considered differential access to "open" development activities relates to outside training programs. Each year many companies send one or more aspiring executives to a prestigious university's executive development courses. Such courses are considered an asset for managers vying for promotion. Historically, few people of color or white women have attended such programs, but now some organizations are recommending more nontraditional candidates for acceptance into them. Patti Watts (1991) indicates, however, that even when company officials encourage nontraditional managers to attend executive development programs, university officials still resist admitting them to their highest-level courses. In one case, an admissions director questioned a female candidate who was at the same reporting level as a man who had been accepted into the course, without question, the previous year.

The evident reluctance of some university officials to open executive courses to white women and people of color, despite their qualifications, may help explain why such developmental opportunities and credentials are still so difficult for nontraditional managers to obtain. Watts (1990) cites data on the proportion of women participating in four-week executive development programs at eight topflight universities, including Harvard, Yale, Columbia, and Stanford. In all but one case, the percentage of female participants in 1989 was the same or lower than it was in 1988 or 1987, and in no case did women represent even 15 percent of the class. Harvard had the lowest percentage of women — a mere 1.2 percent. Such figures suggest that programs that are in theory open to all candidates regardless of sex or ethnicity may in reality be less accessible to nontraditional managers.

Obviously, there is no simple answer to the question of how open a development program should be. Executives who contend that some restrictions are inevitable and even necessary to develop future executives sometimes find an acceptable middle ground either by sponsoring both open and restricted development programs or by including some white men in development programs that are largely targeted at underrepresented groups. They give preference to nontraditional employees because they do not believe that including only a few people of color or white women each year in their organizations' traditional development program is an adequate solution to diversity problems. They restrict access largely to nontraditional employees so that they can prepare them more quickly for advancement. These restricted programs are their choice, for the time being at least, for selectively investing in a small group of exceptional candidates and preparing them for leadership positions.

Program and Participant Confidentiality

The third important question to be addressed in the design of a development program is how "public" or how "confidential" the selection process and the list of program participants should be.

The more restricted a program is, the more relevant the question of confidentiality becomes. When the list of participants or candidates for a program is mandated to include women or people of color, there may be even more reason for secrecy. One manager explained that his organization's compensation system rewards executives who include nontraditional candidates in the succession plan and thus get them promoted into management levels. He then said, "We don't want to tell women and minorities they got in to meet someone's affirmative action goals." This manager would argue that secrecy should apply to the selection process itself, perhaps more than to the identity of those who are selected, to avoid the impression that nontraditional managers are not as qualified as the white men who are included.

If selection to a development program is not confidential, the publicity can be a burden. Simply taking part in a development program demands extra work and extra risk, and the pressure on participants can soar when the names of those selected are made public. A black vice president of a personnel function vividly recalled for us his experience nearly twenty years earlier in an elite development program for newly-hired managers. He, like other graduates of such programs, had felt the constant pressure of watchful eyes on him, even at social events. Managing his own visibility as a participant in the program was a challenge for him. According to this vice president, "A lot is expected of you. There is a little bit of a halo effect, and some built-in animosity, so you quickly have to develop some win-over skills if you want to survive. You have to go into a group of people and learn from them, and they know you'll someday be their boss."

The extra challenge posed by being labeled a "hi-po" (high-potential candidate) may make success harder to achieve. According to one Hispanic manager who has been with his company for fifteen years, some managers might have advanced just fine and would have been far better off in general if they hadn't been set apart as "crowned princes." With expectations so high, one failure can be the "kiss of death" that derails a career. After that one mistake, this manager said, "No one wants to have anything to do with you."

Even though these are good reasons to conceal how management views an employee's advancement prospects, it is important to assess whether the reasons for secrecy outweigh the potential disadvantages and whether the secrecy is designed more to protect the employer than to protect the employee. For example, keeping a list of "hi-pos" secret protects executives from having to tell employees why they are on the list or, particularly, why they are not. While the fear of being hauled into court may be involved, there is also a very real reluctance to give people bad news. Secrecy makes feedback optional, so in many cases, there is no feedback. As we will see later, there are indications that nontraditional managers are especially likely to miss out on the kind of performance feedback that can help them manage their careers.

Just as there are benefits to keeping the selection process and participation in development programs secret, there are also good reasons to make them public, and some programs that are open only by invitation or nomination are known for the deliberate publicity that goes with selection. The prestige of being selected for such programs is highlighted inside and outside the organization to help make participants feel honored and valued. Exposure of this kind adds to the power of a program in which significant resources are being invested in a very few individuals. Participants themselves have sometimes found that the publicity they receive more than compensates for the added demands and challenge of a development program because it gives them more respect and more career options. One Hispanic manager told us that prior to being selected for the company's "hi-po" development program, her repeated requests for a transfer were refused. Once selected, she got several offers to transfer and was able to get the job she had requested.

The issues of confidentiality, structure, and eligibility with respect to development programs pose dilemmas for executives. Decisions about these and other issues that affect the fate of nontraditional managers, as well as white men, need to be connected with the organization's development philosophy. Beyond this, decisions about how development programs (if they are even thought of as "programs") are constructed and operated must be made in a sea of trade-offs.

Mentors and Networks

Mentors and networks of supportive colleagues are extremely important in leadership development and advancement. They provide support, challenges, and recognition in managers' education, experience, and influence as managers wend their way through the tests and decisions that shape their future.

Mentors

According to our study, a lack of mentors and role models is a barrier for many white women and people of color. Nontraditional managers may especially need the guidance, encouragement, and advocacy that more seasoned managers can provide to overcome such hurdles as isolation, lack of credibility, and perhaps a naïveté about institutional politics. Sometimes encouragement alone can make the difference to nontraditional managers who see only white men in the positions to which they aspire and become unsure about their advancement prospects. One executive in an educational institution credits her advancement to the encouragement she received from a former boss. In her words, "He'd say, 'I'll have an administrative opening, and I want you to apply' or 'Did you apply for one of the area superintendent jobs?' When I'd say to him that I wanted to return to the classroom, he'd say, 'No. You'll help twenty-five students, but what about all the others in the world?'"

Mentors are most often bosses, although they can also be helpful colleagues inside or outside a manager's organization. Previous research done at the Center for Creative Leadership on white female and male executives indicates that mentoring may be a temporary partnership that lasts for several months, or it may be a long-term relationship in which the mentor may even take a manager along on every promotion from one division or company to another. Mentors often place a high value on developing people and build this into their daily or weekly routine. A senior executive in our study who viewed himself as a mentor for a newly hired black female subordinate described what he did to pave the way for her. Because the company had few other blacks or female upper-level managers, he called two white female executives and one black male executive and asked them to meet her. He invited her to the company's high-level finance meeting. He regularly made time for her, and after the first thirty days, he deliberately asked her if she was having any problems on the job. At one point, he also helped her stay focused by giving her the unpleasant news that she was getting too bogged down in details. His efforts were intended to help her feel like an informed team member from the start.

A mentor's help is often given informally or unofficially, even when she or he is also the manager's boss. A white male vice president explained to us what he does as a boss and mentor for a successful black manager who has one noticeable problem that could easily derail him. Off the record, the vice president gives him a combination of understanding and criticism that other executives probably would not give him. According to this vice president, "I've had a certain role to play in his career. He has a very strong value system, and he is volatile and mercurial. He will fight very hard for his people, and they love it. . . . He doesn't give a damn what he says. He needs people he works for to really manage him. If his manager let him lose his temper, he'd fall on his sword because others won't tolerate it. I've helped him cool out. I've given him direct feedback on his temper. I'm not threatened by him, but others might very well be."

Mentors who are not bosses can also be supportive in many ways. For example, a black manager we interviewed regularly counsels newly promoted people of color, helping them separate pressures they may feel as a result of taking on a new job from pressures that are tied to racial issues. A government executive encourages other women in her unit by asking them for their opinions in meetings. If they are cut off by a man, she makes sure later that their ideas are heard and identified as their own. She thinks this role is special and necessary because, as she put it, "we're so conditioned that good decisions come from men."

Mentors are sometimes assigned to high-potential managers as part of a larger, formal development program. Their value in this situation may be even greater because the demands on managers can be particularly intense during such a program. Having someone to help them plan and analyze their experiences and their learning can be crucial to managers during this time. Mentors are also assigned to help managers entering the organization get over the initial orientation "humps" and quickly learn about its informal systems and norms. The advantage of assigned mentors is that the mentoring responsibility is clearly for only a specified period of time, which is acceptable to many managers who might resist a longer or more ambiguous mentoring relationship.

The effectiveness of assigned mentoring programs, however, seems to be extremely variable. In some cases, assigned mentors simply don't do anything, and they become known as "ghost mentors." Often others will not fill in for an absent mentor, perhaps because they are reluctant to step into an assigned situation. When this happens, the manager who is meant to benefit has no one to turn to. On the other hand, some people are against any assigned mentors on the grounds that effective mentor relationships must occur naturally. A woman we interviewed in a telecommunications firm argued vehemently against assigning senior white male executives as mentors for women, saying, "Good god, that's letting the fox in the henhouse. Some of these guys you would no sooner want as mentors than the man in the moon. It's got to occur naturally, and they've got to be men who respect women."

Many senior managers who may be considered as mentors are not sensitive to the issues that affect nontraditional managers. As mentors, they sometimes offend women and people of color by saying and doing inappropriate things, often without even realizing it. One human resource manager we interviewed described the executives in her company's formal mentor program as including the "master of the universe" type with traditional attitudes. She noted that one executive mentor, trying to be helpful to a woman who felt her salary was inadequate to live in New York City, suggested that her father help her out financially. The woman immediately came to the human resource staff exclaiming, "Is there a place for women in this company?"

Systematic mentor selection and training may be the key to improving the effectiveness of assigned-mentoring programs. In a few of the organizations we studied, mentors are selected with great care. They are required to have good skills in communication, for example, but they may also be expected to understand and value diversity so that they don't pose yet another barrier for people of color and white women. Another precaution taken in a few of the organizations we studied is to require prospective mentors to receive training in the roles and skills of mentoring.

Requirements such as these take some of the uncertainty out of the mentoring process while providing a structure that may be needed to provide more mentors for nontraditional managers. Simply leaving mentoring to chance may not give these managers the support they need to develop and advance. Some of the organizations we studied use an approach that combines assigned matching of mentors and managers with some leeway for individual choice in the pairing process. This appears to be an effective way to help guarantee that more mentoring will occur.

An important issue is the role of women and people of color who have achieved prominence as mentors for other nontraditional managers. Nontraditional executives are in great demand as mentors, both for formal development programs and for informal activities. Yet while many nontraditional managers have the skills and the inclination to be mentors to other people of color and women, the added responsibility can be overwhelming. Thus, nontraditional managers who feel a special obligation to help others of their sex or ethnic background, often find themselves in a troublesome bind. There is not enough time in the day to meet the high standards for their current jobs, to continue to advance in their organizations, to be active and visible role models in their professions and their communities, and to give others the mentoring help they need.

Another barrier for nontraditional managers who want to be mentors is that mentoring other people of color or white women is often not recognized as legitimate work despite the time and energy required. In some cases, mentoring activities are frowned upon by others in the organization, even by bosses.

One black manager, for example, was accused by his boss of "running a black career counseling service." He refuted the claim by showing his calendar to the boss — of five recent meetings, only two were with blacks. The perception, however, was that he was limiting himself to other blacks and that it was a disruptive activity.

Nontraditional managers must be careful not to be perceived as giving one-sided support or segregating themselves with other people of color or female managers. Several managers mentioned that they had to caution black or female managers not to create a "ghetto" by hiring, promoting, or surrounding themselves with only other blacks or women. Some managers talked about the risk of hiring or promoting even one other female or minority manager. One manager said, "There was an opening in another department headed by a Hispanic. I wanted Rick [not his real name] to get the position for experience and exposure. The department head was concerned about Rick. When I inquired why, he responded that it would be perceived that he brought Rick in because he, too, is Hispanic."

The logical and enthusiastic expectation that women and people of color are the ideal mentors for other nontraditional managers must be tempered with a realization of the conflicts they face in becoming mentors. Otherwise, the burden of mentoring may become overwhelming for them. As more nontraditional managers move into the executive suite, it may be tempting to assign more mentoring responsibilities to them. However, white male executives have proven to be exceptional mentors in a number of cases, and it is important to rely on them as mentors as well. Careful attention to building executives' mentoring capability can help spread the responsibility for mentoring so that no one is given an unfair burden.

Networks and Other Support Groups

Like mentors, internal networking groups provide various forms of support to nontraditional managers; they also provide recognition and challenge to their members. Networking typically involves a less personal commitment than mentoring. Instead of devoting substantial periods of time over a year or two to developing one individual, as many mentors do, managers who network may spend only short bursts of time with people to give them information or to introduce them to a key executive. Because networks reduce the burden on any one individual to help other employees succeed, these groups make it possible to reach more people and provide more kinds of assistance than can mentors alone.

Internal networks are groups of employees that usually form as self-help groups. Groups of women, blacks, Hispanics, Asian-Americans, and Native Americans now operate as networks in a number of organizations. In our study, nine of the sixteen organizations have at least one known internal network or support group, and informal networking activities occur at eight organizations. Groups originally formed as self-help networks sometimes evolve into advocacy groups and take on the additional job of negotiating with senior management on personnel and other business issues. Therefore, it is sometimes difficult to distinguish between advocacy groups and internal networks.

Network groups introduce nontraditional managers to one another so they can serve as counselors, cheerleaders, sounding boards, content experts, and resources in other capacities. Networks also sponsor workshops in skill areas in demand by members. When Asian-American managers in one company we studied identified a need for speech training, for example, the network arranged courses for employees. These groups also host and publicize special events to celebrate their cultural heritage. Celebrations of Black History Month or Cinco de Mayo, for example, focus the attention of all employees on the strength and beauty of a culture not familiar to everyone. When senior executives are involved in these special events, the value of diversity may be reinforced even more.

Through special events and other activities, networks sometimes attempt to bring their members into contact with officials of the organization so that they are seen and better known by executives who can help them advance. Several executives in our study commented on the skills and presence of network members they have dealt with, particularly network officers and members who take leadership roles on certain issues. Both executives and the network members themselves have come to appreciate the skills and savvy of the nontraditional managers who emerge as leaders of these groups.

Networks provide a stage for talented nontraditional managers to show their skills, partly because of the challenges inherent in such groups. In fact, some nontraditional executives we interviewed attribute important aspects of their development to the challenges they faced in these groups. One white male vice president likened the role of network members to that of serving on a city council because of the need to "make presentations on touchy subjects and to bring together divergent and contrary interests." When advocacy is also a function of a network, the challenge can be even more complex. One veteran black group member elaborated:

> [Employee groups] have an awful lot of publics to serve, and a lot of groups to interact with. We get good marks overall, yet if you went to female employees and asked, "How do you feel about the groups?" they'd say the women's group should be doing more. If you're a black employee and you want a promotion and don't get it, then the group isn't helping you. If you're a department head and want to run something by the groups, then you feel OK about them. If you're a department head and the group is telling you that you don't have enough minorities, then you don't like the group.

Network and support groups are powerful forums for the individuals who must develop their skills to manage them, as well as for those who benefit from their sponsorship. These groups sometimes represent a sounding board for top management's proposed changes in personnel policies for other business practices. They sometimes work with senior management to revise and polish concepts before they are announced to the entire workforce. They serve top management as a buffer on sensitive issues, and they share the burden for meeting nontraditional employees' needs. Because of these and other functions, such groups often receive at least limited support from senior management. Support may take the form of funds to hire a facilitator for meetings or the provision of a human resource staff member to assist and serve as a liaison with senior management or permission to use company time and facilities for meetings.

Executives have sometimes only reluctantly agreed to support employee groups, not because they doubt their developmental value to members but because they fear they will become advocacy or lobby groups. Such an evolution has occurred in some organizations, with employee groups building power to make demands of management. While some managers in our study consider this a danger, other managers we interviewed believe it is dangerous to try to squelch attempts by nontraditional employees to organize support groups for people like themselves. They cautioned that if resistance from senior managers causes organizing efforts to go underground, hidden from them, it will leave these executives with a serious lack of information and perhaps a reputation for poor management.

Networking and mentoring are powerful development practices when they are carefully planned and carried out. Certainly their potential pitfalls need to be taken into account, but many managers in our study agree that these practices have enormous potential to contribute to the education, development, and well-being of all managers in an organization. These activities truly complement other diversity practices and, in fact, can bring them to life.

Assessment and Feedback

The programs and other activities described above as development practices are beginning to play a significant role in diversity efforts, as the organizations in our study demonstrate. Executives seem to be turning to these practices to help retain and advance the talented nontraditional managers they have worked so hard to recruit. Two additional tools that affect managers' development are being added to the arsenal of diversity practices used in some of our progressive organizations: assessment and feedback.

Assessment and feedback techniques represent a powerful way to boost managers' development without significantly boosting costs. These tools are valuable complements to other development practices because, as research conducted by the Center for Creative Leadership and others suggests, a lack of performance feedback can block managers' development no matter how much has already been invested in them and no matter how much leadership potential exists in them. One of the accepted norms in many organizations is to protect people from unpleasant information about their capability or their career prospects. When employees who have been moving along the fast track eventually get stuck at some point, for example, their supervisors often don't have the courage (or the responsibility) to tell them what has happened. Instead, such employees are typically left "on the shelf," somewhat baffled by what has happened, stalled in positions that might be better used to develop others.

Even when supervisors attempt to help otherwise talented managers correct deficiencies by sending them to a training program, for example, they do not often tell them why they are being sent or what the expectations will be when they return from the training. Many of the managers who are sent to training programs at the Center for Creative Leadership introduce themselves the first day by saying that their boss sent them, but they don't know why. While it is true that not all flaws can be corrected and not all talented managers can advance beyond a certain point, a lack of feedback can only increase a manager's sense of helplessness. To draw an analogy, imagine that when you have your annual medical checkup, your doctor discovers signs of cancer in your body but doesn't tell you. Perhaps your doctor prefers to postpone judgment for a couple months and schedules an appointment with you then. Perhaps your doctor is afraid you will sue for lack of previous treatment that might have prevented the cancer. Perhaps your doctor sees little hope of controlling the disease and does not want you to live your last days in distress. While all these reasons may be understandable, what would your choice be: to have the information about your possible fate or to be protected from the bad news?

Most managers would agree that people who show signs of derailing should be told what they are doing wrong and given the resources to correct the problem or to find a more suitable position elsewhere inside or outside the organization. Yet as these same managers would probably point out, complicating factors can get in the way of this happening. There are few incentives, for example, for managers to go through the uncomfortable process of giving their employees negative feedback. Many managers have never been trained to give their employees constructive criticism or to help them devise a plan to improve their performance. Some managers may not even be able to figure out what the problem really is; all they know is that their employee's work seems to be unsatisfactory. Furthermore, some managers may be reluctant to confront underachieving employees because even if they improved their performance, there would not be enough promotion opportunities to go around. Many managers do not know how to motivate and challenge employees whose career prospects have become limited because of performance defects or because of downsizing or business conditions beyond their control.

Complications such as these affect all managers' access to feedback, but the problems may be greater for nontraditional managers. White men and others seem to have a more difficult time giving feedback to people of a different sex or ethnicity. One senior executive in our study, a white man, concluded that "women and blacks get a different quality of feedback due to the comfort issue."

In a recent court case reported by Pollock (1991), a black female analyst got her job back by arguing that she had never received a poor performance evaluation. The company officials claimed that they had not told her about problems with her performance because they were afraid she would sue on the basis of racial discrimination. The fear that people of color will sue or that women will cry was also mentioned by a number of managers in our study as contributing to the lack of accurate feedback available to nontraditional managers in particular. "Feedback to them is not the same; it's not honest," one human resource manager commented, "so what they hear is different from what is happening to them." A lack of familiarity with people's cultural differences also contributes to managers' difficulty in giving useful feedback. Personnel specialists such as Prabhu Guptara (1990) and Jim Kennedy and Anna Everest (1991) have written about the problems in communicating across cultures and especially in reviewing a subordinate's performance when issues such as saving face may be involved.

The need to provide better performance feedback to managers in general and to nontraditional managers in particular appears to be a growing concern among executives and human resource professionals. Structured assessment and feedback tools, which seem to be growing in popularity, may help reduce the problems of getting this information to managers. In place of awkward face-to-face confrontations about perceived performance weaknesses, managers may be offered the chance to receive written ratings and opinions about their behavior from their boss, peers, and subordinates and to submit their own written self-ratings. In this situation, instruments listing such managerial skills as delegating responsibility, informing subordinates of business activities, and collaborating with other departments are distributed to co-workers, who send their confidential responses to a third party for consolidation. The manager receives a report of all the responses, grouped so that no individual's responses can be identified. The often detailed information in the report may be far more valuable than any feedback the manager might have received from a meeting with her or his supervisor.

Instrumented feedback such as the foregoing is used as part of some training programs. When this occurs, expert facilitators may be available to help managers interpret the written responses and prepare a plan to overcome weaknesses that may have been identified. Some surveys or audits that are used as accountability practices include a few items that assess subordinates' views of a manager's performance, similar to items that make up these feedback instruments. When used as an accountability tool, the item responses are monitored by management and often linked to pay or promotion decisions. However, the use of more extensive feedback strictly for development purposes may make it easier for many managers to see themselves as others see them and, as they choose, to make some changes. Whether feedback comes from a facilitator, a supervisor, or a mentor, it is a precious commodity for both career and personal development. One executive in our study put it this way: "The real enablers in your career are the people who say, 'Hey, there's a better way to do this.'"

Other techniques are also being used in a few organizations in our study in an attempt to strengthen the ability of managers to objectively assess and report performance results to others and to get better information about their own strengths, weaknesses, and interests. In one organization, for example, some managers are being systematically trained as professional behavioral assessors so that they can help staff the in-house assessment centers used to determine managers' promotability potential. In addition, managers and mentors of women and people of color are being trained to help their nontraditional subordinates and protégés prepare for interviews for higher-level jobs within the organization. Training programs are also provided in several organizations to help candidates for management posts evaluate their interest in management and even to prepare for specific higher-level jobs. Such techniques are still more the exception than the rule, however, even within our group of progressive organizations. Many organizations still rely on more traditional selection procedures, and they send their managers outside to get structured feedback. Nevertheless, a few other interesting exceptions further illustrate how new techniques can be put into action.

One of the most innovative techniques to help managers get and give objective, constructive feedback is used at an educational institution in our study. It involves the use of eight explicit standards for choosing and evaluating managers. The standards include managing the instructional program, evaluating staff, developing good school-community relations, and implementing staff development. Performance indicators for each standard are also specified. Under the staff development standard, for example, a performance indicator is that the strengths and needs of staff members are identified. A panel of judges interview candidates, using the standards as the criteria for selection.

Candidates who qualify are given feedback on their performance against the standards, including two or three in which performance is expected to improve. Candidates then have the chance to work on their performance before they are promoted, sometimes serving as an assistant to someone already at the targeted level. Thus, feedback and improvement are built into the promotion process rather than after the fact.

Less formal assessment techniques are also being tried. One organization with the goal of building more input and precision into the selection process brings groups of candidates together with groups of "judges" for interviews. Specific criteria and responsibilities for the open positions are determined in advance, incorporating input from the employees who will report to the new managers. Also prior to the interviews, an independent consultant assesses the candidates and gives them feedback on their strengths and weaknesses, which they can then use to help them in their interviews. Although the candidates are interviewed individually, group exercises and an evening social event give the decision makers additional information about the candidates.

Other organizations solicit individuals' sustained involvement in their own career planning and development. In one company, for example, self-managed career development is emphasized to all employees, and resources are provided to make that possible. The company provides an entire library of books, career guides, computerized directories of people to consult about jobs as well as publications about jobs, interactive computer programs that walk employees through their interests and qualifications for various occupations, videotapes on self-development, and other training tools. Human resource professionals are also available to guide employees through the process. In other words, in this company, the message (that the employees are expected to take charge of their own careers) and the tools reinforce each other. The tools provided enable nontraditional employees to compete more effectively with their white male counterparts by using these resources to get career information that otherwise might have been available only from mentors or social contacts. While such resources are no substitute for mentors or sponsors, they are available to all employees, and they supplement other diversity activities.

Development tools and techniques are now the focal point in the diversity effort of a number of organizations in our study. Many executives feel that they have to "catch up" on developing managers because development practices have received so little attention over the years in relation to recruitment practices. Like other diversity tools, development practices do not stand on their own; they work in conjunction with other practices to break down advancement barriers for nontraditional managers. Adequate development makes it easier for accountability practices to be used effectively, and recruitment practices are still needed to provide the talented individuals toward whom development is targeted. Some of the more recently adopted recruitment practices are discussed in Chapter Six.

SIX

USING RECRUITMENT TO BUILD DIVERSITY

It is early in the evening, several months after the research team meeting, and I have just returned to La Jolla from a visit to North Carolina. The trip involved a long plane ride from Nashville, so I used the time to read through a backlog of business magazines that always seems to accumulate. When I arrive at the office, I run into the researcher who has been doing most of the data analyses for the GOLD project. I enthusiastically tell her about a Gannett Foundation (1991) advertisement that I read on the airplane. The ad relates to an issue of recruitment that we discovered in our study. It begins this way:

> There's a persistent myth in journalism that qualified black media professionals are hard to find.
> That myth has helped hold the percentage of black professionals in print media to a mere 4.2 percent; 7.9 percent in broadcast media.
> **That's not good for journalism.**
> **Or the First Amendment.**
> **And that's not good for America.**

This ad makes the point that what many managers call a "lack of qualified candidates" when they attempt to hire a person of color or a white woman may actually be a myth. A number of managers we interviewed explained that qualified nontraditional candidates may be harder to recognize and they may be harder to attract, but they may not be in such short supply as some managers imagine.

My colleague is also impressed by the ad and responds:

This ad, in fact, may be an effective recruitment tool to attract nontraditional professionals who may eventually advance into senior management. Do you remember the consultant who told us that senior executives sometimes expect people of color to be grateful for any job offer they get? She called in a human resource manager to explain to one executive that the people of color who were being offered jobs by that company were turning them down for better offers from other companies. It's just not enough any more simply to make an offer; organizations have to invest in attracting nontraditional recruits.

The fact that so many managers in our study said that they "can't find" qualified women or people of color for managerial positions indicates that recruitment is still a key part of any diversity effort. More than 26 percent of the barriers that managers report are related to finding qualified nontraditional managers. Filling the so-called "feeder pool" of nontraditional candidates who will one day be candidates for executive posts is perhaps the most important purpose of recruitment practices. Some of the managers we interviewed, however, contend that recruitment must also immediately and directly address the current imbalance at senior-management levels.

Recruitment tools address all three components of leadership development: challenge, recognition, and support. They are used to attract job candidates at all levels who are able and willing to take on challenging work assignments that are offered to them. They are also used to demonstrate that the organization places value on nontraditional employees and offers them advancement opportunities along with the support systems they may need to overcome barriers that remain in most institutions and in society at large.

Recruitment Problems

Businesses have been struggling with recruitment issues for a long time, and most still have problems finding and attracting the nontraditional employees of their choice. Public sector organizations have an even more difficult recruitment challenge because they are often seen as less desirable employers than private sector firms. Several public sector executives in our study complained that the combination of typically lower salaries and fewer perks makes education, government, and other not-for-profit organizations a poor choice for many talented, credentialed, nontraditional candidates. As one educator noted, any person of color who could be hired as a professor can also be hired into the private sector with a considerably better compensation package.

The compensation for public service can be so disproportionately low that even the children of public servants are easily dissuaded from following in their parents' footsteps. One black woman we interviewed, for example, whose mother had received awards for the innovative procedures she instituted while a government worker for many years, was appalled to discover that her mother's ending salary was a meager $6,000 a year. That was enough to make this woman vow that she would never pursue a career in public service.

Managers in many of the private sector businesses we studied also considered recruitment a continuing problem. Recruitment is difficult, perhaps partly because it looks deceptively easy. Managers can be taken in by its apparent simplicity, and many organizations thus fail to make recruitment effective. The specific mistakes vary, but several are common. Some managers, in their haste to reach parity with the workforce, set extremely high goals for recruitment, mandating that one-third, one-half, or even three-fourths of all new entry-level employees must be women or people of color. In some cases, these goals are far too ambitious. Because of a pervasive expectation that the new recruits will be around for a while, some of the organizations that actually meet such ambitious goals may be in for a shock. Many times turnover requires that the same high goals be set again, and again. One plant manager, commenting on his experience, said, "Our goal at the entry level is that at least 50 percent be females or minorities. But lots of attrition takes place due to disillusionment, bad matches, and so on. Entry-level people get lost. There is 50 percent attrition at that level."

Making the initial intake of recruits pay off for an organization is difficult. Recruitment is often ineffective because of a lack of development or tracking of new recruits. Particularly when a large group of employees is recruited at one time, follow-up to orient, rotate, and monitor them may be virtually non-existent.

Another recruitment problem is that the incentives are either lacking or they focus on short-term quantity. Legal and social pressures have made recruitment of traditionally under-represented groups more acceptable, particularly at the entry level, but there are still inadequate incentives for some managers to recruit them effectively. As a result, many recruitment errors, omissions, and general negligence continue to exclude nontraditional candidates. An example from San Diego State University illustrates the problem. According to Smollar (1991a), a teaching post was created in the psychology department to increase minority enrollment. The position called for a specialization in community minority issues and help in recruiting minority students to the department. University officials appointed a white to the post, a white who happened to be the wife of the department chairperson. Their response to cries of protest that the position should have gone to a person of color was that there were no better qualified applicants — the nationwide search had resulted in only nine applications for the position, and only two of those were from people of color.

In some organizations, short-sighted recruitment efforts consist of telling managers simply to bring in nontraditional people; whether they are able to keep them or employ them to capacity is left to chance. When recruitment has been poorly conceived, the resources that have been poured into the effort have probably been wasted.

The practices used to screen and select recruits are also a problem in many organizations. The criteria or procedures used in recruiting may be considerably biased and therefore not accurately reflect the skills needed to do the job. The weight put on math, science, or engineering credentials, for example, may not be appropriate for many jobs. Similarly, the preference given to military veterans may be a dysfunctional deterrent in recruiting women and other nontraditional employees. According to an article in *Personnel Journal* (Kennedy, 1990), recruitment programs that give preference to veterans of the Vietnam era present a significant barrier to white women. At one government installation, 56 percent of all recruits were white women except when the Veterans' Readjustment Program was used, which bypasses traditional government recruitment procedures; then the percentage dropped to only 6 percent.

Dick Gregory, a black activist and comedian popular in the late 1960s, made an observation on one of his records about how the testing many organizations use in recruitment can systematically exclude people of color. He says, "a white racist system keeps me locked in a black ghetto all my life so I've got to develop a different culture to survive with the rats and the roaches. And when I break out and come to your institutions, you ask me the wrong tests. You don't ask me about the ghetto. You ask me about the Eiffel Tower" (1969).

The obvious problem that Gregory speaks of, of course, is that many blacks have not had opportunities to learn about some aspects of the world, and as a result they may appear to be less qualified than their white counterparts. The less obvious problem is that knowledge of the "Eiffel Tower," that is, white, Western culture, may well be less relevant to job performance than knowledge of the ghetto is. Who can say that the savvy and strategic skills one develops through the toughening experience of living in a ghetto are not as important or not more important for managerial work than less trying experiences of someone with more opportunities, resources, and leisure time?

Employment criteria are too often based on assumptions about what is needed to perform the job, and they often exclude — by design or accident — nontraditional candidates who lack the credentials or previous experience historically included as requirements. A competency-based selection system can help define and eliminate exclusionary practices. According to Sachs (1990), one retail company initiated a competency-based approach to recruit sales managers because 40 percent were leaving within six months. When an "expert panel" in the company prepared a profile of the successful salesperson, they included white traits such as extroverted, aggressive, customer oriented, and having a sense of humor. However, when top salespeople in the company were actually interviewed, the profile came out looking very different. Outstanding salespeople weren't aggressive at all. They were very energetic and time conscious, spent their spare time in sales-related activities, and had other characteristics that portrayed them quite differently from the profile generated by company experts who had not done any research. When the company began using the research-based characteristics to select salespeople, more of the recruits were women and people with no sales background. These individuals proved to be much more successful than their predecessors. Sales increased by more than 15 percent, turnover declined, and the company came out $1.8 million ahead.

Results such as these suggest that the actual skills and characteristics people must possess to do specific jobs need to be assessed more broadly and more accurately than they have been. Basing recruitment on nothing more than traditionally valued characteristics or credentials may well be ineffective. For example, physical characteristics such as height, weight, or upper-body strength that have been traditionally required for some jobs have increasingly come under scrutiny because there is growing doubt that they are significantly related to job performance and because they effectively screen out women and some men of color (such as Asian-Americans). Some executives who are familiar with the occupational demands of police work or fire fighting told us that employees' comfort with technological advances and their interpersonal skills play at least as great a role in on-the-job effectiveness as physical strength does. In one organization we studied, entry requirements for physical strength, considered by top management to be discriminatory, had been suspended for some recruits, who were employed on a probationary basis until they could be trained to pass the physical tests.

None of the organizations in our study had an easy time finding solutions to recruitment problems. Like other organizations, many of ours recruited without any provision for retention, assumed that traditional selection criteria were sufficient, and made other common mistakes. The trial-and-error experience of some of the organizations, however, can provide valuable lessons about recruitment. It is clear that executives in some organizations have put their own lessons to use in creating powerful, innovative tools for recruiting nontraditional employees. Perhaps executives in organizations with less experience in diversity will also learn from this evolution of recruitment from a superficial "quick fix" technique into a much more thoughtful, systematic set of promising diversity practices.

Recruitment Practices

The recruitment practices the organizations in our study found to be most important in their diversity efforts are presented here in rank order:

1. Targeted recruitment of women and people of color for nonmanagerial-level positions (used in thirteen organizations)
2. Selective hiring of women and people of color from the outside for key management posts (eight organizations)
3. Extensive public exposure as a leader in diversity (six organizations)
4. Use of the organization's image as liberal or progressive (six organizations)
5. Partnerships with educational institutions (five organizations)
6. Use of incentives in recruiting nontraditional employees, such as cash supplements for recruits (four organizations)
7. Internships to orient and screen potential full-time employees (three organizations)

Managers in all but one of the organizations we studied mentioned using recruitment to develop diversity, and at least one recruitment practice was judged to be a core part of the diversity effort in nine organizations. A complete list of the eleven recruitment practices managers mentioned is shown in Table A.12 in the appendix.

Of the top seven recruitment practices listed above, the second — selectively hiring outsiders — was reported more often in business than in the public sector. Nine of the twelve businesses but only one of the four public organizations use this practice. Businesses also seem to try to attract potential employees by taking advantage of their progressive image more than government or educational institutions do. Half of the businesses in our study did this, but no managers in public sector organizations mentioned it as an asset. To the contrary, as we saw earlier, the image of many public sector organizations is considered a disadvantage in competing with corporate employers for strong nontraditional managers.

For purposes of discussion, the recruitment practices examined in this chapter are divided into four main types: targeting nonmanagerial recruits, recruiting key managers from outside, using visibility as a recruitment technique, and providing incentives for recruits.

Targeting Nonmanagerial Recruits

Targeting people of color and white women for recruitment encompasses several techniques. For entry-level recruits, a number of organizations decided to decrease their reliance on traditional schools with mostly white male graduates. The obvious first step was to expand their sources of recruits by adding two or three schools with more nonwhite or nonmale candidates. Several organizations added institutions with a substantial number of black students as recruitment sites. If they thought that black students would be eager for any offer they received, however, these organizations were probably surprised to discover the competition in recruiting them. In 1991, 225 companies were reported vying for predominantly black Howard University's 125 engineering graduates (Wynter, 1991). The placement director at Howard has begun to screen potential on-campus recruiters on the basis of their record of hiring people of color and the extent to which they are committed to working with the faculty and investing in the university.

For these and other reasons, organizations that go beyond

simply adding a couple of new source schools may get much better results than those that stop there. Five organizations in our study have become deeply involved in the education process, forging partnerships intended to help both students and themselves. Some began to build relationships with schools—universities and colleges, technical schools, even high schools—to help identify and entice student recruits best suited to their needs. One organization builds relationships with certain teachers at targeted schools, offering them summer employment, for example, so that the teachers understand the organization's climate and work and can help encourage and screen their students for employment. Another organization lent some employees to a school to help design the curriculum so that the students would be better prepared to pass the exams required for employment at that organization. Partnerships such as these can bolster recruitment efforts enormously and help give an organization an edge over competitors in finding young, educated employees.

Three of the organizations we studied also initiated internships and work-study cooperative programs, which offer managers and nontraditional students a chance to "check out" the other before making a long-term commitment. In one co-op program, students are required to apply for a job through the personnel department, and managers interview them just as they do any other job candidates. The students are in the program for two to four years while they complete their education. In some work-study programs, scholarships are also awarded to students to encourage them to complete their education.

One well-known internship program called Inroads is being used by organizations to take advantage of a trial period to get to know young, nontraditional employees. Robert Kennedy, the chief executive of Union Carbide Corporation, wrote a laudatory column in the *Wall Street Journal* about the value of this nationwide organization. According to Kennedy (1990), Inroads operates with corporate support to prepare people of color who are professionals for entry-level management jobs in such a way that they can move on to higher levels. High school students in the top 10 percent of their class are selected as corporate interns. They participate in training workshops, counseling and tutorial programs, and community service projects, while at the same time maintaining their academic and on-the-job performance levels. Kennedy points out that finding qualified young people of color has never been a problem for participating companies because there are two or three high-potential candidates for every available internship. By 1990, the program had become so popular that it had expanded to thirty-seven cities, in which more than one thousand companies sponsor more than four thousand internships.

Another practice that allows employer and employee a "wait and see" period is that of hiring temporary workers who may later become full-time employees. Some organizations in our study target people of color and white women for summer jobs and seasonal work. One large company advertises for seasonal employees in black newspapers and on black radio stations. Another retail company gives bonuses to seasonal employees who stay for the entire season to reduce the normally high dropout rate. Moreover, employees who perform well through the season are often asked to stay on as regular employees.

Employees sometimes initiate new recruitment techniques, nudging their managers into trying them by promising their own participation. Alliances between employees and their managers to recruit white women or people of color more effectively exist in several of the organizations we studied. In one case, an employee group "adopted" a school class, with management's support, to provide tutoring, support, and encouragement to the students. In another company, in which a shortage of female engineers was legendary, a vice president of human resources told us that everyone has pretty much accepted the idea that "they just aren't out there." But then some of the women at the field facilities convinced him and a few other managers to create a development program in engineering. Among other things, the organization began recruiting at technical colleges, and for the next five years 35 percent of the new engineering recruits were women.

In the face of increasingly fierce competition for some non-traditional job candidates, managers have begun to pay serious attention to the recruitment process. Recruiters are being trained in how to conduct an interview, and many recruiting teams are being recomposed to include nontraditional employees as "peer recruiters." At some organizations recruiters have more explicit criteria than they did before so that they can be specific with candidates about performance standards and the rate of advancement they can probably expect. Higher-level managers are also expected to participate in recruiting, both to give them a better idea of what the candidates are like and to demonstrate to the candidates that the organization considers them important. To manage an increasingly complex recruitment process, people are being hired specifically to coordinate nontraditional recruitment or to consolidate an often fragmented recruitment program into a coherent whole. In at least one organization, recruitment centers have been established in various parts of the country to help organize the process.

The investment being made in recruitment today may not be substantially more than it was in the past, but it is certainly more visible and, in some cases, represents a considerable financial commitment. One company in our study, for example, recently earmarked more than $2 million for the recruitment of nontraditional employees. For organizations trying to make a strong start in diversity and for those still recovering from recruitment blunders of the past, that may be a small price to pay. In this case, the $2 million represents less than .03 percent of the company's annual revenue.

Money, however, is not the only type of investment needed to improve recruitment, and it may not even be the most important. The key to recruitment may lie more in the creative, analytic thinking that matches recruitment tools to the desired pool of candidates. A manager in one company in our study started going to conventions to let parents know about opportunities available for young people of color. He reasoned that they would encourage their children to apply to his company rather than to competitors. CEOs of major employers are being invited to at least one predominantly black school to be interviewed by upcoming graduates. Clearly, the financial expense is insignificant compared with the CEO's time and ability to make the company look more attractive than other companies to talented, selective students. Time and creativity are certainly needed to accompany whatever financial resources are devoted to recruiting employees of choice.

Recruiting Key Managers from Outside

Regardless of whether an organization uses special incentives, the process of bringing an outsider into the executive suite is a tricky one; and it is an option many executives use only as a last resort. In fact, several managers we interviewed warned against this approach, citing their own disastrous results with executives parachuted in from the outside. One problem with this option is that insiders may be alienated by such action, seeing it as yet another sign that they have only limited advancement potential within the organization. One female vice president told us how angry women in her organization get when a female executive is hired from outside. "Hiring women from the outside to fill senior management positions sends a negative message to those inside," she said. "There's a flaw if senior management can't develop women from inside."

Another problem with hiring key managers from outside is that they often seem to fail. Whether because of the resentment of inside colleagues or because the new managers are unable to adjust to the culture or simply because limited information about outside candidates results in job mismatches, frequent failures in such placements have scared some executives away from outside hiring. Nevertheless, executives from many organizations with a proud tradition of promoting from within are resorting to hiring one or more executives from the outside.

According to managers in our study, having women and people of color in senior-level line management positions is one of the most important ingredients of an effective diversity effort. Not only are these nontraditional executives important role models, but their individual efforts also shape and vitalize diversity activities throughout the organization. The need to meet goals for diversity at higher management levels represents one driving force that compels executives to hire from outside. Whether internal candidates are truly underqualified because of poor career development or whether they have been prematurely discounted, the only choice in the short run for many executives seems to be promoting a white man from inside or hiring a nontraditional manager from outside.

Executives who have made the difficult decision to bring in an executive from outside the organization have learned some lessons about how to reduce the risk. Extra attention to newly hired executives is especially warranted when women or people of color are involved, as a signal that senior management is committed to smooth and successful integration. At one company, for example, a female executive was introduced slowly and methodically to the staff of her new employer, with careful attention given to the meetings she would attend and with whom. Her qualifications were exceptional, but top management was sensitive to the need for a proper introduction as well. At another company, outsiders are brought in at the middle-management level, which gives them a chance to grow into senior-management jobs more quickly than they might have if they had been hired into entry-level jobs.

Using Visibility as a Recruitment Technique

The portrayal of women and people of color in an organization's communication with the public is likely to influence prospective employees at all levels. A few organizations in our study have taken steps to ensure that the materials recruits receive contain the message that diversity is valued. In at least one company, people of color and white women are recruited with special brochures describing opportunities for them. In other organizations, executives have decided instead to revamp existing public relations materials to better convey that message. Publications such as annual reports now include more text about the organization's commitment to diversity and more photographs of nontraditional employees. Perhaps these executives have realized that potential employees, particularly at managerial levels, are just as likely to form an impression from the organization's general publications as from any special materials they receive.

Advertising the organization as a progressive employer in the popular press is another technique that is likely to attract the attention of nontraditional potential employees. A number of companies now advertise their commitment to promote a diverse workforce in magazines such as *Black Enterprise* and *Working Woman,* hoping to create a more positive image among recruits. A work environment that is more supportive than that of other organizations can be a strong drawing card for white women and people of color. Ads similar to the one mentioned at the beginning of this chapter, which is more indirect as a recruiting tool than many other ads, can give an organization a visible edge as the employer of choice for many nontraditional managers.

An even more desirable method of obtaining visibility through advertising is to be included in published lists of "best companies," such as *Hispanic* magazine's "Hispanic 100: The One Hundred Companies Providing the Most Opportunities for Hispanics," *Black Enterprise* magazine's "25 Best Places for Blacks to Work," or books such as Baila Zeitz and Lorraine Dusky's (1988) *The Best Companies for Women.* Such recognition often provides even more credibility and visibility for companies searching for a competitive edge. At least some of the companies listed have found that the number of nontraditional job applicants has increased.

Managers can also make their organizations more visible to nontraditional potential employees by getting involved in community activities. Clubs, sports leagues, church groups, and committees to organize local ethnic events, for example, offer managers a chance to discover talented individuals whom they would otherwise not meet. Ongoing relationships with school alumnae groups and professional associations provide recruitment avenues at local and national levels. Groups such as the American Association of Hispanic CPAs, the National Black MBA Association, and the American Indian Science and Engineering Society often have national conferences and local chapters through which managers may get involved, develop a positive image for their organization, and effectively recruit managers and professionals.

Providing Incentives for Recruits

Other techniques to aid recruitment are quite controversial, particularly such practices as offering financial incentives to attract nontraditional managers and high-level professionals. The argument for incentives is that offering a "bonus" for nontraditional employees helps the organization attract the cream of the crop. Critics suggest that this type of "bribery" is unfair to other employees. Incentives being used by organizations in our study include cash bonuses given to headhunters who find suitable nontraditional candidates in their searches and bonuses to department heads who recommend nontraditional candidates who are eventually hired into the organization. Sign-on bonuses are sometimes also paid to the nontraditional recruits themselves, along with a salary or benefit package that is more substantial than that offered to white male recruits.

Noncash bonuses for hiring nontraditional employees are also used. Extra positions are allowed, even funded from a separate budget, to increase the representation of nontraditional employees in a department or region. This type of practice may be more difficult to adopt in a government agency, but it is used in education and in business. Here is how it works: if there are two approved openings — say, two marketing representative positions or two lecturer positions in the school of engineering — a third position may also be approved if at least one of the original two is filled with a nontraditional employee.

Yet another controversial incentive tool is the "cookie jar." If a desirable nontraditional candidate is available for hire but no official job opening exists, the person may be put on the payroll and given project work to do until a legitimate job opens up. Some managers consider this a useful technique because it precludes the danger that the candidate will accept work in another organization while waiting for a position to open. The cookie jar may be especially effective in areas with high turnover, where a legitimate job is likely to become available quickly.

Pockets of extreme homogeneity within an organization have also been targeted for the cookie jar incentive, according to one manager we interviewed. Managers caution, however, that judicious use of this tool is essential so that it does not backfire and create a backlash. Temporary "make work" assignments may cause others to believe that nontraditional employees can't handle "real" jobs.

Incentives of any sort that are used specifically to attract people of color or women into an organization are risky, but they can be effective in recruitment. Special financial arrangements have been made in organizations for many years to attract and keep white male managers and other individuals who are considered special. Many companies, for example, have adopted the practice of giving sign-on bonuses to new employees who are particularly desirable, including white men. Some companies now offer what are called stay bonuses, which, according to the *Wall Street Journal* ("'Stay Bonuses' Are Used to Keep Employees," 1991) consist of cash or other inducements to keep valued workers from leaving in the middle of a merger or closedown. As a diversity strategy, however, the challenge is to use recruitment incentives to emphasize that performance, not demographics alone, is the objective.

Recruitment today clearly means much more than setting up a booth at a few elite colleges each spring and waiting for students to walk by. Our research suggests that progressive organizations have made two major changes in their traditional recruitment strategy. They have changed the primary sources for their recruits, and they have adopted different techniques for use with both the old and the new sources.

Part Three describes a step-by-step process for making organization-wide improvements in the recruitment, development, and accountability practices affecting diversity.

LEADERSHIP
DIVERSITY
AS
ACTION

Part Two has described a variety of practices that organizations can use to foster diversity. The question now is how to select and use those that hold the most promise in a given situation. Part Three outlines a process for making the hard decisions involved in designing a diversity effort and moving forward to implement meaningful practices.

The process we recommend here consists of five basic steps that can help managers organize and answer the questions that need to be addressed in creating and carrying out a diversity plan. They are the same steps often recommended for change efforts involving quality improvement, increased responsiveness to customers, and other issues that involve an overall "culture change" rather than minor fine-tuning. These steps are not academic, however; they are based on the successes and failures of organizations in our study in dealing specifically with diversity issues. The mistakes and gaps the companies experienced in their diversity efforts actually helped us to arrive at this process. The five steps shown in the following figure and enumerated below, therefore, incorporate both the lessons of success and the lessons of failure.

> Step one: Discover (and rediscover) diversity problems in the organization. Collecting current information helps counter assumptions about diversity problems and

Five Steps to Develop Diversity in an Organization.

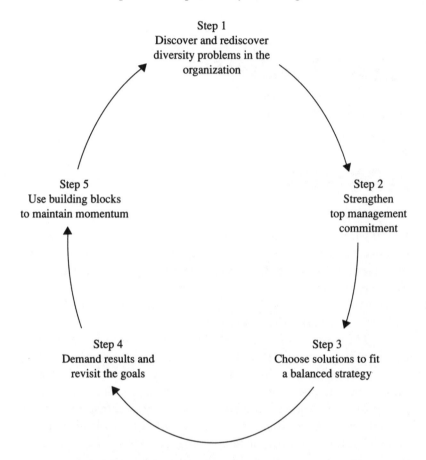

Step 1
Discover and rediscover
diversity problems in the
organization

Step 5
Use building blocks
to maintain momentum

Step 2
Strengthen
top management
commitment

Step 4
Demand results and
revisit the goals

Step 3
Choose solutions to fit
a balanced strategy

progress. What is the best way for managers to collect
the information needed to set priorities for their diversity efforts?

Step two: Strengthen top-management commitment. Top
managers' involvement in a diversity effort can be the
key to success, but there are also some pitfalls to avoid.
What do committed top managers do that promotes
diversity, and what kinds of actions should they avoid?

Step three: Choose practices that fit a balanced strategy.
Although no particular set of practices seems to work

better than others across organizations, the selection
process involves some strategic issues in responding to
current problems. What criteria should be used to choose
certain solutions over others?

Step four: Demand results. Setting specific diversity goals
and evaluating the results of diversity efforts are complicated and often involve debate over quantitative and
qualitative measures. What are appropriate indicators
of progress on diversity, and how should they be measured?

Step five: Use building blocks to continue progress. Managers alert to their organization's traditions, business
situation, and past successes in fostering diversity can
incorporate these into an ongoing diversity effort. What
characteristics can strengthen a diversity effort, and how
can managers keep the momentum going?

The steps are not entirely separate from one another. For
example, analysis of an organization's strengths, which can serve
as building blocks, should occur in all five steps, not only late
in the process. Moreover, the steps are not meant to suggest
a lockstep process; rather, action should flow from one step to
another, perhaps even back and forth in some cases. After choosing a set of practices in step two and monitoring the results in
step three, it may be appropriate to recreate a mix of practices
in response to those results, dropping some practices in favor
of others and again monitoring the results. Likewise, after information is collected in step one and that data is used to garner
stronger support from senior managers in step two, additional
information may need to be collected to further convince top
management to commit to action and also to help determine
which practices may be needed most to solve the most pressing
problems.

Chapters Seven through Eleven offer managers several
guidelines for each step in the diversity development process.
A summary of all twenty-one guidelines is presented at the end
of Chapter Eleven.

SEVEN

STEP ONE: DISCOVER (AND REDISCOVER) DIVERSITY PROBLEMS IN YOUR ORGANIZATION

We are sitting in an executive conference room, overlooking a panoramic cityscape. A senior vice president of operations has been talking with me for more than an hour. He has put his reading glasses back into his pocket and is sipping mineral water as he prepares to answer my next question. He has an unhurried air and seems to be totally engrossed in the interview. He is white, fifty-six years old, and has a bachelor's degree and a certificate from Wharton's advanced management program. He has worked in the same organization for many years. I ask, "Of all the diversity policies and practices you've mentioned, can you identify one or two that you think are most significant?" He answers:

> The single most important driver of change has been our employee groups of minorities and women. One reason for their effectiveness is that over the years they've really done their homework, and they've presented facts and statistics.
>
> One group, for example, demonstrated that average pay increases for four groups—Hispanic females, Hispanic males, black females and black males—were less than those for white males. Black females across the organization had average pay increases that were 63 percent of those for white males. In another case, the women's group raised a concern regarding the hardships of relocation on dual-career couples. With their help, we did a survey regarding mobility and found that anyone

163

with a working spouse will be less likely to move. As a
result, we now give more help with trailing spouses and
additional incentives to move.

Because these employee groups present such
convincing data, we use a lot of what they recommend.

Barriers to advancement affect many nontraditional managers
across many organizations, but the ways in which those barriers operate can vary dramatically from one organization to
another and even among divisions or regions of the same organization. Finding and understanding the most significant problems in your organization (or in your part of the organization)
is a basic first step in making headway on diversity issues.

There are several good reasons to investigate current issues. A benefit of uncovering problems on your own is that they
have special meaning within the context of your company or
institution. When managers and employees are directly involved
in the investigation and have clarified the issues for themselves,
they are more likely to get involved in the solutions. An internal investigation may help convince executives that problems
really do exist. Reports of problems in other organizations may
be dismissed as not relevant, but an inside investigation provides more compelling evidence that is difficult to shrug off.

A Hispanic manager we interviewed was concerned that
Hispanics were not moving up in his company. Although he
eventually got the nerve to approach a senior vice president five
levels above him in the company, he couldn't convince the vice
president that there was a problem. Finally, the manager offered
to provide proof if senior management would then take steps
to correct the problem. An agreement was struck, and the manager started a process that continues today. As this manager
described it, "These senior managers realized they didn't understand Hispanics. Most were from the East and had very little experience with Hispanic people. I got the vice president to
have a meeting that could help educate other managers about
Hispanic issues. It was very risky, but I brought in fifteen other
Hispanics from varying jobs and places to discuss twenty-five

issues of sensitivity. The response was great. The managers didn't want to leave, and they extended the meeting. They took lots of notes."

Keep Assumptions Under Control

Obtaining current, accurate information to dispel myths about diversity problems is the first step toward finding effective solutions. One mistake many executives make, according to managers in our study, is to assume that no news is good news when it comes to hearing about advancement barriers. Assumptions abound because some topics having to do with differential treatment are still considered taboo in organizations. Many people of color and white women do not feel free to comment on the barriers they encounter because doing so often only serves to separate them more from traditional managers. They feel like complainers, not team players, if they bring up these issues. Learning about the current hot buttons in an organization is a difficult but necessary learning process that facilitates follow-up discussions about how to resolve problems.

Another fact we discovered is that some managers continue to assume that nontraditional managers are less competent than traditional managers. In effect, they "blame the victims" for their lack of advancement opportunities. We know from our study that prejudice along with other barriers accounts for at least part of this perception. An imbalance in the components of sustained leadership development may also shape impressions of the competence of nontraditional managers. These factors need to be examined along with individuals' knowledge, skills, and abilities to determine the actual problems that need to be solved in an organization. Collecting information that addresses these factors is an important step in getting beyond assumptions.

Other assumptions about diversity proliferate in organizations. For example, there is no problem because equal opportunity now exists; the problem is this (say, family conflicts for women, or poor education of people of color) rather than that (differential evaluation criteria, or lack of career guidance, for instance); the same problem affects all nontraditional managers equally or in the same way; the most severe problems affect only one ethnic group. Such assumptions need to be tested — and retested over time as situations change — so that any remedies undertaken address the real and current problems.

Although many of the most critical barriers appear to apply to all nontraditional managers, some problems differ for different groups. Several managers in our study noted that white women, for example, have been in management in their organizations longer than people of color, so their major problem may have more to do with promotion or development than with entry. The two groups' problems may, then, require different types of solutions. The history and status of different nontraditional groups vary from one organization to another and may indicate which problems are most critical for particular groups.

Substituting data for assumptions helps prevent situations in which solutions go in search of problems. When senior executives propose solutions to some problems but key groups of employees want other problems solved first, those solutions have little credibility. A good solution to the wrong problem is hardly a solution at all. Catalyst's 1990 report shows that the most common practices organizations use to advance women past the glass ceiling are not directly tied to the most common barriers cited. Overemphasizing work-family programs, for example, at the expense of developmental programs may occur at companies because executives assume that family conflicts are women's main frustration. However, research by Victoria Tashjian (1990) has shown that more female managers leave because of career blocks than because of family conflicts.

The benefits of investigation increase when it is regularly repeated. Regularly asking employees about their concerns is a way to take the temperature of an organization, to identify the issues that are still current, and to identify points that can shape the solutions to diversity problems. An additional benefit of repeated queries is that progress becomes evident. When a problem has been solved between investigations, that information is important to report. Achievements can be good morale boosters that might be lost if repeated inquiries were not made.

Repeated investigations help track problems as they wax and wane in a given organization. For example, several years ago, a company used focus groups of women to identify problems, and the groups cited sexual harassment. The company then took action to curb that problem. In the words of a consultant we interviewed, "Two guys got transferred and were told to clean up their act or go. We identified three high-level men engaged in sexist behaviors, and all of them got on the retirement list." The follow-up investigation that the focus groups held about eighteen months ago revealed that sexual harassment was no longer considered a problem; none of the women identified blatant instances of sexual harassment, so the company's actions had apparently solved the problem. However, another problem — child care — was raised for the first time, perhaps because the women were now more comfortable talking about how troublesome an issue child care is. This company's ability to keep in touch with important issues identified by employee groups has helped focus its efforts toward effective solutions. The focus groups may return to the issue of sexual harassment in the wake of the accusations made by Anita Hill against Supreme Court nominee Clarence Thomas. Periodic investigations allow this and other issues to be readdressed as necessary in the pursuit of diversity.

Monitoring progress toward diversity helps ensure that the practices being instituted are effective. Managers in our study noted that some executives have been going along for years believing that they have done enough for nontraditional managers or that they have done as well as anyone could expect. They have complied with the personnel profile goals set by the government, they have drawn up policy statements against discrimination, they have begun recruiting graduates from a predominantly black college, and so on. Their perception is that they have done enough, and they are surprised when others do not agree. In one company in our study, for example, executives were apparently dealt a stunning blow by some employees who felt compelled to take matters into their own hands. A group of black managers was so dissatisfied with their work situation that they called a press conference to declare the company racist.

Follow-up investigations may enable organizations to uncover problems that are relatively new to them, such as infighting among nontraditional groups, employment practices that don't fit the growing dual-career workforce, or the increasingly creative disguises used to mask differential treatment. Moreover, regular investigations may be one of the most effective methods for tackling what has become the most destructive problem in many organizations, the problem of backlash.

Managers in our study mentioned backlash more than any other problem as a weakness in their diversity efforts, and some managers cited backlash as a barrier in itself to the advancement of nontraditional managers. According to Nelson-Horchler (1991), an *Industry Week* survey showed that 35 percent of male managers believe that their companies discriminate against men to redress past bias against women (only 10 percent of women agreed). Without attention at the discovery stage of diversity development, backlash can become a serious deterrent to diversity efforts. Reverse discrimination lawsuits or sabotage of existing diversity practices, for example, can perhaps be prevented if backlash can be detected early enough to defuse a hot issue. In fact, the data collected in the first step of the diversity effort may be an effective tool to defuse such an issue because the data may well show that white men still get advanced and rewarded more than others. For the white men who fear that all the promotions are going to nontraditional managers, such data can make them feel less threatened while also demonstrating that differential treatment still exists.

In short, periodic investigation of the existing problems in an organization gets information out on the table for everyone to see. Managers can be an organization's biggest handicap in making headway on diversity and that misinformation can be equally destructive.

Collect More Than "Just the Facts" — Perceptions Count, Too

Objective, statistical data are the obvious and primary goal of an investigation. The information needed to document problems often lies in the numbers. Where in the organization are women and people of color not equitably represented? How do promotion rates compare? Are there any disparities in pay among managers within the same pay grade? What proportion of nontraditional managers receive benefits such as incentive compensation, outside leadership training, and the like? Answers to these questions are critical in determining the type and extent of problems within an organization.

Statistical data, however, represent only part of the information an investigation should provide. Perceptions, too, have a role in helping managers discover problems and lay the foundation for solving them. The "why" behind the data must be examined so that the data contribute to a learning process. Internal examinations at Johnson & Johnson, for example, were initiated because of declining progress in advancing black managers, according to vice president Gail Judge (1988). The information collected revealed that the acquisition of new high-tech companies with few black employees had changed the corporate profile and that a shift toward hiring technical specialists had further exaggerated the decline. Shutting down older facilities in historically black areas made the picture even worse. These changes in the nature of the business may have been at the root of the problem, but the perception of black managers in the corporation was that they had less opportunity to be sponsored, to establish social contacts, and to be appraised fairly.

According to Judge, the management of Johnson & Johnson chose to deal squarely with the perceptions of both the white and black managers involved in the investigation. The problem is being addressed by finding better ways to recruit black scientists, conducting performance appraisals the way they were designed to be done, and understanding why the human resource systems are seen as unfair. Had the corporation opted to deal only with the "factual" issues, it is likely that more black managers would have opted out. The perceived inequities were seen as equally important to the loss of opportunities due to documented changes in business operations.

There are many effective ways to conduct an organizational audit to determine which, if any, diversity problems exist and which problems warrant attention first. The sixteen organizations we studied use a variety of methods to identify problems, including surveys, interviews, focus groups, and combinations thereof.

Surveys usually come to mind when people think of investigating problems, and in fact surveys have been effectively used in a number of organizations in our study. Examples of survey research are available in the books of John Fernandez (1981, 1987) and Roosevelt Thomas (1991) and in a number of other publications cited in this book. Surveying employees is a relatively quick and easy way to solicit the views of a large number of people. However, because surveys preclude interaction with respondents, survey data alone can be misleading and can contribute to the problem of misinformation if they are not used carefully. What employees write is what you get, which may be indecipherable, ambiguous, or incomplete. There is no chance to follow up on the responses unless the respondents are identified. In that case, confidentiality concerns may cause employees to slant or limit the information they provide.

Surveys usually involve multiple-choice rather than open-ended responses. To create a survey form, one has to know not only the questions to ask but also the answers employees are likely to give. Most employees are not willing to write extensive, descriptive answers to survey questions. They will check a box or rank order a short list and even occasionally fill in a short answer. If they find the choices to be off base, they may skip the question or mark the choice that seems closest to their answer. Few will go to the trouble of writing an explanation of how their preferred response compares with the options given on the survey form. There is the risk that terms such as *mentor* or *successful* may mean different things to different employees and to the researchers. Interpreting the responses, then, becomes a seemingly subjective process that may or may not reflect the respondents' true opinions.

Interviews are less risky in these respects, but they also have their downsides. They are expensive. Interviews consume far more time and energy than surveys on the part of the questioners and the respondents. Spending at least an hour with each respondent is not unreasonable to achieve the purpose of the interview: to develop a rapport with the employees, to elicit their ideas and experiences regarding diversity, to probe and explore those ideas to get a clear understanding of problems and examples. Because such information is very difficult to quantify, statistical reinforcement is typically sparse; this can be a disadvantage to those inclined toward numbers. Because of the expense, only a small number of people can be interviewed, particularly on an individual basis. Group interviews or focus groups reduce the cost but lead to other potential problems. Employees may be reluctant to speak their minds because of less confidentiality (because others in the group hear what is said and by whom) and the inclination to go along with what the others are saying rather than disagree.

One way around some of these problems is to interview a number of employees first to create the survey questions and response categories. The rich information from the interviews forms the basis for the survey, and the survey method allows far more employees to share their views. Experienced researchers have used this technique in a number of diversity investigations. In one case, a team of researchers led by Clay Alderfer (1980) of Yale University used this combined method to diagnose race relations in a large industrial corporation. In this study, the researchers initially held confidential interviews with twenty-four employees to get their views of black-white relations within the company's management and their help in identifying other employees with very different views. The researchers used the responses to construct a questionnaire that nearly seven hundred employees completed. This two-step process can be an effective way to capture the advantages of each method.

While questionnaire surveys, interviews, and focus groups are the three principal methods used to investigate perceptions of organizational issues such as diversity, each method, as we have seen, has its pros and cons, and no one method is categorically better than the others. Combining two or more methods may be especially effective in some situations. Choosing the best investigation procedure involves a number of considerations, including the goals of the exercise; the influence of past efforts to investigate or solve problems; the time, money, and expertise available; and the urgency of obtaining and using results. A team of people that represents the major constituencies within the organization should weigh these factors.

Ensure That a Team Is
Responsible for the Investigation

Because no technique is perfect, the actual method of investigation is probably not as important as how the method is chosen. A unilateral decision by a couple of managers as to how diversity problems will be identified is definitely not recommended. Instead, involving a diverse group in deciding how the investigation will be conducted will strengthen the process and make the results more credible in employees' eyes. As the first in a series of investments in diversity, the problem investigation step should require the participation of all groups who will be addressed in the solutions. Because the solutions should address all employee groups, including white men, it follows that the information-gathering process should also involve all groups.

The level of involvement in a task force may vary across demographic groups, with some playing a more central role and others being apprised along the way so that they can express any concerns and relevant design issues can be reconsidered. The same may be true across functional groups, with the human resource staff in particular playing a more central role than those in other areas. One danger to avoid, however, is having the process taken over by one group so that others feel the investigation is a "black project" or a "human resource project" and thus has little relevance to their situation.

A task force is often formed at this stage to help ensure full representation. This task force may or may not continue to operate in the later stages, or steps, of diversity efforts. A small task force of six to twelve people who represent the various constituencies within an organization can be a very useful working group, although larger groups are not uncommon. The task force of one organization in our study, for example, consisted of thirty members. This large group split into four working groups, however, to create specific recommendations in the areas identified for action. Even if a large group is needed to ensure adequate representation, it can make speedy and responsible decisions about an investigation, particularly when one or two skilled professionals can aid discussions.

The team or task force responsible for an investigation must first answer three major questions:

1. Who will collect the information? Will outside professionals be involved? If so, to what extent?
2. Whose opinions will be solicited? That is, how broad will representation be across demographic groups, across levels in the organization, and so on?
3. What information is needed to identify the problems accurately and thoroughly and to sort out those that are most in need of immediate action?

Who Will Collect the Information?

There are three reasons to consider hiring outside professionals to collect and analyze data: to gain additional expertise, to safeguard confidentiality, and to speed up the process by means of additional staff. An outside professional or firm may be helpful in constructing the questions to be asked, actually asking the questions, and compiling the results. Outsiders usually take a more objective look at the issues and sometimes bring a perspective based on similar work at other organizations that can add to the value and credibility of the process.

The involvement of an outside organization keeps raw data out of the hands of insiders; this protects employees because none of their co-workers see or hear their responses (unless group interviews are conducted). The responses are grouped, even disguised if necessary, when presented to anyone from the organization so that anonymity is preserved. On emotionally charged issues such as diversity and differential treatment the guarantee of confidentiality can be very important, especially when people at different levels of the organization are involved. Executives may feel that their remarks must fall in line with the organization's official policies regardless of their true views; lower-level managers may fear repercussions from superiors if their opinions clash. Without precautions such as those an outside firm can provide, employees may decline to participate or withhold important information when they do participate. Roosevelt Thomas (1990) suggests that if a comprehensive culture audit is being undertaken, outsiders may be required to sort out the values and rituals that characterize the dominant culture and to help employees envision those that would characterize a desired culture. It may be too difficult for insiders alone to analyze the assumptions and behaviors that make up their own working environment.

The expense of an outside firm should be weighed against the relative speed of its work in comparison with having staff members do the work along with fulfilling their ongoing responsibilities. Inside staff members likely to be most involved in this type of project are those in the human resource functions. The more knowledgeable, trusted, and available these staff members are, the less need there is to go outside for help. The project task force or advisory committee members will also be actively involved, but their role as contributors and overseers may not change significantly if outsiders are called in.

Although many organizations could use additional resources to carry out an investigation, the additional time, coordination, and funding required may not be warranted, particularly if appropriate consultants seem to be elusive. If a cooperative and respectful working relationship between outside experts and the internal investigation team cannot be quickly established, then an internal investigation should be seriously considered. Technical expertise does not automatically outweigh purposeful collaboration.

Whose Opinions Will Be Solicited?

The rule of thumb in regard to whose opinions will be solicited is to err on the side of too much rather than too little inclusion because a high degree of involvement helps ensure that the results of an investigation will be meaningful and believable. Even when employees of certain ethnicities or at certain levels are not obviously tied to some of the issues being examined, their involvement may be critical. For example, let's say that an organization's senior management candidates currently include only white men, white women, and black men. Certainly these individuals should be asked their ideas about "glass ceiling" barriers, but other women and men of color in the organization's so-called pipeline are likely to be valuable contributors to understanding related issues such as the barriers within middle management or recruitment hurdles.

Digging down through the organization's levels to get diverse demographic representation can be helpful until it becomes distracting. Leadership diversity is a different issue from workforce diversity in general. In principle, every employee is a candidate for leadership of an organization, but in practice only some of the workforce has the potential and the impetus to advance to senior levels. Sorting these individuals is an imperfect process, but an investigation may be more powerful if as many high-potential candidates as possible are included. Clearly, grouping individuals' responses by their assessed potential, their level, and other functional characteristics, as well as by their sex and ethnicity, helps in interpreting the results. Comparing the responses of senior-level "hi-pos," lower-level "hi-pos," and other managers of color, for example, may lead to penetrating insights about effective diversity practices.

Geographical location is another factor that can affect diversity and the ways in which employees view diversity issues. The various geographical regions in which an organization operates should definitely be considered in the development of an investigation. The ethnic makeup and even the term *minority* are defined differently in different cities, states, and regions of the country. Blacks represent the dominant minority group in many parts of the United States, but Mexican-Americans and Asian-Americans dominate in California. Cubans dominate in parts of Florida, and so forth. For an organization with wide-ranging operations, diversity problems may be very different from one plant, subsidiary, or region to another. Other factors, including climate, business conditions, and social opportunities, also come into play. Attracting black managers to Fargo, North Dakota, for example, is a very different challenge from recruiting them to Atlanta or Washington, D.C., because of the climate and community factors. Therefore, the input of people who are geographically diverse may be as relevant in identifying and resolving diversity problems as the input of people diverse in other respects. When some managers in our study analyzed results of an investigation, they were surprised at how much employee responses differed from one plant to another and from one region to another.

Concentrating on getting the opinions of viable candidates for senior management posts is one way to limit the number of people when gathering certain types of information. If high-potential lists are not available or consist of virtually all white men, then inclusion may be based on level, function, or location. If participants must be limited, it may be a good idea to focus on people with the most knowledge and potential without automatically excluding those with nontraditional career paths or qualifications that may have ruled them out of contention previously but may not necessarily restrict them in the future. Former employees who were thought to have high potential but who voluntarily left the organization also represent a valuable source of information. Although it may take additional work to track down and convince former employees to participate, several organizations include them in their studies because they, better than anyone else, may reveal ways to keep other high-potential employees from leaving.

What Information Is Needed?

Several types of information, both factual and perceptual, can be helpful in an investigation. In terms of diversity, answers to questions such as the following can provide that information.

> What evidence is there that differential treatment actually exists?
> What policies and practices of the organization contribute to differential treatment, on the basis of sex, ethnicity, or other nonperformance-related characteristics?

What aspects of the organization's culture facilitate or interfere with diversity?

How well are managers doing in supervising and developing their white male and nontraditional subordinates?

What do employees think and feel about their work in general and about diversity issues in particular within their organization?

Evidence of differential treatment includes statistical data such as personnel profiles specifying sex and ethnicity and a number of other measures that are described in more detail in Chapter Ten. Other types of evidence may also be used to assess the type and extent of differential treatment.

In the investigation led by Clay Alderfer (1980) referred to earlier, the researchers examined seven areas of interest in their questionnaire in addition to general race relations: management groups, hiring, advancement, firing, job opinions, actions for change, and reactions to the study. Employees indicated their degree of agreement with statements in each of these areas, and the responses of black men and women were compared with those of white men and women. Among the statements were the following (pp. 154–159).

Good one-to-one black-white relationships are common in XYZ [the designation the researchers used for the corporation].

XYZ screens out assertive, confident black females.

Black managers are often given assignments with the expectation that they will fail.

Reverse discrimination demoralizes XYZ management.

XYZ officers do little to advance the cause of black managers.

The way management movement committees are set up within XYZ, it is almost impossible for blacks to reach upper management levels.

Although this investigation was conducted specifically to assess race relations, techniques and data from research on other, broader organizational issues are often used in an examination of diversity issues. Attitude surveys, for example, often serve as a key source of information. Whether questions specifically directed to diversity issues are included or whether responses to only traditional questions are analyzed according to respondents' sex and ethnicity, the results are often valuable additions to other data on diversity.

Attitude surveys, which measure employees' perceptions of and satisfaction with a variety of factors about their work, working relationships, and employer, are sometimes used as a feedback tool for managers and even as a measure of managers' competence. In one of the organizations in our study, for example, a regularly conducted employee survey is used to inform managers of their strengths and weaknesses and to prompt them to improve their effectiveness as supervisors of both traditional and nontraditional employees. The questions on this survey cover a range of topics that presumably affect employees' performance. Employees are asked to indicate their agreement with statements such as the following:

> I am satisfied with the training I received for my present job.
> My job makes good use of my skills and abilities.
> We have an effective process for identifying candidates to fill open positions.
> I plan to be working for [this organization] a year from now.
> My manager does not show favoritism.
> My manager gives me honest feedback on my performance.
> My manager is effective at
>> discussing the objectives and problems of my assignments with me.
>> discussing my strengths and areas for improvement.
>> adjusting his or her management approach to meet my individual needs.
>> giving me assignments that provide potential for personal growth.

These questions are designed to address the impact of individual managers on their employees' career development and overall well-being. Larger issues concerning the work environment, such as "culture" and systemic factors, may also be important in assessing and correcting problems. While an organization's culture can certainly be explored by means of surveys and interviews, observation and archival records may also be necessary to round out the picture. Similarly, potential systemic barriers may also become apparent only after examining documents as well as polling employees. The impact of the organization's recruitment and selection systems, training and development systems, performance evaluation system, reward system, and communications systems, among others, may need to be assessed with multiple investigative techniques. Other forces that affect the organization, such as economic conditions and standardized business procedures, should also be studied and considered in creating solutions to diversity problems, as the managers at Johnson & Johnson did in the earlier example.

Do Not Get Bogged Down in Collecting or Analyzing Information

Obviously, the discovery process can easily become cumbersome and time-consuming. Although gathering and analyzing information are an essential first step in finding effective solutions to diversity problems, managers must avoid the possibility of getting mired in data. The very process of collecting information about diversity heightens employees' expectations that some action will be taken. Employees will not be content to contribute information and then sit back and wait for something to happen. Therefore, it is important to keep the discovery step driving toward solutions.

The discovery step itself is likely to involve a series of substeps to uncover the roots of problems. Short-circuiting these substeps could jeopardize the diversity effort by allowing a problem to remain disguised, but they should be taken with speed as well as diligence. One task force in our study, for example, used a variety of techniques to uncover some issues until they were satisfied that they had identified the core problem. A series of investigations began when one task force member claimed that the grievance procedures were unfair to people of color. The group decided to check certain company records to see whether the claim was true. The records of formal grievance cases showed that employees of color got a favorable ruling 45 percent of the time, whereas the figure for white employees was 52 percent. The data were not broken down by job level.

When that task force began conducting preliminary interviews with employees to investigate diversity issues further, it included a question on the formal grievance process: "Have your grievances been adequately resolved through the company's procedures?" One person of color commented that he had been reluctant to take his grievances to the committee for fear of reprisal. Because of this comment, the task force revised the question for inclusion in the questionnaire survey of employees to read: "I hesitate to take my complaints to the grievance committee for fear of reprisal. This is especially true in cases of pay inequities, being passed over for a promotion, being sponsored or recommended for developmental assignments, being denied flexible working hours or special benefits, other _____."

The survey results revealed that people of color were more hesitant than white managers to make formal complaints regarding promotions and development assignments. A reexamination of the records showed that, indeed, far fewer promotion and development cases had been submitted by people of color than by whites, and the rulings on those types of cases were disproportionately more favorable for whites than they were for people of color. Further, the task force learned that 60 percent of the white managers who lost their cases for promotion or development had since been promoted or transferred to desirable assignments compared with only 10 percent of the people of color who lost their cases. The task force was able to conclude that differential treatment might be occurring specifically with regard to promotion and development opportunities. Their recommendations could then swiftly address this specific problem.

The selective probing that the task force used to identify problems helped them avoid getting bogged down in collecting data for its own sake. The series of data-collection substeps in the foregoing example uncovered both the facts and perceptions needed to understand the nature of the problems that were occurring. Combining data from employee surveys or interviews and data documenting the organization's actual practices is a powerful technique in diversity efforts. Records about grievance outcomes, promotion rates, bonuses, transfers, travel, and a host of other indicators of career advancement can and should be used to assess the problems and progress within an organization. They represent benchmarks by which an organization measures progress. Appropriate benchmarks vary, depending on the situation. Certain indicators are more important in some organizations than in others and at certain times than at others. Certain indicators are more credible than others, and certain ones are more meaningful than others. Being selective about the benchmarks, the indicators of progress, and the questions asked of certain employees concerning leadership diversity is one of the task force's most important functions.

Because an ideal process for gathering data is not always available, in some cases it will be difficult to collect any information let alone risk becoming bogged down with data. Choosing the most relevant indicators is even more important in these cases; a few revealing pieces of data can constitute a very effective investigation.

Summary

The first step in the diversity effort, discovering and rediscovering problems, helps managers dispel divisive myths in organizations. The collected data help focus attention and remedies on those specific areas where perceived or actual differential treatment is a problem. The investigation team, whether it is composed entirely of insiders or includes outsiders, has the challenge of forcing momentum in collecting and analyzing relevant information that will result in speedy, concrete solutions to real problems. The team must build on the information it has collected, peeling away layers of symptoms, to get at the roots of problems.

The investigation team works in a pressure cooker of sorts. Team members must be responsive to employees' raised expectations that an investigation creates, yet they must also be thorough and precise in their analyses. Members must tap into the full range of diversity issues so that some do not fester and grow more destructive, but they must also quickly narrow the priorities to issues that are most pressing and inclusive. In doing this, they must advocate the unique needs of their particular constituency but also effectively collaborate with other team members to resolve overarching issues. Clearly, the teams that carry through a successful investigation deserve recognition and support for the challenge they take on.

Actually solving the problems uncovered in this first step of the diversity process is the goal of later steps. However, before remedial action can effectively begin, top management's commitment to diversity must be secured or strengthened. That second step is the subject of Chapter Eight.

EIGHT

STEP TWO: STRENGTHEN TOP-MANAGEMENT COMMITMENT

The setting is a corner office in the corporate headquarters building located in a suburban office park. The field sales manager was delayed by a previous meeting, and she has had to interrupt our interview twice to take phone calls. Despite her obviously hectic schedule, she is graciously giving detailed answers to my interview questions. The manager is an Asian-American in her mid forties who joined this company just after she finished college. She has been in her current position for about three years. Because of her history with the company, I am eager to hear her opinion about whether there has been a change over the past several years in the way that women and people of color, particularly those in the management ranks, have been treated. Her response is consistent with those of several other managers who have already been interviewed:

> Only in the last two years have we made significant progress regarding people of color and that is because of the commitment by senior management to make it go forward. Two years ago, diversity became a priority. Our business grew rapidly in the seventies and early eighties, but then we hit a bumpy time. We reduced staff and that included a lot of women and people of color because diversity wasn't a priority then.
>
> When business improved later in the eighties, we had a chance to regroup and focus on our commitment to diversity. Diversity is added value. I don't believe our competitors really recognize that we have a global econ-

omy, but our senior managers are aware of the diversity of customers and employees who are potential management candidates. Over and over, they have said that to compete in a diverse world market, we have to start at home.

The commitment of an organization's leaders to diversity is so important that it warrants emphasis as a separate step in the diversity process. This does not, of course, mean that commitment occurs only at this point in the process. The spirit and actions that characterize commitment are needed at every step. To take the first step of discovering diversity problems without any semblance of commitment from top management would indeed be foolhardy; identification of the problems without any follow-up to solve them would undoubtedly increase the problems. In fact, some management experts would recommend not collecting any data unless top management is willing to act on the information. One question for executives to ask themselves even before the first step begins is "Am I willing to take the findings seriously and act on them?" The words and actions of commitment apply broadly to the entire process of effectively increasing diversity. Commitment is included here as the second step instead of part of the first only because revealing problems related to diversity sometimes increases leaders' commitment to solve any problems unearthed and to pursue the next steps with focus and vigor.

Commitment from the top of an organization to reduce differential treatment and to foster diversity at higher management levels may be the most important factor in the success of a diversity effort. The commitment of top management was the only key element of the diversity effort that managers in all sixteen of our organizations reported. Other ingredients, such as the growth and profitability of the organization, the availability of resources for this initiative, and the capability of the individuals involved, were also mentioned as important contributors to the diversity effort, but not as often and not by representatives of all the organizations.

Top management's role includes defining the fundamental approach the organization is to take in regard to diversity. The five types of strategies outlined in the introduction to this book range from the "golden rule" approach to a "multicultural" approach. To encourage commitment throughout the organization, whatever strategy is behind a diversity effort should be explicit and widely known. Although there may be considerable disagreement over the strategy chosen, even an unpopular strategy, if explicit, may be preferable to an ambiguous one that promotes confusing or conflicting actions because of differing assumptions. Choosing a strategic approach should precede action planning.

Position Diversity as a Key Business Issue

Many managers in our study were adamant that top management must treat diversity as an important aspect of the organization's ability to continue doing business. This is because diversity must be viewed as a central issue worthy of managers' time and resources. The diversity mission needs to be explained again and again and reinforced regularly to ensure commitment down the line. The commitment of top management is critical in emphasizing how diversity is linked to the overall promise of the organization and, therefore, to the future prospects of every employee.

The benefits of diversity outlined in Chapter One were extolled by top executives and other managers in the organizations we studied. Some of the business reasons for diversity can be effectively used to convince top managers to become active in promoting diversity, perhaps because achieving business goals often appears to be more central to the role of management than pursuing social or moral goals. The top managers in our study seemed to be convinced that business reasons were the primary incentive to promote diversity and that these reasons were the best way to convince others to support diversity. Their own commitment was at least partially a result of the business needs they recognized.

What, exactly, does a committed executive do? Commitment can take many forms, and executives have only so much time to devote to any one issue. Perhaps the most significant way that top management can express commitment is through responsiveness.

Be Responsible for Diversity by Being Responsive

Before urging top management to be responsive, one caveat is in order. Managers in our study encouraged top managers to heed the data and to listen and respond to the opinions and suggestions of others. Nevertheless, it is at least as dangerous for a CEO to make quick assumptions about nontraditional managers' problems and barriers as it is for anyone else in the organization to do so. Therefore, top managers must fight the urge to take too much initiative in moving ahead with solutions until they are assured that those solutions — as well as the problems they are meant to address — are consistent with the facts and are agreed upon by others in the organization. It may seem strange to check the natural inclination of top management to act quickly on this issue. Yet for many action-oriented senior executives, the discipline needed to put aside their own ideas and get behind others is an indicator of the extra effort invested in diversity.

This means that top management's best bet for long-range solutions may be to support the recommendations of a task force or employee groups that represent large numbers of employees by providing the necessary resources. Top management should participate in defining and interpreting the issues surrounding diversity in a way that allows others to shape the direction of the effort. Top management should also clearly outline for the task force any resource or advocacy limits so that others can choose priorities and recommendations with full knowledge of the level of support they will receive. Senior executives may, for example, nominate a task force to make recommendations for retaining people of color and white women in management, suggesting the questions that should be addressed and stipulating that a certain amount of funding will be allocated for promising solutions.

Listening and responding to employees on diversity issues is a big part of top management's role in fostering diversity. Top managers also take other actions that contribute to their being seen as the major factor in whether a diversity effort succeeds or fails. What else do committed top managers do? For a variety of examples, let's look at how one white human resource executive in a large corporation described his top management team to us:

> Our leaders are saying things like "Are you working on diversity? I am interested in diversity." "The next time we do an operations review, I want you to tell me about upward mobility for Hispanics." There are special projects that are corporate goals, such as finding a female sales manager. If the excuse is given that no women are qualified here, their answer is, "Then go outside and get one, if you can't grow your own." For an annual award we give, they explicitly ask units to consider in their recommendations women, blacks, Hispanics, and so on. The survey feedback we get includes items on how women and minorities are treated. They attend meetings with minority employee groups. Our senior officers go to Washington, D.C., to be keynote speakers at weekend conferences sponsored by minority groups. This has been going on for years. Name me another company where that happens.

This description illustrates the variety of actions that committed executives take. They include providing resources of various sorts to support diversity activities, modeling ways to manage nontraditional managers, and providing the rationale and incentives to keep at the job of fostering diversity.

Allocating resources to diversify activities is the prerogative of top management; it is an indicator of the value executives place on the issue and one determinant of how successfully intentions can be transformed into actual change. The use of resources to encourage diversity can be even more controversial than policy decisions, and committed top executives are further burdened with the task of resolving the conflicts that arise. For example, if extra money is set aside to find and attract nontraditional managers, there will probably be some disagreement about whether to fund a separate (and expensive) recruitment effort for nontraditional managers. On the other hand, debate will probably grow much more heated over issues such as whether or not to reserve funds so that women and people of color can be paid more than white male recruits to join the organization. Top management is often forced to choose between making exceptions to standard pay levels to attract talented or experienced nontraditional managers or following the rules at the risk of losing nontraditional candidates who are in great demand by other organizations. Advocates on both sides of this choice are likely to be extremely opinionated and vocal, making this an awkward and risky decision for most senior executives.

Decisions about the allocation of resources come up over and over again, and many of them are no easier to resolve. Management jobs, for example, represent a valuable resource that can be a more sensitive issue than money, and holding positions open for nontraditional managers is another controversial diversity technique. When top executives refuse to accept a white male candidate for a key job that has been "reserved" for a nontraditional manager, they face the angry arguments of some subordinates who find themselves overworked from the continued effort to fill the post and to do the job themselves until someone else is brought in. Anger and controversy also confront senior executives who encourage nontraditional candidates to be brought in and "held" until appropriate permanent positions open up, as well as executives who demand that new positions be found for managers whose current positions could be used as development paths for nontraditional managers. Tipping the applecart like this is upsetting to many people who are not accustomed to making such concessions to women and people of color (and perhaps not to any white men either) and who must struggle to plan the details of such accommodations.

Senior management must also be responsible for allocating other types of resources to help ensure the success of diversity. Consultants or facilitators may be needed to help manage the work of task forces and employee groups. Instructors, facilities, and materials for diversity-related training programs involve additional expense. Awards for managers' diversity efforts may include some monetary recognition. Even awards that involve no money require resources to plan and publicize them.

Although diversity efforts often involve considerable monetary expense, the most valuable resource needed for diversity may be time. Even when budgets are tight and funding for out-of-pocket expenses is limited, managers can still do a great deal in terms of diversity simply by spending time. Committed senior executives we interviewed and those who were described to us in our study justify expending the organization's time on diversity issues, and they also spend their own time on them. They allocate meeting time for their highly paid management committee to discuss diversity goals and progress. They expect managers to use their time to master the "people management" competencies that diversity efforts often require. In short, top managers have redefined their managers' jobs to include responsibility for diversity and the resources to get the job done. Because fewer resources are available to solve other organizational problems while the diversity effort is absorbing time, money, and energy, top managers must have the courage to deal with their managers' possible confusion and resentment along with their questions about priorities.

Diversity is a long-term effort, and managers are easily distracted from diversity activities by short-term priorities. One responsibility of top management is to keep diversity uppermost in their employees' and associates' minds. The president of a retail company pointed out the difficulty—and the necessity—of doing this. In his words, "I never forget that I have to increase sales, but I may forget about recruiting women and people of color. More regular discussions with the senior management group would make this issue more top of mind, more part of our daily reality. We can make that happen. We just have to set it as a priority within the context of our limitations. We can spin only so many pie plates, but we have to manage the process of developing our human resources."

The senior executives in many of the organizations we studied made diversity a priority in part by setting an example for others to follow. They did what they expected others to do, showing their managers how diversity can be practiced. These are executives who "walked their talk" by personally taking action to accomplish what they said was important to them and to their organization. One executive in an educational institution, for example, made the diversity message more powerful by constantly backing it up with deeds of varying significance. According to one of his employees, "Whenever he speaks to the group, he will include something about minority achievement. He communicates that these people are important. Teachers and administrators perceive that he values black people. He selects blacks and women for key roles, and he suggests that they are 'in.'"

Committed top managers described in our study constantly remind managers to follow the policies and to focus on the goals for diversity. The actions that these top-level managers take are geared to getting others to take action. They confront, hassle, cajole, and praise the managers who report to them about diversifying the management ranks. The top executives at our sixteen model organizations "stay in their managers' faces" about the issue, relentlessly nudging and pushing managers to recruit, promote, delegate, challenge, recognize, and support women and people of color within their own domain of the organization.

Another way that top managers can set the tone is to meet with an employee group. Some committed top managers carve out the time to sit down with the officers or representatives of an internal advocacy group to hear their concerns and suggestions, sometimes on a regular basis. It may be a very uncomfortable experience, but these executives see their availability as a symbolic as well as practical measure to solve problems. They know that demonstrating such commitment to diversity is more painful and riskier than merely talking about commitment. Using dramatic, symbolic events that become part of the organization's oral history is one way to give diversity shape and meaning.

Sometimes senior executives must take drastic measures to convince managers that they are serious about diversity. The executive team of one company decided it was important to rely on more people of color and their firms as vendors. These executives followed the normal route of becoming active in minority professional associations and more visible to the black professional community. But that wasn't good enough for them. They did two other things to signal the company's interest in business relationships with people of color. One was to take five corporate vice presidents to a black professional meeting. The other was to encourage their white vendors to hire people of color. They did this by sending a letter to all the white professional firms with which the company was working. The letter made two points, in the words of one senior vice president: "First, we are receptive to working with blacks. Second, we insist that you have black professionals to handle our work."

Some senior executives committed to diversity take the dramatic action of disciplining and even firing otherwise high-performing managers because of their negative behavior toward nontraditional employees. A Native American manager we interviewed was impressed that senior management, for the first time, had begun punishing managers who violated the organization's diversity guidelines, including a policy prohibiting harassment. She said that several middle-level managers had been fired for sexually harassing secretaries, being abusive, and making slurs against homosexuals. "The message comes through the grapevine," she said, "and then it comes down from the vice presidents to their managers that inappropriate behavior will not be accepted."

On a larger scale, downsizing poses a difficult problem for senior executives, and some have handled it in a dramatic way to show their continued support for diversity. In an interview published in *Financier* (Lee and Mark, 1990), CEO William Lee talks about his difficult decision to lay off 1,800 white male workers from Duke Power Company instead of cutting according to inverse seniority, as was the custom. He used what he calls reverse discrimination "to preserve the progress that we had made toward nondiscrimination" (p. 31). After many discussions, he still had to face the men he laid off. "I went eyeball-to-eyeball with the white males," he reported, "and said that to the extent that I and my predecessors have been guilty of discrimination in history, we are not now going to take a backward step, and you suffer because of it" (p. 31).

Similar action was taken in at least one of the organizations we studied. A human resource manager praised the "willingness of top management to stay the course in bad times as well as good" when thousands of layoffs had to be made. White men with more seniority than others were laid off to maintain the representation of people of color, white women, and workers over the age of forty. Top management accepted the risk involved in reverse discrimination by doing this, but only one lawsuit was filed. "Our method saved us," this manager told us; "our policy could be demonstrated."

Less dramatically, senior executives also demonstrate their commitment to diversity by giving special assignments to their managers, including everything from putting a policy into written form to filling a certain key position with a nontraditional manager. A number of top executives in our study put pressure on officers to select women and people of color for director-level and even officer-level openings. They insist on seeing nontraditional candidates on the list for each opening. They require all their general managers to identify, describe, and develop high-potential nontraditional managers in their units. And they don't accept excuses.

Some chief executives make sure that diversity is on the agenda of key meetings, and they regularly attend to the demographic mix of people at all the meetings they attend, whether they are annual meetings for managers above a certain level or breakfast meetings to get better acquainted with a new crop of high-potential recruits. Their feedback, publicly or privately given, on how the mix reflects the organization's diversity goals is another reminder to managers that their bosses are paying attention to the issue.

Many top executives in our study sometimes use public pressure as a tool to keep themselves and their managers on track, showing continuous movement toward diversity goals.

Some chief executives have touted their organizations as being on the leading edge, outstanding examples of choice employers because of their policies on work and family issues or the diversity already achieved in their management ranks. A number of top executives accept invitations to speak to their peers as champions with a track record on diversity issues. They commission recruitment brochures and advertisements that document significant advances made in their organizations. They set up themselves and their organizations for public scrutiny, and they use the attention from the media, potential recruits, and the public in general to force themselves to keep pushing for new breakthroughs that will satisfy the expectations they have created.

While some of these activities are rather glamorous and courageous, most are tedious, awkward, and frustrating. The dedicated effort senior executives invest in making progress on diversity is legendary in many of our model organizations. Their personal intervention in activities to promote diversity has played a major role in moving their organizations ahead of many others. A hard lesson for some of these executives, however, is that their personal effort is not enough to guarantee sustained progress, and in fact it can even interfere with long-term results.

Make Diversity a Pervasive Part of the Culture

Although it is critical for senior executives to provoke change in the ways described above, it is also essential for them to make it possible for others to manage the process of change. This means building diversity into the organization's ongoing systems. When diversity is institutionalized in an organization, support has a better chance of continuing even after personally committed top executives leave.

A rarely recognized downside of top management commitment is that it can turn into a one person show. One manager we interviewed was blunt about the impact of the chief executive. If it weren't for his personal demands, she said, "I think we'd limp along until we had a major suit." But the question must be asked: What will happen when he leaves? And in the meantime, will his managers give him more than temporary solutions to diversity problems when they know he will be retiring within a few years and the pressure will be gone?

For impact to outlast the chief executive's tenure, progress must be linked to something beyond one individual's personal interventions, as important as those interventions are. In one of the organizations we studied, the members of the management team give ratings to each promotion candidate. One manager declared that some managers always give women the lowest ratings. Fortunately, these ratings serve as advice only to the boss, who has been willing to override them and give promotions to women and people of color. But what if the next boss isn't willing to take such risks or wants to keep nontraditionals out of management? The promotion system will still be in place to exclude candidates on the basis of prejudice or for other subjective reasons.

The commitment of the executive in this example is commendable, but simply going against his managers' recommendations is not an adequate strategy to ensure long-term progress. There are several ways that this individual can help ensure continued progress on diversity after he leaves. One way is to choose as his successor a manager who is also committed to diversity. Another way is to reform his management team by educating those who discriminate by sex and ethnicity or replacing them with managers who do not discriminate. Still another way is to change the promotion system so that more objective criteria or raters are used to assess candidates. Any of these techniques can help decrease dependence on the personal influence of one senior executive and balance it with institutionalized support.

Executives in fifteen of the organizations in our study described the administrative systems they had revamped or targeted for review as part of their strategy, including promotion and evaluation systems. Some executives are making a deliberate effort to select managers who share their vision so that by the time they leave they will have developed a cadre of replacement candidates who have similar views and intentions regarding diversity. These executives are supplementing the action they are currently taking on problems and are probably helping consolidate diversity progress.

Other Influential Leaders

Top management is usually thought of as the CEO or president of an organization and perhaps some or all of those who report directly to him or her (executive vice presidents or senior vice presidents, for example). In fact, top-management commitment typically refers to this small group of executives. There are, however, other executives who sometimes wield considerable power over the extent and pace of diversity within an organization. They include members of the board of directors, as well as managers who control a substantial unit of the organization, such as a region or subsidiary.

The board of directors can affect progress on diversity in various ways, according to managers we interviewed, including putting diversity issues on center stage for an organization. For instance, directors sometimes have the option of approving the appointment of certain key executives and may choose to demand demographic diversity within the senior management team. Board members may also initiate or approve basic organization policies, such as those related to employee bonuses or benefits. Moreover, directors may insist that new or existing administrative policies be reconstructed to help foster diversity.

Another positive role board members play is asking tough questions of the organization's executives. By demanding that executives dig for information about how business practices are designed or carried out, particularly when a complaint is filed or other problems arise, directors may help keep subtle forms of discrimination from going unnoticed. Board members of educational institutions may be particularly active in examining diversity issues, partly because of the strong local representation on school boards. One school principal, in describing the approach her board takes, noted that board members can sometimes be too inquisitive, to the point of being meddlesome, but that the result is to keep diversity issues alive. "The school board asks hard questions when we don't do well with minority achievement," she told us. "They get people looking for answers about what worked and what didn't versus giving us a mandate and walking away. They choose the statistics they want. They don't just accept the numbers they're given regarding, for example, the gap in test scores between whites and blacks. Maybe that's unreasonable, but they pay your salary, and this keeps everyone interested in the issue."

The mandated activities of formal board committees, even those associated with major corporations, also help keep diversity in the forefront of managers' minds. Although some board committees are set up specifically to govern the diversity process, attention to this issue is more commonly allocated to a standing committee on personnel policies. Such a committee can make a difference by requesting data of management, by digging for information about how promotions or pay scales are determined, and by regularly placing diversity in the limelight.

The composition of the board may be a major factor in determining how active the board will be regarding diversity issues. Some of the CEOs of organizations in our study made it a point to see that their boards represent their workforce or their marketplace. They actively recruited women and people of color to serve as members of the board, knowing (or hoping) that these individuals would have the inclination and the energy to keep diversity a top priority issue. Demographic diversity alone is no guarantee that directors will support diversity goals. A board of white men may actively promote diversity to the same extent as a diverse board. Nevertheless, a demographically diverse board of directors does have symbolic value. In one of the organizations we studied, for example, a vice president complained about the lack of women and minorities on her board, noting that "the board doesn't reflect their own policy suggestions."

Perhaps a more important factor in ensuring board support for diversity issues is to choose board members who actively pursue diversity goals as part of their work or community activities, regardless of their sex or ethnicity. We were told that certain CEOs, clearly looking for active advocacy from directors to buttress their own efforts, have specifically recruited people with a track record in heading advocacy groups or efforts in other organizations. Sometimes these people were very visible, nationally known individuals who, as directors, would be expected to pay special attention to diversity issues.

The other group of influential organizational leaders who can have a major impact on diversity within an organization are the managers in charge of business units. These managers can make a big difference in fostering diversity if top management is not opposed to diversity. General managers who have a fair amount of autonomy in running a plant, region, business unit, or function can do many of the same things in their bailiwicks that their bosses do throughout the entire company or institution to make diversity happen.

Starting Without Top-Management Commitment

Many people outside our study who understand the importance of top management commitment to diversity are discouraged because the CEOs or presidents of their organizations give little more than lip service to diversity. They want to know what options are open to them to move their organizations forward in this area. One possibility, particularly in decentralized organizations, is to rely on the heads of certain operating units to make progress in their parts of the organization. Progress in such units at least gives women and people of color opportunities there, and it sometimes spreads to other parts of the organization. Eventually, a change in the organization's top leadership may make it possible for the nontraditional managers who have stayed and succeeded in these vanguard business units to move higher into the organization's central executive ranks.

Several organizations in our study benefited from diversity activities that began in "pockets" of the organization rather than at headquarters. The managers who value diversity and who have had considerable freedom in running their own units have modeled the practice of diversity for others in their organizations. These managers have battled differential treatment in a number of ways. One regional manager, known throughout the organization for his strong advocacy, described a variety of methods he has used to promote diversity. Shortly after he took the job, he held an off-site meeting with those who reported directly to him to share his expectations concerning affirmative action and equal opportunity among others. He put

his expectations in writing, and he asked his managers to put
their commitments in writing. He continues to monitor these
and give managers feedback on their progress. He also believes
in personal involvement. He or his assistant sits in on interviews for all two hundred management slots in his region, even
those at the entry level. The interviews always include questions about the candidates' position on equal employment opportunity and their feelings about it. If candidates seem anti-
EEO, they aren't selected. As this manager put it, "Since all
managers go through this for selection, EEO gradually grows
in importance."

One regional director of a government agency contributes to diversity by directly intervening in the promotion process.
Not only does he select people of color for jobs that are open,
but he also challenges his managers when they choose white men.
"Show me the ones you didn't select," he often instructs his managers, according to one executive we interviewed. "That's where
all the minorities are sometimes," the director continues. "That's
where you find the criteria are different." By probing to see
whether the criteria are indeed different, this director may effectively be reducing subtle forms of bias that creep into selection
decisions in his region. When managers transfer from there to
other regions, perhaps they will continue to monitor themselves
and others for bias in selection decisions.

Whatever specific goals such managers pursue to achieve
diversity in their parts of the organization, their accomplish-
ments are often recognized by the public. Outstanding achievements in certain pockets can give the entire organization widespread publicity, even when the rest of it is not following along.
The publicity sometimes translates into a competitive advantage for the organization in attracting customers and employees.
When progress in these organizational pockets is applauded and
rewarded by top management, similar advances can spread
throughout the organization.

Some have argued that independent activities in particular parts of an organization are not only desirable but may be
a necessary early step in a successful change effort. Beer, Eisen-

stat, and Spector (1990) argue that allowing departments to "reinvent the wheel" in terms of their approach to a problem is a better option than ordering specific changes from headquarters. Once some experimentation has been done with various techniques, then and only then should new procedures be institutionalized across the organization. While top managers should set high standards for the changes they want and hold their managers accountable for meeting them, they should allow them to choose their own methods. Encouraging a grassroots approach to organization-wide problems is one way in which top management can be responsive. Eventually, this responsiveness must shift to standardizing procedures that have proven their worth in one pocket or another.

Long-Term Commitment

A hard lesson for many executives has been that well-intentioned efforts don't always get results over the short term. Commitment must go on and on because the issue is a strategic issue of change. Creating change in an organization boils down to creating conflict — conflict after conflict — and opening the system enough to allow people to face one conflict after another until a series of resolutions has put the organization on a new course. The new course involves dramatically different norms about who gets selected and rewarded in the organization. Even working hard to achieve diversity for five or ten years may show remarkably little change. Why, then, do some chief executives and their key managers add this awesome burden to their already overwhelming agenda? Because despite the frustration and the wrong turns and the expense, they see a big payoff then or twenty years down the road. The benefits of diversity, described in Chapter One, may not come quickly, but they may help an organization gain a competitive edge in the long term.

Top-management commitment goes far beyond personal initiatives, yet it requires sustained, relentless action on diversity over a period of years, if not decades. Commitment that matters is more than wishing away differential treatment, more than ordering equal opportunity and walking away. The commitment we have seen by senior executives in the organizations we studied involves a willingness to subject oneself to the awkward, painful, draining, discouraging business of slowly giving diversity respectability and value in the organization. This kind of commitment is an essential ingredient in a serious diversity effort. Without it, progress will occur even more slowly, and the progress that is achieved will be potentially less lasting. Once the commitment is there, the focus should shift to choosing solutions to diversity problems, the subject of Chapter Nine.

NINE

STEP THREE: CHOOSE SOLUTIONS THAT FIT A BALANCED STRATEGY

I glance out the office window and enjoy the river view even on this cloudy, windy winter day. Seated in an armchair across the coffee table from me, the senior vice president of human resources is nursing a cup of coffee. She has been thoughtful, taking time to reflect before she answers each question. She is forty-seven years old and white. She has a Ph.D. in organizational development and has been with this company for fourteen years. I ask, "What can you tell us about the constellation of current policies and practices that benefit people of color or women in your organization? For example, how did this mix come about?" She responds:

> As women began to appear in greater numbers in business school in the sixties, the company hired them. They were good women, but they didn't make it; they plateaued. The recruiters didn't make it clear that the career path to senior management required several relocations, including international ones. When it came time to take a new assignment, the women said, "We can't do that." Two issues were at stake. First, these women were in dual-career couples and their husbands were unwilling or unable to interrupt their career paths. Second, the women were not sure the moves would pay off. They told management, "We don't see any women at the top."
> Because of my experience at another company, I was brought in to change this situation. I realized that a number of systems needed to be changed. We revised

our selection procedures. Now the women we hire have backgrounds that include cross-cultural experience, and they often have language skills. We tell them clearly that the route to senior management will involve relocation. We reorganized our development program to include experience in several field locations. We built relocation in early.

We addressed the management side, too. We hired women from the outside for both line and staff positions at the senior level to be role models. We didn't just parachute them in and hope they made good. We planned and supported their entry process.

We also dealt with the perception bias by making sure that the board of directors includes women. I arrange for a group of our high-potential women to have breakfast with them each time the board meets. This informal opportunity for visibility and networking has been important in changing perceptions.

In other words, we looked for several ways to attack this issue, not just one.

A vast array of diversity practices exists. However, it is difficult to choose some practices over others as solutions to diversity problems when virtually all of them have merit. As noted earlier, we found that the sixteen organizations in our study have used fifty-two different practices, each of which some managers believe has value in increasing diversity. Nevertheless, some practices, or solutions, have been used more frequently than others to break down barriers to diversity. Again, as reported in Part Two, the top seven practices found in our study are as follows:

1. Top management's personal intervention and influence to promote diversity (used in all sixteen organizations)
2. Targeted recruitment of women and people of color for non-managerial positions (thirteen organizations)
3. Internal advocacy groups or task forces for women or ethnic groups (ten organizations)
4. Emphasis on equal employment opportunity statistics or personnel profiles (nine organizations)

5. Incorporation of diversity into performance evaluation goals or ratings or the review process (twelve organizations)
6. Inclusion of diversity in the management succession or replacement planning process (ten organizations)
7. Revision of promotion criteria and the decision-making process to reflect diversity goals and to help counter institutionalized barriers to advancement (eleven organizations)

There may be a temptation to adopt the solutions used most often by the model organizations in our study. It is certainly worth considering whether these frequently used solutions could be successfully applied in your organization. However, there are other equally important factors to consider as well. Every one of our model organizations relies on a unique set of diversity activities. In terms of specific practices, they are more different than alike. Even if your organization were to look like, act like, and feel like one of these organizations, simply copying its practices would exclude the involvement and limit the acceptance of many employees. Short-circuiting the process of formulating solutions is likely to result in unraveling during implementation.

Finding an effective mix of solutions is a tricky exercise. The mandate to match solutions to the most pressing current problems is full of complexity. Emphasizing accountability as a remedy for prejudice, for example, covers hundreds of techniques that are interactive and sometimes elusive. Even when specific problems can be pinpointed through an investigation, the process of solving them is not necessarily easier. If prejudice, for example, were limited to the act of excluding black women from field assignments despite their qualifications, how easy would it be to choose one specific solution to that problem? More likely, a battery of possible solutions comes to mind, including ways to keep prejudiced managers from taking that action, rewarding those who treat candidates with equal respect, finding black female candidates with obviously better qualifications than their competitors, and so on.

The existing panoply of options is necessary because no single solution is likely to have a significant, lasting impact on diversity. Yet the dilemma is clear: although concentrating on only one or two practices will have only a limited or temporary effect, spreading resources too thinly over a number of practices will doom them all. How can you choose a reasonable set of solutions? Fortunately, there are a few guidelines that can take some of the frustration out of this process.

Match Solutions to the
Organization's Data and Culture

Without a special effort to formulate solutions that address the specific diversity problems identified in the earlier discovery step, it is likely that the solutions will be too general to make an impact or may even be unrelated to the problems discovered. According to Catalyst (1990), the practices reported by human resource managers did not address the lack of certain career opportunities that they and their CEOs identified as primary barriers for women's advancement. Their "priority strategies" rarely include close monitoring (only 2 percent of respondents reported this), line experience for women (4 percent), or succession planning procedures (8 percent). Even something as basic as targeted recruitment of women was reported by only 16 percent of the human resource managers surveyed. Catalyst (p. 24) concludes that "companies have not developed programs that would enable women to move up from the lowel-level ranks of management to senior positions in corporations, as the identified programs do not coincide with the identified problems."

Not only do solutions need to be logically connected to the problems, but the solutions must also capture the support and conviction of the many constituencies integral to their success. These constituencies include top management, key line and staff managers, both traditional and nontraditional high-potential managers, and a host of others. Because both credibility and accuracy are needed in this step, as in the first step, entrusting this job to a carefully selected task force is a good place to start.

The pooled effort of a task force helps ensure that many different perspectives will be considered in the choice of solutions. The task force would naturally include employees of both sexes, different ethnicities, and other diversity characteristics. The task force might also include people who are knowledgeable about the history of the organization and those who are aware of the factors likely to influence how readily certain solutions will be accepted throughout the organization. In a service-oriented, innovative organization, for example, where employees have generally been valued and invested in, employees at all levels may easily accept the use of training programs or job rotations to foster diversity. Chances are these practices have become commonplace tools for development in general or in regard to other issues, and they may be used with little fuss. On the other hand, in an organization steeped in the tradition of never fixing anything until it breaks, the likelihood of employees accepting the same solutions is probably quite low.

Task force members who have broad knowledge of the organization can be instrumental in indicating where and how solutions are already being used in certain departments or locations so that the same solutions can be more widely applied. Peter Drucker (1991) warns against trying to change the corporate culture to solve problems. Instead, he writes, use the culture by doing the things people know and preach already. He explains that when the Marshall Field department stores ran into trouble in the 1970s, a succession of CEOs fruitlessly tried to change the culture. Finally, a new CEO asked, "What do we have to produce by way of results?" All the store managers knew they had to increase the amount each shopper spends per visit. When they analyzed the few stores that were already doing this, they discovered that these few stores were simply doing what was in the policy manuals. The foundation was already there, in the culture, for managers to produce the results they wanted.

A task force that includes members with a historical perspective may have the best chance of choosing solutions that will be readily accepted by managers and other employees. If, for example, there was a past instance in which a training program failed or a nontraditional manager was promoted into a key spot only to flounder there, managers may be reluctant to try something similar without extensive preparation. Past confrontations with unionized workers may have made some executives reluctant to accept employee groups of any kind, so other negotiating partners may need to be found. Because historical events such as these influence how acceptable some solutions will be, such events should be taken into account.

The task force mandated to choose solutions may be the same one that discovered the problems, or a new task force may be formed. In either case, if it does not include any members of top management, then the task force should have direct access to them. Part of the commitment of top management is to be a resource to this group and to attend to the difficult process of identifying and putting into place the initial pinions of a diversity plan. One of the worst things that can happen at this point is for top management to be perceived as being uninterested in this process or in the issue as a whole.

It is a good idea to rethink the composition of the task force and gear it to the task at hand. If the existing task force members were reasonably active in the previous step of discovering problems or if that step continued over several months, some members may be eager to return to their other (perhaps somewhat neglected) job responsibilities. Past members who were not effective contributors should be replaced. Perhaps there are potential new members who could bring additional information or influence to the group. For example, the manager of a business unit that has made great strides in advancing nontraditional managers would be an ideal candidate for the task force. Even if the task force is reconstituted, however, it is important to retain some earlier members so that previous work is incorporated into this step.

The information collected in the discovery step may reveal that the problems existing now are widespread and not limited to one level or function of the organization. Likewise, attending to the development needs of nontraditional employees without regard for the needs of their white male managers and co-workers may not lead to an optimum mix of solutions. Making changes at the upper levels, where key administrative decisions are made, may be at least as important as developing nontraditional candidates. Likewise, examining different levels of the organization to determine how different groups of employees contribute to the problems identified and how they have and could contribute to the solutions may be a useful way to determine where to target remedies initially and later. As mentioned earlier, if some remedies have already been adopted in certain parts of the organization, they may be models for remedial practices that can be phased into other parts. Building on the positive actions already being taken helps ensure that aspects of the organization's culture that are compatible with diversity will be incorporated into the diversity effort.

Involving people in the mission of the task force and more generally in the goal of formulating effective solutions to problems of unequal opportunity is a major goal of many managers engaged in diversity efforts. Managers need the understanding and buy-in of many employees to carry out most remedies. Emphasizing the potential benefits of the task force recommendations to all employees or all managers is one way to get everyone involved in contributing.

Emphasizing the role of task force activities in the organization's growth or profitability is another way to garner support from a wide array of employees. It also helps move the diversity issue into the mainstream. One task force we learned about got the go-ahead to formulate a set of recommendations only after agreeing with top management that all of their recommendations would increase business as well as foster diversity.

For Sustained Leadership Development, Select Solutions That Address Challenge, Recognition, and Support

A key goal of leadership diversity, as explained in Chapter Three, involves developing leadership potential over a substantial period of time. The key elements of leadership development — challenge, recognition, and support — may be provided through the fifty-two practices identified in our study and enumerated in the appendix. Establishing a balance among these three elements is recommended over the long term. In order to do this, however, an organization's practices may lean more toward one or two of the elements at any given time.

It is difficult to be precise about which individual practices affect which elements of leadership development. A development program for high-potential managers, for example, may offer participants challenging assignments, the recognition of being included in an expensive program for an elite group of up-and-coming managers, and a network of supporters in their fellow participants and the staff who carry out the program. Depending on the emphasis and the types of activities involved in the program, one or two of these elements may dominate. While it may be impossible to accurately dissect the areas of impact of a given program (50 percent challenge, 35 percent recognition, and 15 percent support, for example), an assessment of the primary and secondary impacts should be made. This information can be useful in moving toward a balance when one particular program is combined with other diversity activities planned or already in place.

Select Solutions That Include the Use of All Three Components of the Diversity Strategy: Education, Enforcement, and Exposure

Solutions to problems identified in step one should represent a balanced diversity strategy. Achieving a balanced approach over time, not necessarily at any given moment, may be the best way to address diversity issues.

Education is geared toward two goals. One is to increase the sensitivity of (primarily) white male managers to the nature and value of cultural differences and to help them become more aware of how institutional practices discriminate against nontraditional employees. In a number of the model organizations we studied, top executives rely on education to convince traditional managers that diversity goals benefit the organization as a whole and therefore are in their own best interest. The second goal of education is to better prepare nontraditional candidates for advancement by helping them acquire the knowledge, skills, and savvy considered to be important for high-level management posts. Although some short-range results may come from educational efforts, these are primarily tools to promote change for over the long term.

Enforcement of standards for nonexclusionary behavior helps ensure that at least some forms of differential treatment will be quickly extinguished. Executives often monitor and attempt to correct managers' behaviors that tend to exclude nontraditional employees or treat them unfairly, and they establish procedures to reinforce new behaviors over time. This approach is similar to that used to ensure safety. Most of us, for example, are familiar with traffic laws. Were it not for enforcement, how many of us would obey every traffic law, even though we understand (and even agree with) the reasons for doing so? Enforcement often involves incentives for adhering to behavioral standards, regardless of one's personal beliefs, as well as costly or embarrassing discipline for violating the standards.

Education and enforcement, as described here, are much like the planned-change strategies described by behavioral scientists Robert Chin and Kenneth Benne in 1976. The three strategies used to effect planned change are the empirical-rational, the power-coercive, and the normative-reeducative strategies. The empirical-rational approach involves educating people about the benefits that will accrue to them from a change; in the power-coercive approach, powerful individuals influence others to accept a change. Chin and Benne caution that the second approach yields compliance only as long as rewards and punishments occur. The normative-reeducative approach assumes that sociocultural norms, attitudes, and value systems must be reoriented to support a change. Peer pressure, however irrational, is an important factor in shaping behavior.

Perhaps there is another approach that contributes to acceptance of change, an approach that some of our model organizations use in combination with other approaches to foster diversity. That approach is to expose traditional managers to nontraditional managers who operate as peers in their organization. In terms of the planned-change model, this would foster change in the normative-reeducative approach by changing the peer group itself and consequently some of its norms. Such exposure can give many traditional managers the evidence and the incentive to move beyond their stereotypic beliefs about people who are different from them in terms of sex or ethnicity. For example, one man recalled for us that in the 1960s he had

been skeptical about whether a woman could handle the job of
going to people's homes to collect past-due bills. "I thought it
was dangerous," he said, "too tough for a woman. After all, we
don't carry guns; we carry ballpoint pens." It turned out that
on her first assignment, a woman got the full amount owed in
only one contact. "My myths were dispelled," this manager said.
"She had them eating out of her hand."

Working side by side with a white woman or a person
of color sometimes helps a white male manager discard the myths
he grew up with as he comes to know and respect that person
as an individual. Such a personal revelation is a powerful supplement to the larger-scale, but often abstract, impact of education and enforcement. When the individuals involved are at
high levels of an organization, serving as role models for many
managers at lower levels, the impact on the organization can
be enormous. A black woman we interviewed talked about her
long-term association with a white male executive: "For a long
time he thought I was a thorn in his side. Then I became his
direct report. We spent a lot of time together, and he's become
one of my strongest advocates. This is happening throughout
the company now — white men are associating with women and
blacks."

Managers have very different opinions about which approach, or component of the diversity strategy, will best conquer
the prejudice that still permeates many organizations. When
we asked managers in our study about how to stamp out prejudice, for example, some emphasized the need to change people's attributes (to which education and perhaps exposure would
contribute), indicating that changes in behavior would then follow. A black manager asserted, "To get integration, you must
first change the attitude of whites that blacks are intellectually
inferior, that women and minorities cannot be managers. Selection decisions affect this; they make it possible."

Other managers claimed that changing people's behavior
will, in the long run, change their attitudes; enforcement would
be the preferred approach in this case. A white male manager
we interviewed believes that in making cultural changes, the
toughest issues are in changing behavior. "You have to change

behavior first, he declared. "Don't use that language. Don't forego that opportunity." A related approach recommended by managers in our study is one of simply changing prejudicial behaviors without worrying about what people's attitudes are. These managers argue that shaping behavior is as much as one can expect in the workplace and that employers shouldn't be concerned about attitudes. They don't care whether employees' attitudes change so long as prejudicial behavior stops. Some of these managers would be perfectly happy with prejudiced employees who behave as if they were not. A white male senior-level manager we interviewed said, "You could wear a white sheet at night KKK-style, but at work you had to perform EEO." Again, these managers would emphasize an enforcement approach.

Research on the role of education, enforcement, and exposure in diversity efforts is sparse. The survey data from one investigation (Fernandez, 1987) indicate that the frequency of work contact with people of color has little effect on racist stereotypes, but frequent social contact does moderate racist attitudes of white women. Fernandez also discovered that level of formal education has minimal impact on white men's perception of race discrimination, although higher education does affect the perceptions of white women and people of color. Fernandez's conclusion that racist and sexist stereotypes have a powerful influence over many white male managers supports the notion that a combination of exposure, education, and enforcement may be required to create change on diversity issues. These three approaches to change complement one another, and they have the potential to create an effect in combination that they could not achieve sequentially. There is probably no proof that one strategic approach to diversity is better than another, but there is some indication from our research that an effective overall strategy is a balanced one.

Nearly all the progressive organizations in our study appear to take advantage of a "gestalt" effect from combining practices that support each of the three strategy components. It is difficult to analyze the constellation of practices in this way because only some of the diversity practices identified in our study can be easily categorized according to one of the three strategic approaches (education, enforcement, or exposure). In most cases, different elements or aspects of a given practice seem to fit different approaches. A development program for high-potential managers, for example, typically involves education, but it may also involve exposing senior and high-potential managers to others who are of the opposite sex or of a different ethnicity. Revamping a performance appraisal system to take better account of individuals' diversity efforts is mainly an enforcement practice, but it may also involve education about managing people in general or nontraditional employees in particular. New recruitment procedures may be aimed mainly at exposing traditional employees to newcomers who are "different," or they may be seen as a way to attract young, talented people who can be educated in-house as they begin their careers; these procedures may also be linked to enforcement that involves numerical goals for entry levels.

Because of the complications involved in sorting practices strictly according to the type of strategy component they support, it is probably a good idea to conduct a more informal assessment of the overall thrust of the practices being used or considered. Thus the goal should be to include practices that support all three components. We don't know if the organizations in our study deliberately sought the balanced approach that appears to characterize many of their diversity efforts; it is even possible that executives in these organizations are unaware that a balance has been achieved over the years. The reason that six of the seven highest-ranked practices are in the accountability group and reinforce the enforcement component may be that these organizations have attempted to counterbalance practices that emphasize the education or exposure component.

The combinations or constellations of diversity practices used in two of the businesses we studied help illustrate how balance can be achieved by choosing some activities over others. Business A, a multinational service company, is based on the East Coast and has more than 100,000 employees. Business B is also a service company, but it is based on the West Coast and has only about 25,000 employees. The major barriers in both companies appear to be fairly typical, including the prejudice and discomfort of some white male executives who have been socialized to undervalue women and people of color, as well as weak career development and poor working conditions for many nontraditional managers.

The principal practices that these two organizations are using to break down barriers are very different. Listings of all the diversity practices that managers from the two companies mentioned show that Business A uses more practices (twenty-four) than Business B uses (twenty). (See Table 9.1.) Moreover, practices at Business A promote recruitment and external visibility more than do those at Business B, whereas practices at Business B highlight development a bit more than do those at Business A. (The two companies use enforcement tools to about the same extent.) Business A relies on two "core" practices that form the heart of its diversity effort. Core practices are so central that they have been given a weight of 3, which has affected their standing in the rank ordering of all diversity practices. In this case, top management's intervention and the high-potential development program used in Business A are so strong and pervasive that they are considered keystones that shape and permeate other diversity activities. Business A also relies on four "priority" practices, which are considered to be more critical to the diversity effort than the other practices listed; these have been given a weight of 2 because their impact on diversity results is considered to be greater than that of other, unweighted practices. The diversity effort at Business B, in contrast, involves only a two-tiered array of "priority" and other practices.

Despite these differences, however, both companies appear to have combinations of practices that address all three components of sustained leadership development (challenge, recognition, and support) and that use all three diversity strategy components (education, enforcement, and exposure). The first step in determining the balance within each of these two sets of factors is to assess each practice in terms of how well it contributes to each set. In terms of the threefold diversity strategy, for example, the actions top management takes to spread accountability for diversity among managers is primarily an enforcement technique, but the actions also involve educating man-

Table 9.1. Constellations of Diversity Practices in Two Companies.

Practices	Business A	Business B
Core	Top management's emphasis on accountability for diversity Entry development programs for high-potential managers	None
Priority	Targeted recruitment of nontraditional managers Targeted recruitment at nonmanagerial levels Board of directors activities that support diversity goals Public exposure as an organization active in diversity	Top management emphasis on accountability for diversity Development program for "hi-po" women and people of color Job rotation program Career planning process (advisers, workshops, resources) Succession planning process that includes diversity activities Performance appraisal goals that include diversity
Other	Succession planning process that incorporates diversity goals Performance appraisal goals and review that include diversity Development program for high-potential employees Work/family policies Partnerships with schools Partnerships with ethnic/professional groups Community involvement of key managers Publications and PR materials that highlight diversity Targeted assignments for women and people of color Diversity training program for all managers Informal networking to expose "hi-pos" to senior executives Award for people management Internal publications that feature women and people of color Active AA office (for selection of people of color and so on) Internal diversity task force Selection preference for minority vendors Progressive corporate image (liberal, philanthropic, caring) Child-care resources for employees	Targeted recruitment of nontraditional managers Targeted recruitment of nontraditional nonmanagers Board members who promote diversity Development program for all "hi-pos" Work/family policies Key outsiders hired into executive positions Job posting Informal mentoring Informal support groups Employee attitude survey data Bonus tied to AA goals for all managers Outside seminars and tuition reimbursement Internal training (English, AA for supervisors, and so on) Use of task forces for major issues

agers about the importance of diversity goals and keeping that issue at the front of their minds. These actions do not appear to relate closely the use of exposure to nontraditional individuals to break down other people's stereotypic prejudices.

In terms of the components of leadership development, top management's actions appear to emphasize recognition of the strengths and potential of people of color and white women. Furthermore, through their advocacy, some top-level managers might be considered part of the support system for nontraditional managers. Although providing challenge may also be involved in the recommendations of top management, this function is probably less direct than the other two.

Table 9.2 shows how the "core" and "priority" diversity practices in these two companies contribute to a balance in the three-part diversity strategy and to a balance in the three components of sustained leadership development. An asterisk indicates that a practice contributes to the component of strategy or leadership development under which it appears, and a double asterisk indicates a stronger contribution. In Business A, for example, top management's personal intervention in making diversity a priority contributes to two components of a balanced diversity strategy, although more strongly to the enforcement component than to the education component. Top management's intervention also contributes to two components of sustained leadership development, but more heavily to the recognition component than to the support component. The judgments in Table 9.2 are based on the information available from each company, including descriptions of the goals and results of the practices. However, some interpretation is still needed, so these judgments are both subjective and approximate. The combined judgments provide a picture of the balance in each set of practices, that is, whether the three parts of the diversity strategy are used to about the same extent and whether all three leadership development components are being evenly targeted.

The judgments concerning core and priority practices in Table 9.2 could, of course, be extended to the other practices that the companies use to provide a more complete assessment.

Table 9.2. Balances of Components of Diversity Strategy and Sustained Leadership Development.

Diversity Practices (top 6)	Diversity Strategy			Sustained Leadership Development		
	Education	Enforcement	Exposure	Challenge	Recognition	Support
Business A						
Top management's personal intervention	•	••			••	••
Entry development programs for high-potential managers	•				•	••
Targeted recruitment of nontraditional managers			•	•		
Targeted recruitment of nontraditional nonmanagers			••	••		
Board of directors' activities that support diversity goals		•				
Public exposure as an organization active in diversity					••	
Business B						
Top management's personal intervention	•	••			••	••
Development program for high-potential people of color and white women	•		•	•	••	••
Job rotation program	•		•	•		
Career planning process (advisers, workshops, resources)	•	•	•	•	••	
Inclusion of diversity in succession planning process		•			•	
Inclusion of diversity in performance appraisal goals		•			•	

This limited assessment, however, reveals a couple of potential trouble spots. Support systems may not be getting enough attention at either company. Only two of the priority practices seem to contribute to support, and both of these also contribute to other outcomes. Both companies may need to give more attention to providing support through priority practices. Meanwhile, other practices may help restore a balance among the three components of sustained leadership development. In Business A, additional support may be provided by the other development program for "hi-pos," work/family policies and child-care resources, diversity training, the internal diversity task force, and informal networking. Some of these same practices are also used in Business B.

A second potential trouble spot lies in a possible imbalance in the use of strategy components at Business B. Exposing employees to outstanding nontraditional managers does not seem to be given as much weight as the other two components of a diversity strategy. Again, some reshuffling of the priority practices may be warranted to correct the balance, but other practices may also help. Targeted recruitment and key outside hires may be very effective ways to give existing managers exposure to talented nontraditional managers and refute stereotypes.

Making an assessment such as this on current or future practices can reveal strengths and gaps in the balance of the plan. While the array of diversity activities chosen must relate to the problems identified, there must also be a deliberate effort to address an overarching balance in approach and targeted outcomes. The long-term success of a diversity effort may hinge on an ability to blend specific, short-term solutions with other, more general practices. Over time, for example, an organization may choose to phase in one strategy approach over another, for example, highlighting education early in the diversity effort and concentrating more heavily on enforcement and exposure later. With regard to leadership development, some organizations may initially address support systems and later emphasize challenge and recognition. There is no one best way to balance a constellation of practices at any given time; and there is no foolproof way of assessing the balance in the first place.

There will always be a degree of ambiguity (and faith) in a diversity effort. However, continued attention to balance and an appreciation of how the various factors work together are likely to make any diversity effort substantially more effective in the long run.

Reach as Many Employees as Possible with Each Solution

Finding inclusive ways of defining and implementing diversity practices is no longer a luxury but a necessary part of any effort. The failure of managers in the past to accept the idea that white men are also placed at a disadvantage by differential treatment practices and that white men need to be included in forging solutions to the problem of unequal opportunity has helped make backlash the biggest new obstacle to promoting diversity. Similarly, resentment and defensiveness on the part of certain nontraditional groups have been fueled because they have not been included in some diversity programs. Hispanics, Asian-Americans, and Native Americans, for example, may not be considered in "minority recruitment" efforts that involve only predominantly black colleges. Infighting among members of nontraditional groups gets in the way of progress. Both backlash and infighting discourage senior managers from experimenting with new techniques to remedy long-standing differential treatment in their organizations.

If the goal of diversity is to improve productivity and build better, more collegial teams, then changing the outlook and the skills of traditional managers will benefit them as well as people of color and white women. Strengthening the organization as a whole means that gains are not limited only to nontraditional employees. Packages of solutions are needed to help break down the we-versus-they mentality that pits white men against nontraditional managers and divides members of various nontraditional groups. A more inclusive way of developing diversity solutions may be to redefine barriers so that comprehensive corrections can be made. Increasing the organizational savvy of aspiring executives, for example, is not a need peculiar to women or people of color. The needs — and perceived needs — may differ from one ethnic group or sex to another, as noted in the description of specific barriers to advancement, but everyone, including white men, would benefit from some improvement. Instead of focusing solely on the particular needs of a given subgroup (for instance, language or articulation skills for certain immigrant people of color or greater awareness of their own social privilege for white men), a little attention to the deficiencies that cross sex and ethnic lines (lapses in strategic thinking or self-objectivity, for example) can help transform what have been characterized as problems of nontraditionals into management issues that affect the organization as a whole.

It may be that many so-called "minority problems" are actually problems in how people in general are managed in organizations. A frequent revelation in the organizations we studied was that practices installed originally for the benefit of nontraditional managers turned out to be good practices for people in general, and they were often extended to all managers at the levels or units in which they were initiated. Incorporating "people development" criteria in managers' performance appraisal criteria and revising the criteria for promotion into certain management positions are but two of the changes that proved to be valuable for both white male managers and nontraditional managers.

In his book *Racism and Sexism in Corporate Life,* John Fernandez (1981) makes the point that the styles and values of the "new breed" of managers require changes in the management-employment system regardless of employees' sex or ethnicity. The components of this system include work design, performance evaluation, evaluation of potential, career planning, and training and development. All of these practices need to be revamped to take into account the demand from all managers to have more say in when, where, and how they fit work into their lives and the greater need of all managers today to have significant, satisfying work. Poor career planning may be brought to executives' attention as part of an investigation of "glass ceiling" issues for nontraditional managers, but the same poor career planning may also be depriving many white men from reaching their full potential. Remedies that can improve career planning for all managers, regardless of their sex or ethnicity, will be more valuable to the organization and valued by more employees.

The need to find inclusive solutions to diversity issues does not mean that some practices cannot be limited to certain groups of people. The desired effect of eventually benefiting everyone in the organization can still be achieved. A special developmental program for high-potential managers, for example, may be limited to only twenty people each year. However, the new job rotation schemes used in that program or the assessment and feedback techniques created for this small group may well be applied to other managers later to benefit a much larger group. In the same way, programs reserved for nontraditional managers may have the same impact and, at the same time, help accelerate the advancement of potential role models and active recruiters who can help the diversity effort in a variety of ways.

As a general guideline, it is probably better to develop solutions that are not restricted to nontraditional managers when the potential benefit to others is apparent. In reality, it is not unreasonable to find a blend of solutions that, as a whole, help improve management practices in general even if some of the practices in that blend are first limited to only certain groups. Such practices may fit well with other, broader practices that together will have a substantial impact on the entire management or employee population.

Provide Training and Preparation for Each Solution

Diversity efforts extend over a period of many years partly because each step requires extensive preparation. Managers and other employees must be readied for new practices by being adequately informed and instructed about their use. For solutions to be successful, it is essential that people understand the rationale behind any new practice and practical ways of implementing it.

Training and preparation should be part of the investment of time and other resources that any organization change requires, and careful thought should go into selecting the techniques that will support the change being proposed. Consider, for example, the introduction of a new voice-mail system into a corporation. This is an expensive proposition, because the research needed to select the best system is often extensive, new equipment is sometimes required, and service fees can be substantial. Although the system requires a major investment and has the potential to increase efficiency, the system is only as good as its users. All employees need to be taught to understand how it benefits the corporation and themselves, and everyone needs to be trained to use it.

Investing in diversity activities is much the same. People need to be motivated to try new practices and trained well enough to take some first steps on their own. In some organizations, how-to training is postponed for up to a year until employees have a chance to digest the concept itself and appear to be mentally prepared to implement a new practice. Awareness training may be used during this period to alert employees to the need for additional practices. Mental readiness can be an important asset in initiating new procedures, particularly when some parts of the diversity effort can be introduced later, after employees have become more accustomed to the idea.

Training is a critical part of the preparation stage and also figures prominently in later stages. Ongoing consultation, for example, is sometimes necessary to keep practices in tune with the needs of employees and the organization as a whole. As employees get involved in carrying out a new practice, an initial dose of training may require follow-up to answer their questions, resolve dilemmas, and keep them informed of changes being introduced to make the practice easier or more effective. As noted earlier, systematic follow-up for some types of awareness training programs or core groups may be especially important in helping employees constructively confront their own and others' feelings about diversity issues.

Ongoing consultation builds employees' confidence and skill in a new practice and helps managers stay informed about how its implementation is progressing. Such consultation also serves as an early warning system. If a new practice seems to be triggering backlash or infighting, for example, the built-in consultation process may be able to detect this early and give management a chance to intervene by making changes or providing additional training.

Agree on a Modest Start

The diversity task force needs to narrow the array of problems and issues identified in the discovery phase to a few immediate priorities that address the needs of at least the major employee groups in the organization. A consensus may be necessary on the first steps to take and also on later steps that focus, for example, on other ethnic groups or extensions or evaluations of initial practices.

Some managers in our study emphasized that the investment they made initially to find extremely strong nontraditional managers had proved to be worthwhile because these individuals represented the infrastructure of their diversity effort. One choice as a starting point, then, may be to focus on recruitment or the identification of outstanding internal nontraditional managers. The effectiveness of that choice, however, may hinge on specifying follow-up techniques geared toward keeping those outstanding managers. A big mistake in many organizations has been to attract outstanding managers without any provision for retaining or advancing them, which has resulted in losing them. Planning ahead for the next steps is an important part of the task force's mission, but practices can often be sequenced so that the process is manageable.

Ideally, the practices first implemented are chosen to create a positive effect on the bottom line. While it is extremely difficult to demonstrate increased revenue as a result of greater diversity, it is often possible to show a decrease in expenses. Reduced turnover, for example, translates into financial savings that can be linked to the bottom line. Such evidence for the utility of diversity practices can be used to generate more support for continuing and extending the practices. Many diversity practices are expensive, and showing that the money and time are being well spent is likely to be an unstated if not explicit condition for continued support. Diversity will not be permitted to override the organization's financial health; financial indicators must be maintained while the diversity effort goes on. Therefore, even if a net return cannot be shown, it may be important that the practices do not have a substantially negative impact on the organization's bottom line, especially during the start-up period.

It is also important, however, that managers not have unrealistic expectations that diversity activities will immediately and obviously pay off. The test period for any new practice should be long enough to allow the benefits to develop. For example, according to Karr (1991), Carl's Jr., a California-based restaurant chain, began to pay college expenses for employees. After two years, the company had spent $90,000 on tuition and fees, but the savings in turnover costs had exceeded $145,000. Had the test period been only one year instead of two, the practice would probably have shown a financial loss and might have been abandoned. Diversity activities, like others, need time to be given a fair test.

As in any change effort, the diversity starting point may consist of a pilot project in one part of the organization. If a certain division or region of an organization has progressed farther than others, it may represent a good pilot site in which to add techniques to those already in place. On the other hand, a particularly troublesome business unit can also be used as a pilot site if there seems to be a reasonably good chance that changes will be accepted there. Any unit headed by an influential manager who could be a champion for expanding diversity activities throughout the organization is a good candidate for a pilot site. It is far easier to phase in a set of new practices in a small, somewhat discrete part of an organization than to tackle the entire organization at once. A pilot test may even allow more practices to be introduced at the same time than would be possible to do in the entire organization.

There are many ways to confine the early stages of a diversity effort to a manageable set of practices while keeping in mind the longer-term strategy and goals. Whatever way is chosen, it is critical that the decision process not drag on. Once the investigation of issues is completed, quick, decisive action must be taken to resolve the problems identified. People are expecting something to happen, and they will get increasingly frustrated if they see nothing being done. In this regard, initial solutions that are fast and reasonably good will have a more positive effect than better but slower solutions. To be able to communicate a sense of urgency through quick action adds credibility to the entire process and keeps inertia from gaining the upper hand. Inertia poses the danger of increasing the cost and the difficulty of taking action later.

Many considerations go into choosing what action to take. Although this is clearly a critical step in making progress, the selection process should not be allowed to become overwhelming. There are no perfect answers, so taking any reasonable step is often better than studying the situation endlessly. Once actions, or solutions, are chosen, however, they must be supported—given a chance to work and followed up. As we'll see in Chapter Ten, to be effective any solution must produce results.

TEN

STEP FOUR:
DEMAND RESULTS
AND REVISIT THE GOALS

I have been ushered into a small, tastefully furnished office and offered a soft drink by a secretary. Within a few minutes the vice president of compensation arrives, apologizes for the delay, and collects from his desk the notes he made on the interview questions. During the first ninety minutes of the interview, his responses to the questions are so extensive that my hand is aching from trying to take complete notes.

This executive is black, has an M.B.A., and has been with the company for seventeen years. He describes in detail several of his company's diversity practices, such as the annual day-long succession planning meeting to determine who is eligible for senior management positions. He discusses the requirement imposed by top management that people of color and white women be included on the "promotable list" for each position. In addition, he describes the company's goals in the area of representation of women and people of color at all levels and in all functions. Specifically, the company aims to have the same demographic percentage of people at each higher level as at the level below. This executive also notes how the company tracks the representation of white women and people of color in each function, such as operations, marketing, and finance, and goes on to describe the compensation guidelines that have been issued. His animated gestures reveal the excitement he feels about his own role in the diversity effort.

"What is there about these practices that makes them work?" I ask him. "That is, are certain key ingredients responsible for their effectiveness?"

He answers without hesitation, "You have to demand results. This year we sent managers' salary recommendations back to them

a number of times before we would approve them. There was no equity in the way they assigned merit increases to blacks versus whites,
for example. This sends a message to white managers: Fix it until it's
right. I don't think we'll have to go through that again next year."

The degree of emphasis that organizations place on results may
separate those that succeed in their diversity efforts from the
field of hopefuls. When revenue or profit is a goal of a business
function, progress is regularly measured and managers are held
accountable for the results. When quality improvement or customer service is a goal, measures are devised to indicate progress,
and managers are evaluated against them. When it comes to
diversity, however, there is strong resistance to establishing indicators of progress and holding managers accountable for measurable results. This seems to be a major reason why many organizational efforts fail.

The simple rule that "what doesn't get measured doesn't
get done" applies as well to diversity efforts as to other activities. However, the way that progress can and should be measured is probably the most emotionally debated aspect of the
diversity issue. Adopting sensible measures is necessary to overcome the resistance to focusing on concrete outcomes. The guidelines provided in this chapter should help defuse the measurement debate. But first the resistance needs to be understood.

The resistance to measuring diversity comes in large part
from managers' negative reactions to government regulation of
equal employment opportunity. From the start, managers have
resented the goals and timetables the government has required.
According to a number of managers in our study, those goals
and timetables have proved to be disastrous in promoting the
interests of nontraditional managers. Accountability for meeting hiring or promotion goals prompted many managers either
to fill positions with unsuitable women and people of color or
to withhold support from the nontraditional managers they
promoted. These mismatched and unsupported individuals were
seen as failures, testimony that forced integration is a sad and
costly mistake. The "quotas" at the heart of government regu-

lation have consequently come to represent a measure to be avoided at all costs.

The term *quota* is likely to raise eyebrows and heart rates among many groups of people, even though individuals define it differently. Some managers in our study think of a quota strictly as a percentage goal (we need 15 percent more Hispanic sales managers by next year), while others see it only as a simple head count (three more female vice presidents). Some define a quota in relation to population statistics (the percentage of black professionals should match the percentage of blacks in the standard metropolitan statistical area, or SMSA), while others believe that any numerical goal is a quota regardless of whether or not it conforms to population statistics. Generally, we found that managers used the term *quota* when they objected to a measure, whatever it was. The negative connotation was clear. According to managers we interviewed, the term *quota* conjures up images of traditional executives in the private sector buckling under the pressure of government regulations, along with pictures of seemingly less qualified nontraditional managers taking their reserved places in management and eroding their organization's capacity to perform. Those managers are therefore reluctant to use statistical performance measures that even approximate quotas.

The reaction among nontraditional managers is more mixed but no less emotional. Some insist that quota measures are the backbone of any diversity effort because the numbers have to change if progress is to occur. In fact, the affirmative action requirements for government contractors did prompt visible progress, according to statistics presented by Leslie Dunbar (1984). Between 1974 and 1980, for example, government contractors increased their employment of people of color by 20 percent in contrast to only about half that by other companies. Parallel figures for the employment of women were 15 percent and 2 percent. Other nontraditional managers shy away from quotas because of the stigma attached to them. If these managers get promoted under a quota system, they fear that they will be perceived as less qualified or capable than their white male counterparts simply because the quota exists. Moreover, their vulnerability to this negative attitude is sometimes exploited. For instance, sheets posted across the campus of the University of California at San Diego in 1991 by the local chapter of Young Americans for Freedom maliciously queried nontraditional students, "Were you accepted to UCSD in order to fulfill its goals?" (Smollar, 1991b).

The emotional sting of quotas is evidenced by its impact in political campaigns around the country. For example, according to Phillips (1991), controversy over the use of quotas may have given the lead to North Carolina's incumbent senator Jesse Helms over his black opponent, Harvey Gantt, in 1990. Helms emphasized that the civil rights bill then under consideration in Congress would mean that race comes before qualifications in hiring or advancement. An advertisement targeting quotas and run during the final week of the campaign may have put Helms ahead. The ad depicted a white man crumpling up a job rejection letter while an announcer intoned: "You needed that job and you were the best qualified. But they had to give it to a minority because of a racial quota. Is that fair?"

Diane Feinstein's campaign for the California governorship may also have been damaged by her announced plan to earmark government jobs for women and people of color. Her opponent, Pete Wilson, attacked the plan, indicating that such a quota is imposed at the expense of better qualified people appointed on the basis of merit. Feinstein's reaction, according to an article in the *San Diego Union* ("Feinstein Job Quota for Women, Minorities Decried," 1990, p. A24) was that "it is insulting to believe there are not enough qualified women to hold jobs in proportion to their numbers in the state." However, the negative connotations of a quota system may have contributed to her eventual loss in that race. President Bush's opposition to a civil rights bill that involves measures sometimes described as quotas is further evidence that many statistical measures are offensive to many people, perhaps because of the prejudicial assumption that nontraditionals are not as meritorious as white men.

Quotas based on ethnicity or sex have been justified by some people as a necessary and fair solution to past injustices and as being virtually no different from other forms of preference that have been used and accepted for many years. Leslie Dunbar (1984) and others point to a variety of cases showing that group identity is systematically used as a criterion for selection, as when a university gives preference to applicants from certain states or to children of former graduates, when veterans receive preference for jobs and special benefits, when children of cabinet members are given help to find government jobs, or when balance is sought in putting together a political slate. Using race or sex as one criterion among several is not such an unusual practice considering the many other versions of preferential treatment that are regularly used, even among white male candidates. According to Dunbar, the rationale for using race in particular as a preferred characteristic may even be more justified than other forms. Remedial preferences for people of color are a small price to pay for the brutal discrimination they have suffered under Jim Crow laws and practices. Says Dunbar (1984, p. 67):

> The preference may take away some benefits from some white men, but none of them is being beaten, lynched, denied the right to use a bathroom, a place to sleep or eat, being forced to take the dirtiest jobs or denied any work at all, forced to attend dilapidated and mind-killing schools, subjected to brutally unequal justice, or stigmatized as an inferior being. Setting aside, after proof of discrimination, a few places a year for qualified minorities out of hundreds and perhaps thousands of employees, as in the Kaiser plant in the *Weber* case, or 16 medical school places out of 100 as in *Bakke*, or 10 percent of federal public work contracts as in *Fullilove*, or even 50 percent of new hires for a few years as in some employment cases—this has nothing in common with the racism that was inflicted on helpless minorities, and it is a shameful insult to the memory of the tragic victims to identify the two.

As explained in the introduction to this book, the intense personal feelings with which the diversity issue as a whole is debated make it difficult to resolve; emotions run deep, particularly in regard to statistical measures of diversity. The following guidelines should help separate the measurement issue from the powerful historical events that contribute to its emotional impact.

Create Meaningful Numerical Goals and Use Them

Numerical goals and statistical measures are needed to help managers focus on results rather than on effort or intent. If outcomes are not emphasized, it is quite possible that well-intentioned diversity efforts can cost an organization a great deal of time and money and yet not create any significant, lasting change. Numerical goals, when properly used, reinforce the idea that diversity is tied to core business objectives and, over the long term, contributes to the organization's very survival.

Many of the progressive organizations in our study have discovered alternatives to government-imposed statistical goals, alternatives that capture progress on key aspects of their diversity activities and avoid at least some of the problems associated with traditional EEO measurement techniques. These alternative goals do three things: they focus on specific levels and functions of an organization, they highlight retention and development as well as recruitment, and they sometimes separate small groups of exceptional high-potential individuals from other employees.

A number of the organizations we studied monitor personnel profiles in some detail, using level and function categories that are more specific than those required by the government for federal contractors. Instead of looking at broad categories such as "officials and managers," which may account for thousands of managers throughout the country (and beyond), they break down the profile into significant levels of management. Some organizations profile clusters of managers in certain pay grades (grades 13 to 15 compared with grades 16 and above, for example) or with certain titles (directors compared with vice presidents, or officers) or those with certain privileges (managers eligible for bonuses or stock options). Examining separate levels of management makes it possible to track the upward movement of women and people of color once they become managers. This kind of tracking is important to organizations that have the goal of advancing nontraditional managers through management layers. Some organizations also regularly look within pay grades to see whether nontraditional managers are distributed throughout the pay range (and not all in the bottom quartile of the pay range, for example) to determine whether pay is also increasing with level of responsibility.

Some organizations also monitor personnel profiles outside the management ranks but above entry level. In one organization in our study, for example, professional, technical, and sales positions are monitored to be sure that nontraditional employees are adequately represented. These are the higher-paid jobs for individual contributors, and they represent an important part of the pipeline for management roles. Furthermore, in some organizations, jobs in certain functions such as production or finance are reviewed separately if they represent historical "trouble spots" in terms of adequate representation of women or people of color or if they are exceptionally good tracks to senior management positions. Separating these types of jobs from those at lower levels or in more peripheral functions is one step in checking how well the pipeline is being filled with nontraditional candidates. Goals for these particular job categories may be different from those for other jobs in the organization. In at least one organization in our study, profile goals are not used for lower-level jobs. The hypothesis is that by concentrating only on higher-level jobs, representation in lower levels is practically assured. Until the higher-level jobs were targeted, some managers noted, nontraditional employees were hired only at lower levels.

Regional differences are also considered in setting personnel profile targets. The SMSA or appropriate recruitment region, is used as the basis for targeted personnel profiles in an organization's different plants or subsidiaries so that representation in job categories reflects the ethnic mix of the pool of candidates in those locations. It would not be reasonable for an operation in Minneapolis or Atlanta to have the same targeted profile as an operation in San Francisco or San Antonio, at least for positions that are typically recruited for locally. At higher levels, however, the profile goals may be quite similar if candidates are sought nationwide.

Besides creating specific goals for specific groups of jobs, some of the organizations in our study also base goals on upward movement. In some organizations, personnel goals reflect the philosophy that it is just as important that nontraditional managers are being advanced to their potential as it is to assume that they represent a certain proportion of the managers in their job group. In one company the percentages of "promotable" women and people of color in each department are reviewed annually and compared with the percentages of women and people of color in that department and in the SMSA. If, for example, the percentage of women considered to be promotable is lower than their percentage representation in the department, then a "glass ceiling" to advancement may be present. Goals would be set to increase the promotable group to more closely equal their representation.

Goals are also used in some organizations to compensate business unit heads who develop nontraditional managers and then lose them to other units. In a traditional calculation, these managers' profile numbers would decrease because of transfers, and they would be penalized under many affirmative action programs. However, in this case, they are given credit for the number of people they have developed, including those who have been transferred or promoted into other units. This modification helps keep managers from holding onto their nontraditional employees when they should be sending them away for the broadening experiences that will help them qualify for executive posts. The measurement system reinforces the kind of behavior and achievements that aid career development for nontraditional managers.

Another precaution that some of the organizations in our study take is to use statistical goals to factor hiring and promotion opportunities into their profile calculations. Managers whose profiles do not improve throughout the year because they had no turnover or new openings in their units or departments should not be penalized. Therefore, numerical goals in some organizations are based on how many opportunities existed to improve the personnel profile. Managers record who got the job when an opening existed, including the person's sex, ethnicity, and whether she or he was an internal candidate or hired from outside. These data are then distributed monthly or quarterly to upper-level managers. These goals put the responsibility where it belongs, on managers who have some control over the mix of their personnel.

Managers who leave for one reason or another also affect numerical goals in some organizations. Terminations are included in profile reports in at least one company, along with hiring opportunities and beginning and current percentage representations. Other organizations regularly calculate the percentages of nontraditional managers who leave, voluntarily and not, and compare these with the figures for white men. This information is important in determining how well the organization is retaining nontraditional managers.

Retention goals, like advancement goals, apply more significantly to a single subset of managers, regardless of their sex or ethnicity. A reasonable goal is to retain and develop those managers with the most talent and the most potential. It is possible to incorporate this consideration into some calculations by, for example, counting the number of "promotable" or "high potential" managers who leave and comparing the rates for nontraditional groups and for white men. However, in some organizations, the information collected goes beyond group numbers and into individual assessments, some of which are impossible to quantify. For example, an annual review in one company involves a total of about two thousand general managers and their direct reports. Of all those who left during the past year, the organization identifies those it wished to retain. Executives review the proportion of these in comparison with other groups, but they also consider individual circumstances in assessing reasons for departure. In some cases, the organization decides to interview high-potential managers who left so that it can interpret the data on turnover and perhaps shape the goals for the next year. Techniques such as these allow organizations to mon-

itor individuals and small groups of managers who are special
in some way, as well as larger groups of managers who are special in some way, as well as larger groups of managers separated by demographic characteristics, making the measures more
relevant to the development, retention, and recruitment goals
of the diversity effort.

Alternative and more functional numerical measures of
progress such as those just described are more meaningful to
managers because they are designed by the managers and therefore better fit the organization and its diversity goals. Because
of this and because they are at least partly self-directed, such
measures are often more acceptable — and enforceable — than
government measures. More progressive companies give managers as much input and leeway as possible in creating and reinforcing statistical goals. In one company, the human resource
staff originally evaluated managers on their diversity progress.
As the process and the criteria became better understood over
the years, however, the managers were eventually given the
responsibility of assessing themselves; since progress has been
made, their self-reports are now required every six months instead of every quarter. In another company, executives are experimenting with a range instead of a specific target number
of personnel profiles so that managers can regulate themselves
from one period to another and still meet their yearly and long-
term numerical goals.

Tailoring numerical measures to the organization's goals
and giving managers more control over them are approaches
that many of our model organizations are using to take the heat
out of the measurement controversy. Although the numerical
goals they use are not popular with all managers because they
are still difficult to attain, the techniques seem to have helped
overcome some resistance to measuring outcomes, and this is
a critical aspect of any diversity effort.

Supplement Personnel Statistics
with Other Outcome Measures

The impact of a diversity effort involves far more than personnel statistics. While these are important, they are not a sufficient

measure of progress, and they are not an adequate incentive for managers to pursue diversity over time. Other outcomes must also be regularly examined to complete the picture of how much progress is being made and to evaluate the effectiveness of the diversity effort. Outcomes often relevant to diversity goals include measures of productivity and profitability tied to diversity efforts; employees' attitudes and opinions concerning their work and co-workers; and indications that the organization's culture provides a satisfying working environment for members of both sexes and all ethnicities.

Productivity and Profitability

Standard measures of productivity or profitability are sometimes used in organizations to show that diversity is good for business. While these measures can be useful in demonstrating that increasing diversity does not damage the bottom line, it is very difficult to prove that diversity is the reason for a rise and fall in standard, organization-wide business. Even when one can show that the organizations that are the most progressive on diversity issues are also outstanding profit makers or leaders in quality, as many of the organizations in our study are, there is still no clear evidence that diversity rather than a host of other possible factors is the primary cause.

More specific indicators of effectiveness are often used to strengthen the link between diversity and bottom-line results. Data on turnover is probably the most frequently used indicator in this regard. Organizations that are trying to improve the retention rate of nontraditional managers often use turnover rates to gauge their progress. Comparing overall turnover rates prior to and after diversity activities provides benchmarks for judging progress, and comparing the turnover rate of one group of managers to the rates of others (blacks compared with whites, women compared with men) pinpoints who is leaving at a higher rate. Goals for reducing the turnover of nontraditional managers, who have a historically high rate of departure, are not uncommon.

Subsets of managers can also be tracked; this can be done, for example, by separately reviewing the turnover of managers from key functional areas, those lost from line versus staff positions, or high-potential managers who may have been pirated away by competing firms. While the cost of replacing any manager is high and cuts into profits, the loss of key managers and key candidates is particularly damaging for an organization because of the significant investment that has often been made in their development. Statistics on these subgroups help monitor progress, but additional information on individual cases may also be needed to determine what particular problems are or are not being solved and why.

Data on absenteeism are also sometimes used to gauge effectiveness. Like turnover, absenteeism is expensive for organizations, and it represents a compelling reason to go forward with diversity if that expense can be cut. When diversity activities can reduce the stress and dissatisfaction that many nontraditional managers associate with the workplace, then the savings in turnover and absenteeism costs can be significant. Absenteeism, however, may be of limited usefulness at management levels because managers often travel and have considerable freedom to choose their own hours, and so it is harder to determine when they are avoiding the workplace.

Another indicator of effectiveness that is related directly to the bottom line is reduction of lawsuits. Discrimination lawsuits can be very costly, as the examples presented in Chapter One demonstrate. The Texaco case involving a $17.65 million award to a single employee is probably the most dramatic example of how much a lawsuit can cost. John Rebchook (1990) claims that fired employees win 70 percent or more of their cases that get to court, and that juries typically award $250,000 to each. To the extent that diversity efforts can reduce lawsuits, considerable expenses may be saved. Comparisons from one year to another or from one three-year period to another may indicate progress in reducing lawsuits. Organizations in which employees are being encouraged to use an internal grievance system may only monitor grievances filed with outside agencies so that managers do not feel pressured if internal grievances increase during an initial period of a year or two. The number of suits or grievances filed outside, including the number lost by the employer, may be useful measures of effectiveness and financial impact. A closer, nonquantitative examination of those cases — where they originate, and the nature of the complaint, for example — may again reveal the kinds of problems being solved or not solved in an organization.

Other measures of productivity or profitability are more difficult to link to programs on diversity. There is probably no direct evidence to link increased diversity to increased productivity, although many organizational researchers see a theoretical basis for the connection. It may be that the data now being collected by organizations will help confirm that connection. Some educational organizations, for example, are optimistic that increasing diversity among teachers and administrators will lead to increased diversity among the student body. Some educational leaders in our study are looking at the percentage of nontraditional students who graduate as a key indicator of effectiveness, along with the percentage who go on to college or to graduate school. Higher standardized test scores among students is another indicator relevant to educational institutions struggling to diversify staffs and student bodies.

The argument that diversity increases productivity and profitability is still based more on faith than on statistics. The diversity issue, however, is hardly unique in this regard. What direct evidence do we have that better customer service is directly related to the bottom line? Do we know for sure that product quality increases profits more than clever advertising? Can anyone prove that one product or market will be more lucrative than another over the long term? Businesses operate on a host of assumptions, some based on sound theoretical premises, that drive the way they spend money to make money, but few can be conclusively proved. The lack of a guarantee is hardly an excuse for not taking action.

Numerical links between diversity and the bottom line are simply not a sufficient basis for creating or evaluating a diversity effort. Although diversity activities may indeed improve managers' skill in supervising and developing their people and consequently improve their productivity, we probably will not be able to prove it. For example, performance appraisals originally developed for use in special development programs for non-traditional managers may eventually be used throughout the organization and improve the way all managers are developed and evaluated, thereby increasing their contributions to the organization. Yet statistical measures may not capture the impact of that particular change. Demonstrating results from a diversity effort can and should incorporate whatever quantitative measures are available on profits and productivity. However, other indicators of effectiveness are also needed to assess the more subtle forms of progress that can be made in organizations, in the short run and over the long haul. The fact that these changes have not yet been linked to the bottom line may say more about our methodological limits than the relationship itself.

Attitudes and Perceptions

Employees' perceptions about whether they are being fairly treated are an important indicator of progress. In the first step of investigating problems, executives often discover that perceptions differ dramatically from one demographic group of employees to another. Research by John Fernandez (1981, 1987, 1991) and internal organization studies have shown that white men at all levels feel better than any other group about how they are treated in their organization. Some organizations have set clear goals to improve nontraditional employees' perceptions of treatment, while also maintaining the good feelings of many of their white male employees. Perceived inequities and barriers can be as powerful as any that are proved to be actual; they may affect motivation, concentration, retention, health, and a variety of other factors that have effects on employees' work.

Management consultant John Hinrichs (1991, p. 77) notes that "the impact of employee actions on a company's financial health can be truly staggering" and that much of that impact is tied to "what goes on inside people's heads." Hinrichs' study of a Fortune 50 corporation linked employee commitment—coming to work, staying with the firm, caring about deadlines and the quality of their output—with bottom-line performance areas. A survey question about employees' intention to stay with the firm, for example, can be translated into actual cost figures. Hinrichs reports that 36 percent of employees who respond that they will probably leave the company actually do quit (compared with only 13 percent of those who say they don't plan to leave); at an average cost of $10,000 per person, the total projected turnover cost can be calculated. Absenteeism costs can also be calculated on the basis of employees' survey responses. Those who respond that they are not satisfied with their company have a 50 percent higher absentee rate than employees who are satisfied. With an average absentee rate of eleven days per employee per year, at a cost of $100 per incident, the total projected absenteeism cost can be computed.

Whether all executives can project exact costs that stem from their managers' and other employees' dissatisfaction and lack of commitment is not clear. What is clear from this analysis is that employees with lower commitment cost an organization more and that components of their commitment can be measured by employee surveys. Regularly surveying employees is a common technique for monitoring the effectiveness of diversity activities. Focus groups and interviews with current and past managers are other tools often used to tap into employee attitudes. In addition to the questions already mentioned, some specific indicators of effectiveness that should be considered in measuring perceptions of fair treatment include the following:

How likely is it that a manager will receive an accurate and thorough evaluation of her or his work at least once a year?

Is each manager's pay (base and bonus) in line with his or her contributions and the pay of co-workers?

Does each manager receive information about opportunities to advance or to increase her or his potential to advance?

Are there any significant consequences for managers who harass or discriminate against co-workers? For managers who practice affirmative action?

Does each manager have a fair chance of being sent to a prestigious training program? Of being assigned to a high visibility task force or project team? Of being reassigned laterally when advancement opportunities are limited? Of getting a line job instead of a staff job?

Some executives in our study believe that employers ought to make employees happier in their work, and they would expand surveys and interviews to assess happiness. While there is probably overlap between the perception of fair treatment and what executives call happiness, the latter includes satisfaction of a personal nature as well as professional satisfaction, morale, and easy bonding with colleagues for a sense of belonging. These factors, executives argue, have as much to do with employees' potential to contribute as those dealing more specifically with their feelings about fair treatment. Since it is very difficult to determine which perceptions and feelings affect employees' level of performance or potential, all are potentially useful indicators of effectiveness.

Employees' attitudes are important because they can potentially affect their decisions to stay or leave, to invest in learning, to nurture their subordinates' learning, and so on. Increasing the pool of managers who trust their colleagues and are willing to work in partnership with their employer is a goal that may help fill an organization's pipeline to the top. Organizations may even want to tap the perceptions of potential recruits or customers with respect to diversity issues to assess the image and reputation of the organization to key audiences among the public.

Culture Change

Some executives in our study were adamant about wanting to change their organization's culture. They do not feel that they can rely on personnel profiles or even statistics from attitude surveys to assess their goal of making the culture one that values diversity as opposed to one that resists or even merely tolerates diversity. Assessing the extent of culture change is a challenging and worthwhile goal, but it is important to find indicators that will help executives know how well they are doing. As the culture changes, it may be necessary to shift indicators of effectiveness to reflect the changes already made.

Many managers in our study had a hard time explaining what a changed culture would look like. Some defined a culture of valuing diversity as one that provides a better work environment for all employees regardless of their sex or ethnicity. One executive feels that in a better environment a black manager would not be reminded so often that she or he is black. Other executives suggested that a changed culture involves widespread awareness of how differences in background and culture contribute to business objectives; as a result, managers put more effort into creating and supporting diversity.

If culture change does involve changing certain values and behaviors of managers and their subordinates, then those values and behaviors should be assessed to determine how widely and how fast the culture change is taking place. It is not enough to dismiss other measures of effectiveness because they do not reach the core of the matter; one must add or substitute other indicators that come closer to capturing one's true goals for diversity progress. However, assessing culture is in itself a rather fuzzy process, and accounting for varying interpretations of the link between behaviors and values adds to the complexity of the analysis.

Evidence that increased value is being placed on diversity might be partially captured in attitude surveys. Because managers' support for diversity would presumably be reflected over a period of time in a more diverse group of direct reports and high-potential candidates, personnel profiles would presumably also partially reflect progress in this area. As women and people of color become more familiar in an organization and are thought of more often when promotion opportunities come up, promotion rates should correspond to the change. Thus, it seems that even though some numerical measures tap into only some of the more obvious attitude and behavior changes, such measures should not be abandoned.

Other indicators may supplement the more popular measures in addressing culture change, but some managers are unclear about the direction in which these indicators should go. For example, as part of the change process, will the number of diversity training programs increase or decrease? Will there be more interest in training as awareness grows, or will employees simply stop going to training programs as they outgrow the need? How about the number of special programs, task forces, or advocacy groups for women or people of color? It is tempting to say that these activities will become obsolete as the culture change takes hold, but at what point should they be phased out without jeopardizing the progress already made? Even tracking personnel profiles is sometimes seen as a short-run solution to diversity. Advocates of phasing out this form of monitoring argue that increased awareness of the value of diversity should move us away from statistical measures and from rewards such as bonuses based on numerical measures. Two of our model organizations have, in fact, uncoupled managers' personnel profiles and their compensation for fear that continued emphasis on the numbers will interfere with real progress in changing the culture.

    These are tough issues, and they illustrate the difficulty of defining goals that can be tracked and that may change rather dramatically as progress occurs. No doubt some heated discussions will take place in deciding what outcomes are appropriate and what measures of those outcomes are functional. Those discussions, among task force members and management committee members in particular, are probably necessary to final agreement on some realistic goals and indicators of effectiveness in reaching those goals. The indicators should help managers determine whether changes are in the desired direction. If participation in diversity training decreases, for example, are there other measures to assess whether this is occurring because most employees have already been adequately trained or because many employees who need training are refusing to attend or because the training is not as good as it used to be?

Evaluating Specific Diversity Practices

Evaluating the effectiveness of specific practices is another sticky issue that many managers apparently duck rather than confront. While all the organizations in our study paid attention to some measure of overall effectiveness, only a few attempted to evaluate the effectiveness of specific diversity practices. In fact, it was surprising how few of the managers we interviewed could give us concrete examples of how the effectiveness of practices such as training or developmental programs could be assessed. It seems that very little is being done in the way of evaluating particular practices and their contribution to the organization's overall diversity goals.

In evaluating individual practices, there is a risk that their true contribution will be over- or underestimated because of the effects of other practices and other factors that determine outcomes. Trying to assess one practice, such as an advocacy group or a new set of performance appraisal criteria, out of context, can be a waste of time when other important factors are not considered. The impact of downsizing or the appointment of a person of color to a senior executive post may outweigh the effect of a training program, for example. Yet it seems wasteful to invest in diversity activities without regard for the results they contribute. Some effectiveness measures should certainly be considered for any diversity practice, even if they have to be viewed in light of other contextual factors.

Some managers in our study did suggest indicators of effectiveness for training and development programs, including relatively simple techniques such as asking program participants about the value of the experience and even asking their bosses about any differences they noticed before and after a program. Such inquiries can be made at different times following a program (immediately after, two months later, and six months later) to determine its sustained impact. Although the ratings and comments may have to be taken with a grain of salt, they can sometimes be helpful in deciding whether to revamp, expand, or continue a program. Gathering data for training programs that are handled very confidentially and separating short-term or superficial "smiles test" data collected at the end of programs from longer-term impact data can also be difficult. Here are some other suggested measures of effectiveness.

• Are department heads or business unit managers nominating more of their high-potential managers for the program year after year, or are they increasing their spending for such programs? This indirect measure suggests how valuable these managers perceive the program to be.

• Are participants being promoted after completing the program? If a major goal of developmental programs is to advance the participants, then tracking their movement (perhaps in comparison to others who did not participate) may be appropriate. When promotions are limited by business conditions, adding in lateral moves and special assignments may give a more accurate picture of how participants' careers are progressing.

• Are past participants using the networks they were presumably building during a program, and to what extent has that helped them contribute more effectively? This kind of assessment is appropriate for programs that involve a group of participants meeting together during the course of a year, with one goal being to build ties with colleagues.

• Are participants staying with the organization longer? Programs that help orient employees or managers to the organization, including internship programs or programs to employ people initially on a temporary or seasonal basis, may be assessed in terms of their effect on retention.

These are only a few of the types of indicators that may be used to assess particular practices. Although not all practices lend themselves to assessment, there are ways of evaluating many of them on their unique contributions to diversity goals. While the interaction among practices and other factors must be considered, the analysis of individual practices can go a long way in helping managers shape the diversity effort to be most effective. Because of the costs involved in a diversity effort, it seems likely that executives will begin to require that effectiveness measures be used more often to assess specific diversity tools.

Expect Results That Managers Can Deliver

The demands made on managers and executives should be consistent with the control they have over the outcomes. As mentioned earlier, during times when managers have no hiring opportunities in their unit, it may not be reasonable to expect their personnel profiles to change (unless selective layoffs or natural attrition changes the mix). Along the same lines, holding managers responsible for hiring goals in other business units or at their own level may also be unreasonable unless there are clear ways for them to recruit, transfer, or promote people into available positions.

On the other hand, some managers argue that although organization-wide profitability is equally uncontrollable by many managers, at least some of their rewards (merit pay and bonuses, for example) are typically based on that profitability. Similarly, customer service or customer satisfaction may be outside an employee's area of control yet accepted as an evaluation criterion. Holding managers accountable for diversity results outside their own unit or department may also be justified and widely accepted, but only if managers understand how they can influence those results, say, by helping in recruitment or internship programs, by serving as mentors, or by giving more rotational assignments to their staff.

Results need to come from a variety of managers within an organization, at the top and lower levels, in line and staff positions. Tailoring at least some expectations to each manager's sphere of control is likely to increase the efficiency of a diversity effort. Senior executives may be expected to make a few key placements on their own, but they may also be expected to influence their managers to develop and promote the nontraditional managers who report to them. Human resource managers may be expected to target recruitment sources for those managers. Line managers may be expected to participate on task forces and create nuts-and-bolts career management programs for use throughout the organization. When managers' unique contributions can be explicitly factored into a set of overall expectations, the process is likely to be, and to be seen as, under control.

Managers' ability to produce results should also be considered. Many organizations have made the mistake of equating ability and control. Some managers want to build a more diverse team and to treat women and people of color more fairly and sensitively, but they don't know how. Organizations that provide human resource counseling, options for training that are not too threatening or embarrassing, or useful systems for recruiting can help these managers improve their ability to contribute to diversity goals. Incompetence should not be tolerated; however, because it usually takes time to build diversity skills, a grace period during which new procedures or expectations are introduced may be helpful in allowing managers to learn.

Fitting expected results and consequences to managers' ability and extent of control is an important part of getting things done. Managers' success or failure in achieving diversity results is often strongly related to their perceptions of the appropriateness of the demands being made on them.

Structure a Realistic but Ambitious Time Frame

Diversity goals can be made more realistic and acceptable by expanding the time frame for achieving them, but too many extensions will only deter progress. Goals should be challenging but achievable with planning and discipline within a specific period of time. Goals set too far into the future may be as unrealistic as those set too close to the present.

Diversity plans, like many strategic plans, often rely on a dual time frame that combines long-term and short-term goals. As emphasized earlier, achieving diversity takes a long time: ten or even twenty years. For example, several years ago one company set goals for ten years in the future; the goals largely focused on targeted personnel profiles for the entire organization. Given those long-term goals, the company also set short-term numerical goals for each year, as a step-by-step progression toward the ultimate goals.

Combining short-term goals with long-term objectives makes sense. The time frames, however, require serious thought. Several managers in the company with ten-year goals, for example, complained that the length of time is dysfunctional. The company's one-year goals have never been met, they noted, perhaps because there is no feeling of urgency in achieving them. In other words, the ten-year mark may be so far in the future that it fails to motivate managers to create more immediate changes. Another problem with long-term goals is that managers have difficulty envisioning the world that far in the future, and the goals set are likely to be out of sync with the trends and events that occur between now and then.

Strategic planning around other business objectives suffers from the same problems. How can managers foresee the technology of the future or the markets or the political and social landscape that provides the context for their business? Although a degree of foresight is essential to keep a business thriving, some organizations have decreased the time horizon used for planning from ten years or more to somewhere between three and five years. While yearly goals are set, planning is often done in three-year blocks, with revisions made every third year for the coming three-year period. This kind of rolling plan may be the most effective for diversity goals and activities. It is a useful and perhaps necessary exercise to create a vision around long-term goals, recognizing that the vision may need to be reviewed as the years go by. Specific goals for that long-term vision may not be part of the planning process. Instead, shorter-term goals that lead toward the vision form the backbone of a one-year and three-year plan.

Depending on the type of goals set, other time frames may be more appropriate. If, for example, an organization-wide attitude survey is conducted every two years, the results may be used as soon as they are available to revise some or all of the diversity goals rather than waiting for every third year. There should be enough flexibility in the process to accommodate related organizational processes and unexpected events, although excuses that goals could not be met because of a moderate business downturn or recruiting problems must often be put aside to ensure continued progress.

A time frame that is too short also poses potential problems in making progress on diversity. Goals that are simply too ambitious for a given period of time spark frustration, sabotage, and distrust of the entire process. Involving managers in setting their own diversity goals and analyzing the factors that could potentially help or hurt them in achieving the goals within a certain period can help make the time frame feasible and acceptable.

Summary

Demanding results from diversity efforts is essential. The results should be as clear and as measurable as possible but not limited to personnel profile data or other strictly numerical criteria. Indicators of the effort involved in diversity and the overall process of organizational change must also be recognized as important outcomes of diversity activities. Making demands consistent with managers' spheres of control and their ability to influence both specific and overall outcomes — within a reasonable period of time — helps reduce resistance to including outcomes as an expected part of managers' roles in making progress on diversity.

The methods used to create expectations and produce results on diversity issues interact with one another, especially over time. Making headway involves many factors, some of which can be controlled. As we will see in Chapter Eleven, greater awareness of these factors can help organizations use them to advantage in building on the successes already achieved to sustain and even accelerate progress.

ELEVEN

STEP FIVE:
USE BUILDING BLOCKS
TO MAINTAIN MOMENTUM

The human resource director has just shown a series of overhead slides to the two of us who are interviewing people in this organization. He explains that the data and recommendations concerning diversity activities have recently been presented to the executive committee. He is obviously pleased that the most recent personnel profile showed more demographic diversity than previous ones and that most of the recommendations have been approved by that group. The director is a thirty-nine-year-old Latino who is studying for an M.B.A., and he has been with the company for thirteen years. We ask him a pointed question: "Overall, on a scale of 1 to 10, how effective do you think the policies and practices now in place are in advancing women or people of color toward senior management?"

After a few seconds, he responds:

> Right now, I'd say about a 6, maybe a 7. Our focus has changed over the years. We've built on our successes and our failures over the years. The earliest efforts began in the early eighties with a focus on increasing the number of black male managers. We started with a small development program for black males, and we were able to phase out this special program after about five years once we increased the pool of high-potential black males. But the chairman wanted more than "potential"—he kept asking about results. Last year he demanded that we set hard targets for putting black males into top jobs. The combination of the development program and hard targets may work well.

Another experience we learned from is that in the mid eighties we noticed that the new M.B.A. women we pushed into visible top jobs were crashing. There was no support for them. We realized that many of our talented women were derailing seven or eight years into their career because of child-care issues. So we took a public stance on child care and women's issues, and we're experimenting with job sharing. But we also have to address the senior management culture here. The attitude is "If you don't want to work seventy-hour weeks, you're a wimp."

This year we are continuing to spotlight success in the area of diversity. We are giving an award for the first time to recognize those managers who have made the most difference in achieving diversity. It's a symbolic, very visible award, and it helps us recognize successful efforts when the promotion rate companywide has slowed. We have to keep the momentum going even when our resources are shrinking.

The impact of contextual elements and the sequencing of events in a diversity effort may explain why there is little consistency in the mix of practices used by the model organizations in our study and little agreement on what has worked and what has not. When we asked managers what they would do differently to improve the diversity effort in their organizations given their experience in fostering diversity to date, there was no overriding uniformity in their recommendations. The same techniques were mentioned again and again — training and preparation, accountability for results, support groups for employees, and so on. However, the perceived importance of each technique varied sharply from one manager to another; they even disagreed on whether the techniques had a positive or negative impact.

The disagreement among managers on recommended practices is probably due to a number of factors, including the mistakes and achievements their organizations made in using (or overlooking) a particular technique. The achievements often came about when the organization's unique culture, history, and needs were taken into account in building a diversity effort. In many success stories, the pieces built upon others like building blocks. Organizations' experiences with diversity practices represent a building block effort of sorts, for they allow us to review the actual use of practices, not just their intent. Several guidelines can be formulated around this building process.

Plan Beyond the Short-Term
Impact of Diversity Practices

Some diversity practices chosen only for immediate results have amounted to something worse than a waste of time because they actually interfered with the building process. The most obvious of these is the early recruitment approach that organizations used in an attempt to comply with government affirmative action requirements. In the short run, the numbers were sometimes met, but turnover was so high that the results did not endure. Managers we interviewed realized that the recruitment effort could have been salvaged if it had been supplemented with such support activities as orientation training, coaching and performance feedback, or assignments that exposed newly hired employees to more senior managers who might have become their allies. As it happened, recruitment as a lone remedy failed to have a long-term effect in many organizations or even a significant short-term impact in some. Moreover, some managers came to view recruitment as a tool to be avoided.

Training and development, as a stand-alone activity, also often failed. Training programs often suffer from a variety of ills, such as unintentionally reinforcing stereotypes or defensiveness about racism and sexism; their use as a one-shot attack against differential treatment poses additional problems. In one case, for example, outside training was provided for high-potential blacks, who upon completing the program were pirated away by competitors. Managers wondered whether these departures would have occurred if other activities, such as support groups or career planning, had been operating to build on the training itself and make the organization a more appealing and satisfying workplace.

Limiting practices only to certain groups, such as people of color or women, is sometimes criticized as a short-term Band-Aid approach that may interfere with longer-term progress. A developmental program for blacks that includes some rotational assignments along with group seminars, for example, may have a dysfunctional effect if managers see participants as trying to substitute that program for the "right" experience and credentials. Furthermore, white men along with people of other ethnicities may act out their resentment that such an opportunity is closed to them. Nevertheless, a small, exclusive program does have some potential long-term benefits. In the short run, such a program experiments with ways to prepare and advance individuals who have at least a historical disadvantage; what executives learn about that process through such a "pilot test" they can later use to help others grow. On the basis of their experience with small, closed programs, executives have made significant improvements in human resource systems that benefit all managers or employees, including better performance review practices and career planning techniques.

Sometimes it is necessary to overlook the short-term impact and simply focus on the long-range goals. For example, managers in one organization determined that the selection criteria being used for entry-level nontraditional employees were creating later problems in moving them into higher-level jobs. The criteria were adequate for the initial jobs, but they were not encouraging selection of people who could handle higher-level responsibilities such as strategic planning and polished interaction with outsiders. The entrants, therefore, were often stuck in the lower-level jobs. Changing the initial criteria to include factors important to later career advancement might, of course, make entry-level selection more difficult, at least for a while; the long-term results in upward mobility, however, might be worth that price. Some organizations already use such an approach when selecting managers for the fast track.

The practices that have both short-term and long-term benefits are the most valuable to an organization. The building process involves finding them or creating them and then capitalizing on them in the diversity effort. In creating them, it is sometimes possible to extend short-term benefits into the longer term. If a diversity awareness training program has only a short-lived positive impact, for example, perhaps the benefits can be extended by translating the training principles or insights into other organizational systems. One manager, for example, suggested that the pro-diversity behaviors discussed in the training program be incorporated into the participants' yearly performance evaluations to keep diversity at the front of managers' minds over time. That is one way to combine the potentially interactive effects of education and enforcement in bringing diversity to life.

Employee surveys represent another tool that has the potential to affect diversity over both the short and long terms. Initially, an employee survey can help identify problems and strengths to be targeted in a diversity effort. That initial assessment becomes a benchmark for later polls as a way to measure progress in a given period of time. Later surveys may also provide managers with feedback on how far they have come in managing diversity issues. When that feedback has consequences for managers' pay or career prospects, whether formally or informally, then surveys may be another example of how use of the same basic tool can combine education and enforcement.

A practice that has already impressed a number of executives as having significant short-term and long-term benefits is that of moving nontraditional managers into key, visible, high-level posts. In cases where managers are promoted from the pipeline, they represent concrete success stories of advancement. Even when nontraditional managers are hired from the outside, they are personal examples for their peers and colleagues, helping to increase awareness of diversity and to break down stereotypes about women or people of color. Their symbolic value often has the immediate effect of shaping the perception of other managers and employees that top management takes diversity seriously. Over the longer term, nontraditional managers often act as mentors and otherwise guide and advise other nontraditional managers coming up through the ranks. Their support of other nontraditional managers and of diversity issues in general also increases the success of recruitment efforts for still other nontraditional employees because more candidates see advancement possibilities for themselves.

The impact of high-level recruiting has different elements that build on one another in a way that can generate better results than each of the elements could separately. Each successful element adds leverage to the practice as a whole. Successful high-level recruits are effective recruiters themselves, even when they don't try. With a little help, short-term successes can sometimes create long-term successes, as we see next.

Leverage Successes and Progress

A little success goes a long way in fueling continued diversity efforts. Managers need continuing incentives to put their resources into diversity, and successful results are a powerful motivator. It is therefore important to build successes into an ongoing diversity plan and to use them to move forward so that all employees are better able to see the benefits that accrue to themselves and to others.

Perhaps one of the most essential first steps in a successful diversity effort is to identify and recruit strong, talented nontraditional managers. Eleven of our sixteen model organizations consider hiring the right people in the first place a key element in the diversity effort. The managers we interviewed pointed out that these recruits are closely watched because a great deal is expected from them, so their talents must be equal to the challenge. In addition, the larger the number of strong candidates for higher-level positions, the more likely it is that one will be chosen for promotion. Therefore, success in initial hiring can translate into faster promotion and simplified recruiting in the future.

To increase the chances for success, particularly early in a diversity effort, when success may be crucial to sustain the organization's investment, goals for specific units or groups may be chosen before broader goals are set. Goals for all types of change projects have been broken down into manageable parts and the steps to achieve them then taken in sequence. Revamping a performance appraisal process, for example, might be divided into four phases: the executives' system the focus for the first twelve to eighteen months, followed by the systems for middle level managers, for supervisors, and for nonmanagement employees. With regard to diversity efforts in particular, a number of organizations have taken a somewhat different tack by targeting as a starting point either known trouble spots such as a division or a job category or by focusing initially on making additional headway in an area that already represents a pocket of progress. In either case, a successful effort stands to get considerable attention.

A Canadian company decided to tackle a few troublespots that were linked to one another and also to the company's business expansion. According to Bob Brown (1990), president of Imperial Life Insurance, a conference of company women in 1987 identified three key goals as a starting point to improve the status of female employees: (1) to increase the number of women in senior management; (2) to increase the number of women in sales positions, specifically sales representatives, since these line positions represent a feeder pool for senior-level posts; and (3) to increase business with women by increasing the number of female policyholders. By the end of 1990, some progress had been made in diversifying the senior ranks and filling the pipeline with female candidates for future promotions. Women made up 35 percent of Imperial Life's officers, up from only 10 percent in 1987. At the same time nearly 25 percent of the sales representatives were women, up from 7 percent in 1987. Sales manager positions were also filled by women during the period: 45 percent in 1990 compared with none in 1987. Significant gains have not yet been made in tailoring products and selling techniques to female consumers, but the changes being made in the roles women play in the business may well aid progress in this area in the future. Meanwhile, the impressive gains that have been made in the other key areas have been communicated to employees, who are likely to feel optimistic about and support continued progress.

Corning Incorporated also targeted a troublespot in kicking off its diversity effort, but this trouble wasn't inside the company. According to Koretz (1991) Corning began working with officials of Corning, New York, to make the town of 12,000 more attractive to a diverse workforce. Since then, a black TV station

has been added to the cable offerings, and there are plans to
conduct diversity training for local school teachers. However,
the company's initial diversity phase also included related goals
that could yield more immediate results, such as reducing the
attrition rate for women and people of color and the company's
$5 million yearly cost for hiring and training. Using mentor
networks, training courses, and compensation tools, Corning
has cut attrition for women from 16.2 percent to 7.6 percent
and for blacks from 15.3 percent to 11.3 percent in three years.
Because these numbers represent success that can be carried to
the bottom line, they encourage managers to press onward in
pursuing community changes and making additional internal
changes to promote diversity.

Targeting the organization's pockets of progress is yet
another way of approaching diversity. If one part of a business
is already doing an exceptional job of fostering diversity, then
there is a good chance of learning what kinds of philosophies
and techniques contribute to that success. Because such progress
is happening within the organization, one goal should be to reinforce and expand those aspects of the organization culture that
already contribute to success. As Peter Drucker (1991) points
out, it pays to use aspects of existing corporate culture to help
achieve your objectives.

Managers in our study identified some of the aspects of
an organization's culture and operations that seem to aid diversity. They mentioned certain obvious characteristics, such as
a growing business that has plenty of growth opportunities for
employees, an open climate in which employees have direct access to senior managers to air their concerns, being located in
an appealing community whose members are well educated and
diverse, and having no established career path to the top. Sometimes traditional values can also help, such as when a pool of
nontraditional employees supports a "promote from within"
philosophy or when a people-oriented business approach also
includes emphasis on results. Even turmoil can sometimes help;
deregulation, increased competition, turnover at the top, and
downsizing have made some managers more open to change
and willing to try new methods of managing.

Several managers we interviewed noted that a large, decentralized organization can provide more opportunities for diversity when committed managers have authority to take the initiative in hiring or rotating employees. By building a part of the organization into a visible, noteworthy model for diversity, the organization as a whole may enjoy positive publicity that encourages all employees to apply diversity principles to their own parts of the organization.

Many executives would like to be in the position of receiving media attention and free publicity for their organizations' diversity successes. For a few organizations in our study, the use of public relations is an important part of the diversity effort because it can significantly leverage their own internal diversity activities. A positive public image and a reputation as a fair and satisfying place to work are valuable assets for any organization. This kind of public attention also affects employees; if the publicity is largely true, then employees may be more inclined to stay and to work through problems as they arise.

Managers we spoke with also recognize the value of internal communication for clarifying and emphasizing diversity goals and for calling attention to successes as they are achieved. To help people see that their efforts are paying off, it is important to report regularly the results of diversity activities, recognize the leaders, and urge everyone to continue the process. Feedback is an effective tool in drawing attention to the gains that are being made and encouraging greater, continued participation. Using the organization's grapevine to quickly spread the news of progress being made is sometimes encouraged by giving current information to particular employee groups, who get the word out to others. Early (and later) successes in fostering diversity need to be communicated not only to those who contributed to them but also to those who have the potential to contribute in the future.

Use Business Opportunities to
Retire Traditional Practices

Donald Kanter and Philip Mirvis (1989) report that most American workers believe that they can be more productive. Most

American workers also believe that their employers lack innovation, competitiveness, and efficiency. There are clearly all
kinds of improvements to be made in the way ideas, resources,
and people are managed in U.S. organizations. But it is usually
easier to keep the status quo than to make changes, so systems
and procedures remain in place long after they become obsolete. Changes are often made only as an act of desperation,
prompted by a crisis or the promise of one. This is also true
of diversity issues. A number of the organizations in our study
were inclined to begin diversity efforts only after a crisis or a
clash among employees, in the aftermath of lost business opportunities, or as market share plummeted.

It is difficult to think of a business downturn, a boycott,
or another hardship as an opportunity. An economic squeeze
can stall even long-standing diversity efforts, and downsizing
frequently has a disproportionately negative effect on nontraditional workers. Yet these events do provoke managers to analyze their philosophy and behavior and, in some cases, to scrap
their old ways. Tough economic periods, therefore, present opportunities to inspect and revitalize organizations in a way that
may be more difficult in times of prosperity (although a frantic
growth period may also prompt managers to abandon traditional
practices). These windows of opportunity should be used to retire outdated practices, including those related to diversity, that
may have been crippling the organization and could continue
to do so.

A tight labor market, for example, has posed problems
for business and has prompted many employers to consider a
variety of flexible work scheduling arrangements, including what
was unthinkable until recently—job sharing in management.
According to Hymowitz (1990), Aetna has become the insurance industry leader in innovative work scheduling, with about
70 employees paired into jobs that include management. Of
Aetna's 45,000 employees, 70 percent of whom are women,
about 1,200 work part-time and hundreds telecommute from
their homes. It is not incidental that this company's reliance on
women as workers has spurred innovations as the labor market
shrinks. Managers are making the difficult adjustments in part

because more women are managers and need the same kind of accommodations that they are giving their subordinates. However, "flex management," as it is being called, is an approach that suits the values and life-styles of many employees, women and men. It is increasingly a factor in attracting and keeping the most talented and most demanding workers.

When employees are keenly aware that business is slowing or that labor and consumer markets are shifting dramatically or that competition is erupting, organizational leaders have the chance to reshape policies and practices with less resistance. As profits plunge, for example, there is greater acceptance of eliminating such long-standing practices as simply cutting 10 percent of employees across the board or firing those hired last; instead, employees tolerate, if not expect, selective cuts and layoffs that weed out peripheral functions and poor performers. In such tough times, some chief executives have taken the risk of maintaining the representation of nontraditional employees in their personnel profile despite massive labor force cuts, countering the traditional method of "last in first out" that would have left only white men remaining. Adding the personnel profile to the criteria of performance and career potential in terminating employees, is a dramatic change that some organizations make as they struggle to regain profitability.

A related change in personnel practices is that of firing or laying off employees who are poor performers. It is generally acknowledged that managers find it extremely difficult to terminate marginally performing subordinates, so they are often transferred to unsuspecting colleagues or put "on the shelf," in positions where they can do little harm. This is true of white men who work with their buddies and of nontraditional managers whom other managers are reluctant to confront because of affirmative action goals. When trouble strikes and action is finally taken to cut these employees from the payroll, managers may realize that there is a way to prevent the same thing from happening again. Ill-conceived promotions can be prevented in some cases without embarrassment or penalty by allowing employees to try out for a job for a time without a commitment from either side until an employee's interest and competence are assured. This is a far cry from how promotions have typically been handled, but it has been used with some success as part of at least one diversity effort. The technique seems to be appropriate for situations that involve white male employees as well as nontraditional employees.

Traditional career paths must also be scrutinized if an organization is to maintain its competitiveness. Following the same career path as that of existing senior executives may not be the best route for future leaders. Yet the popular notion of "mainstreaming" nontraditional managers involves giving them the same experiences as their white male predecessors so that they will be credible candidates for their posts. It is possible that some experience that has traditionally not been emphasized in executive development may be critical for executives to lead effectively in the future. To lead organizations through the next ten to twenty years, executives may need expertise in public relations or human resource management, experience in mentoring or facilitating teamwork, or sustained involvement with flexible organization structures or community groups far more than an engineering or finance background. Although the "fast track" may need an overhaul, that is likely to be resisted by executives who advanced on the traditional one.

Again, while crises are rarely welcome, they are windows of opportunity to make changes that may otherwise not be made to help an organization emerge stronger and better able to use the potential that a more diverse workforce presents. If nothing else, slow business periods give managers a better chance to investigate barriers and plan actions that can be taken both now and when business conditions improve. Managers who are able to seize these moments to institute changes that may be long overdue contribute to the future vitality of their organizations.

Add Diversity to Diversity

Sex and ethnicity are only two of the variants of diversity that can help organizations deal with future challenges. Managers are increasingly becoming aware of the differences among people with different cultural backgrounds and their potential value in solving problems, in developing new products and customers, and so forth. As awareness continues to grow, managers will be on the lookout to integrate more diversity into their teams by looking beyond sex and ethnicity for other forms of diversity that they can call upon to increase the effectiveness of their operations. Many diversity efforts begin with a focus on sex and ethnicity because the stereotypes and emotions associated with them are so powerful, perhaps more powerful than those associated with age, religion, or physical challenge. To appreciate diversity fully, in its broadest definition, it may be necessary to first put to rest negative assumptions and feelings about men and women and about whites, blacks, Hispanics, Asian-Americans, Native Americans, and members of other ethnic groups that appear to have clouded people's judgment for a very long time.

Once an organization has managed to overcome barriers that are placed in the path of people of color and white women, progress can go farther. The lessons learned from managing sex and ethnic diversity can help an organization expand its efforts to other forms of diversity, including age, nationality and language, religion, physical challenge, and sexual preferences and orientation. Along the way, one lesson will probably be that an individual's group identity can include many other things as well. We group people together and characterize them, appropriately or not, according to whether they have a Ph.D. or whether they are extroverted, obese, southern, wealthy, bald, artistic or possess a host of other attributes. Using such categories to stereotype people can be as dysfunctional as using stereotypes based on sex, ethnicity, or age, for example. Another important lesson is that group identity (Latino, Jew, epileptic, extrovert, blonde) is not an adequate predictor of an individual's perspective, behavior, or potential contribution. The full range of an individual's characteristics and experiences must also be taken into account.

Advanced levels of awareness may call for further changes in organizational practices suited to fostering diversity. Training and education will need to be revised to highlight the value of diversity beyond sex, ethnicity, or other demographic characteristics, calling more attention to other group and individual differences. Educational efforts should also include such factors as creativity or cognitive style, tolerance of ambiguity, readiness to learn, and other individual traits that may differentiate managers only temporarily or situationally. By noting all of these factors, managers will be able to assess themselves and others more accurately so that they can better match human resources to both short-term and long-term business objectives.

Further changes in employee groups may also be called for in the broader conceptualization of diversity. Even in organizations where ethnic employee groups are rated as very effective, there is an anxiety that the short-term benefits may be outweighed later if the groups continue to remain ethnically separate and refuse to incorporate other forms of diversity. So far, groups have simply multiplied as they have become organized. Continuing along this path could lead to a plethora of groups that might each be devoted to advocating only its own form of diversity at the expense of all others. Perhaps as diversity efforts progress, employees will feel less need for such groups to support, challenge, or recognize them. Some managers want to substitute a single free-floating employee group composed of representatives of existing major employee groups, including white men, to perform many of the same functions that a variety of employee groups now perform. Probably, however, more employee groups will be formed over the next few years to fulfill needs that existing groups cannot yet meet. Despite the possible awkwardness that employee groups pose in the transition to a longer-term approach to diversity, it would be premature to curtail the activities of employee groups in most organizations today on the assumption that these groups do not properly represent full-scale diversity.

To achieve a state of full diversity, we must first achieve sex and ethnic diversity. Nevertheless, building diversity upon diversity, thoughtfully and selectively using tools proved useful in earlier phases, and adopting new techniques as transitions occur are key ways to keep an organization progressive and attractive to the workforce of the future.

Summary of the Diversity Development Process

The five steps and twenty-one guidelines for fostering diversity are summarized as follows.

Step One: Discover (and Rediscover)
Diversity Problems in Your Organization

Guideline 1.1. Keep assumptions under control.
Guideline 1.2. Collect more than "just the facts" — perceptions count, too.
Guideline 1.3. Ensure that a team is responsible for the investigation.
Guideline 1.4. Do not get bogged down in collecting or analyzing information.

Step Two: Strengthen Top-Management Commitment

Guideline 2.1. Position diversity as a key business issue.
Guideline 2.2. Be responsible for diversity by being responsive.
Guideline 2.3. Make diversity a pervasive part of the culture.

Step Three: Choose Solutions That Fit a Balanced Strategy

Guideline 3.1. Match solutions to the organization's data and culture.
Guideline 3.2. For sustained leadership development, select solutions that address challenge, recognition, and support.
Guideline 3.3. Select solutions that include the use of all three components of the diversity strategy: education, enforcement, and exposure.
Guideline 3.4. Reach as many employees as possible with each solution.
Guideline 3.5. Provide training and preparation for each solution.
Guideline 3.6. Agree on a modest start.

Step Four: Demand Results and Revisit the Goals

Guideline 4.1. Create meaningful numerical goals and use them.

Guideline 4.2. Supplement personnel statistics with other outcome measures.

Guideline 4.3. Expect results that managers can deliver.

Guideline 4.4. Structure a realistic but ambitious time frame.

Step Five: Use Building Blocks to Maintain Momentum

Guideline 5.1. Plan beyond the short-term impact of diversity practices.

Guideline 5.2. Leverage successes and progress.

Guideline 5.3. Use business opportunities to retire traditional practices.

Guideline 5.4. Add diversity to diversity.

The five steps for developing diversity described in Part Three are complicated, time-consuming, and expensive. They also overlap; what happens in one step may happen again after a later step, and some of the same decisions may need to be made in various steps. Although the ways in which these steps are woven together are affected by the people and organizations using them, they incorporate the following principles, which are essential in making substantive changes on the diversity front:

- Benchmarks against which progress will be measured are essential to identify the current situation in an organization.
- The responsibility and responsiveness of top management with respect to diversity together form the single most valuable ingredient in a diversity effort; capturing such support by means of data or other forms of education is extremely important.
- Choosing a combination of diversity activities that combines the effects of education, enforcement, and exposure to nontraditional managers is critical in ensuring the long-term leadership development of a wide range of employees.

- A diversity effort without measurable results is a waste of time, but the measures used must be consistent with the goals and supplemented with qualitative indicators of effectiveness.
- Success begets success; building on progress already made can be accelerated; past achievements can be used to extend diversity beyond sex and ethnicity issues into the full range of diversity.

As far as we were able to determine, none of the organizations in our study followed all of the steps and guidelines outlined here. Many omitted the discovery step, and others relied too heavily on the initiative and judgment of top management. Some were too ambitious about making speedy changes, some put too much hope on changing managers' attitudes, and others violated many of the guidelines. Nevertheless, the five steps and twenty-one guidelines recommended are a composite of what the organizations did right, sometimes the second time around, and what managers believe are the strengths of the actions they have taken. Despite the complexity of this plan of action, our study indicates that this is the process that all the organizations in the study would choose to follow if they had to start over again.

MEETING THE CHALLENGES OF LEADERSHIP DIVERSITY

Developing diversity is a struggle. The time and other resources required to make diversity come to life in an organization are truly staggering. What's more, there are no guarantees that certain practices will indeed foster meaningful diversity, and there is no proof that diversity will pay off for an organization. Yet some of the largest, most profitable, and most admired organizations in the United States have made diversity a priority. Their leaders are convinced that the struggle is worthwhile.

The reasons executives give for pursuing diversity are largely related to business objectives. In the context of a changing U.S. population, there are indications that diversity efforts can increase an organization's productivity, innovativeness, market share, and overall competitiveness. For some executives, the habit of choosing future leaders from the pool of white men makes far less business sense than it once did because that pool is shrinking to what will soon be only one-third of the workforce. Some also find that habit to be morally inappropriate and counterproductive. The potential benefits of diversity are compelling to many executives.

The roadblocks to diversity are substantial, and the solutions are still rather vague. No one knows the definitive cure for prejudice or for haphazard career development or for the other barriers that prevent many nontraditional managers from advancing. The efforts that some organizations have already made, however, show that these barriers are not insurmountable. Top executives and their teams have made headway on diversity issues by using information and their own judgment to create solutions that fit their situations. The steps and guidelines described in this book form a process to tailor solutions to the diversity problems inherent in many different situations. As in any change process, this is a long-term effort.

We have been able to learn a great deal about fostering diversity from a number of organizations that have been struggling with this issue and, at least in some respects, are conquering barriers that have kept white women and people of color from fully achieving their leadership potential. These leading-edge organizations and their leaders have not had an easy time of it. They have made plenty of mistakes along the way, but they persist in recovering from them. What happens after risking and failing in trying to solve diversity issues is no different from any other type of risk — you pick yourself up and go on. That's what leaders do.

Now that you have read this book and are poised to act, what might you do? Depending on your role and your resources, the first thing you might do is hand the book to a colleague and recommend that she or he read all or certain parts of it. Or you might convene a meeting of your department to begin action planning. You might review the results of your last companywide employee survey or compare this year's personnel profile with the profiles of previous years. We hope that this book has provided some useful ideas about how to develop diversity within your organization. Ideas, however, must be put into action. That is up to you.

THE GOLD
RESEARCH PROJECT

In the following pages I present a more in-depth look at the GOLD Project, including brief biographies of the members of the GOLD Research Team, a description of the team's research procedures, and a series of tables that present supplementary data that may be of interest to readers.

The GOLD Research Team

Kristen M. Crabtree is a full-time CCL staff member in San Diego. Crabtree has a bachelor's degree in anthropology from the University of California at San Diego and is working toward a master's degree in international business at the University of San Diego. As research assistant for the GOLD Project, she created and organized the data bases, conducted statistical analyses, managed the resource materials and reference list, and prepared tables and sections of the appendix.

Diane Ducat has been an adjunct staff member in research and training at the Center for Creative Leadership since 1985. She has a doctorate in counseling psychology from Columbia University and serves on the faculty of the City University of New York. Ducat was also a member of the data analysis team for the original research on "Breaking the Glass Ceiling." She was the site manager for two organizations in this study, interviewed at another site, and helped develop the vignettes used to introduce the chapters in this book.

Karen M. Grabow is director of human resource planning and development for Target Stores in Minneapolis. Her Ph.D. in industrial/organizational and counseling psychology is from the University of Minnosota. Grabow's dissertation research has incorporated and tested aspects of the "glass ceiling" project and other work done at CCL. She managed one organization in the GOLD Project.

Carol S. Y. García (formerly Carol Green) is an administrative assistant at CCL. As project administrator for the GOLD project, she scheduled interviews and meetings, distributed interview materials, arranged travel, handled inquiries and correspondence, and performed an array of other duties.

Nur D. Gryskiewicz has been an adjunct CCL staff member for several years. She has a doctorate in occupational psychology from the University of London and is on the faculty of the University of North Carolina's Business School in Greensboro. Gryskiewicz shared the management of one organization and interviewed at one other site as well.

Kay Iwata is president of Pacific Resources Education Programs in San Francisco, which specializes in diversity training and interventions. She earned her teaching certificate at San Francisco State University. Iwata managed three GOLD sites, interviewed at another two, and consulted extensively on the classification of the descriptive data used in our analyses and the development of the vignettes in this book.

Edward W. Jones, Jr., a former corporate executive, has headed his own consulting firm since 1983. Nationally recognized for his work on race in organizations, including his widely read 1973 and 1986 articles on black managers in the *Harvard Business Review,* Jones helps CEOs and other leaders analyze and improve their organizations. He graduated from the Harvard Business School as a Baker Scholar. He conducted interviews at one site that is not included in our principal data base of sixteen organizations but that served as a useful reference in interpreting the data.

Libby C. Keating is a self-employed consultant based in New Jersey. She is affiliated with a spousal relocation assistance firm, has a private career-adjustment counseling practice, and teaches at the College of St. Elizabeth. Keating was formerly on the staff of Catalyst, a women's career development organization in New York. Her master's degree in education is from California University of Pennsylvania. She managed two GOLD sites and interviewed at one other.

Karen McNeil-Miller is a program associate with CCL's education and nonprofit group in Greensboro, North Carolina. She has a master's degree in education from the University of North Carolina at Greensboro and is now working toward an Ed.D. degree at Vanderbilt University. McNeil-Miller managed three organizations in this study and interviewed at one other site.

Richard A. Morales is a research and program associate with CCL in San Diego. He has a doctorate in sociology from the University of California at Berkeley, and his specialties include international labor markets. Morales managed one site in this study and interviewed at another four. He also provided extensive critiques of several drafts of this book.

Ronald Stratten is cofounder and vice president of Key Technologies International. His background includes athletic administration and coaching as well as assessing and counseling young retiring athletes. Stratten has a master's degree in curriculum and instruction from Kansas State University. He was the site manager for two organizations in this study and interviewed at another two.

Judy A. Weir, research analyst for the GOLD project, has a master's degree in sociology from San Diego State University. She managed all of the data bases, advised us on computer resources, consulted on many complex statistical questions, and helped prepare sections of the appendix.

Research Procedures

The GOLD (Guidelines on Leadership Diversity) Project is best described as structured field research. We used managers' responses to a set of interview questions to identify both problems and solutions related to diversity. Our intent was to capture the richness of a case study approach without limiting the applicability of our findings only to certain situations. To collect meaningful details and also detect patterns across organizations in the way a large-scale survey might, we used a structured interview format to gather detailed information from managers in various organizations and converted their responses into numerical codes for statistical analyses.

Some of our colleagues in the research arena would prefer to believe that a project such as this is inspired by curiosity alone, with objectivity and distanced emotion. It would be professionally comforting to say that we adhered to an "ideal" research position, seeking only to discover and having no point of view. But that is not the case. Each of us on the research team has an abiding interest in helping organizations foster diversity because we are members of groups underrepresented in management. We also believe strongly that differential treatment is unjust. Our strategy was to seek rigor in collecting and interpreting the data, not by attempting to transform ourselves into creatures of objectivity but by relying on our professional discipline and by subordinating our individual biases to the process of collaborative understanding. We chose to invest in this research because we want to change the practices that prepare and advance potential executives. Perhaps others who have no such motive would have done this research differently. Or perhaps it would not have been done at all.

Selection and Description of the Sample of "Role Model" Organizations

Over a period of nearly a year, we chose sixteen organizations that we believe are role models in developing diversity in management. The selection criteria included both "hard" and "soft" evidence of progress. The hard evidence typically consisted of the numbers of white women and people of color in upper-management positions. For example, at one $15 billion company, 18 percent of those at the vice president level and higher were people of color and 6 percent were women; at one of the educational institutions, corresponding figures (at the executive level) were 17 percent people of color and 8 percent women. At another business 17 percent of those at or above the level of regional vice president were women and 17 percent were people of color. In one company with revenue of over $3 billion, three women reported directly to the CEO. In the large government agency we studied, 10 percent of those at or above the GS/GM 15 level were people of color and 9 percent were women.

Only one of the organizations included in our study, however, was headed by a woman or a person of color, and most of the organizations had very few nontraditional executives. Rather than relying solely on numerical criteria (after all, how many is enough to qualify as a role model?), we also used "soft" evidence to select organizations: uniqueness and thoroughness of the practices being used, depth and logic of the outcome measures, and thoughtfulness behind the process used to achieve diversity. Moreover, basing our selection criteria on numerical data alone could have ruled out organizations using newer, more innovative, and possibly more effective diversity practices simply because there had not been enough time for the new practices to show concrete results.

Another goal of the selection process was to include organizations in a variety of industries and regions and in both sectors. Therefore, we chose companies located in all parts of the country that appeared to be diversity leaders within their industries and four public sector organizations—two government agencies and two educational institutions—for the study. Past research done by the Center for Creative Leadership and other institutions has often been criticized for focusing exclusively on either the private or the public sector. What many people want to know is "Will it work here?" By including a broad range of organizations, we hoped to be able to generalize our findings across industry, region, and sector lines. Of course, any major differences in responses from one sector to the other are noted because they may affect the guidelines presented.

We created an initial list of candidates for this study by gathering names of organizations cited in books and periodicals as those most progressive in diversity. These sources included *Black Enterprise* magazine's list of "best companies for blacks," the companies listed in Baila Zeitz and Lorraine Dusky's (1988) *The Best Companies for Women,* and winners of Catalyst's annual awards to companies. My colleagues and I evaluated this list, added other organizations we knew of, and began contacting managers in those organizations. As we progressed with the interviews, we eliminated some organizations from our list and used an extensive network consisting mainly of human resource experts to investigate other organizations as candidates for our list. One of the interview questions, in fact, addressed diversity practices that are being used effectively at other organizations. We continued to make selection decisions up until only a few months before the interviewing was complete.

As noted earlier, of the sixteen organizations chosen to participate in the GOLD project twelve are businesses, two are educational institutions, and two are government organizations. Of the twelve private businesses, one is a not-for-profit firm and two are subsidiaries of larger corporations. In this description, data on the parent companies are used.

The twelve businesses consist of three industrial conglomerates, two telecommunications firms, and one company each in consumer goods, finance, health care, publishing, retailing, transportation, and utilities. Ten of the twelve businesses are ranked in the Fortune 500 Industrials or the Service 500. Information from *Fortune* magazine (April 22 and June 3, 1991) shows that their revenues range from $3.5 billion to more than $130 billion. The average annual revenue for all twelve is about $23 billion. The number of employees in each of the twelve businesses ranges from fewer than 18,000 to about 140,000; the average is about 60,000. (Most of these businesses are relatively large, perhaps because large corporations have felt more pressure from the government to take action on diversity and thus are where progressive practices emerge. Undoubtedly, some small companies have also adopted a number of innovative diversity techniques, but we were not as aware of them.)

The two educational institutions in the GOLD Project are smaller than the businesses, one employing about 15,000 and the other about 20,000 people. Each of the two has an average annual budget of $950 million. In contrast, the two government organizations are very different from each other. One is a nationwide agency of the federal government that has more than 100,000 employees. The other is a branch of a county government that has only about 100 employees.

These sixteen organizations are headquartered all across the United States. Six of the businesses and one each of the education and government organizations are headquartered on the East Coast. Four businesses, including the not-for-profit firm, and one other government agency are headquartered on the West Coast. Two businesses and one school are headquartered in the Midwest.

We offered confidentiality to all the participating organizations to encourage them to join the project and to help ensure that the information we gathered would be accurate. Because our research approach does not depend upon describing the characteristics of a given organization, the identities of the participating organizations are incidental to the findings. Many of the organizations are publicly known for their policies or practices in fostering diversity. Most of them are listed in the acknowledgments with their consent. While we appreciated the chance to publicly thank the organizations that contributed to this research, we also recognize the advantages of their remaining anonymous. In either case, no practices or comments throughout the text are attributed to an organization by name, which helps preserve the confidentiality of the individual managers who were interviewed.

Selection and Description of the Sample of Managers Interviewed

Our initial contacts at the participating organizations, usually human resource executives, agreed to provide us with a beginning list of managers to interview. Our interviews with these managers sometimes led to their recommending other managers to be interviewed. The 196 managers in our final sample were selected on the basis of their knowledge of the diversity issues and practices used in their organization; their demographic diversity was also a consideration. Most are executives (37 percent) and upper-middle-level managers (43 percent).

Demographic Characteristics. This section includes information on the sex, ethnicity, age, marital status, and level of education of the managers interviewed.

Table A.1. Sex and Ethnicity of Managers Interviewed.

Sex and ethnicity	Managers		Number of organizations
	Number	Percent	
White men	59	30	16
White women	56	28.5	16
Black men	29	14.8	12
Black women	25	12.7	12
Hispanic men	10	5	7
Hispanic women	3	1.5	1
Asian-American men	2	1	2
Asian-American women	5	3	5
Native American women	1	0.5	1
Other men	1	0.5	1
Other women	2	1	2
Unknown ethnicity	3	1.5	3
Total	196	100	

Managers were asked to identify themselves in terms of their ethnic background as part of the interview. As with all interview questions, they were given no categories from which to choose, and their answers were recorded verbatim. After their responses were analyzed, we formed six ethnicity categories: white/Caucasian, black/African-(Afro-)American, Hispanic, Asian-American, Native American, and other.

More than half of the managers we interviewed were white. Those in the white/Caucasian category include those who specified white, Caucasian, European, Canadian, and Jewish.

Some of these subcategories were too small to analyze separately. White individuals who identified themselves as "Southern" or "American," or according to another regional identification were grouped under the white/Caucasian category. "Heinz 57 variety" and "American mutt, fourth generation" were coded as white (European) because of these interviewees' extensive discussion of their European heritage. Europeans included interviewees born in Europe and those who specifically said they identified with their European heritage, however distant.

Blacks, or African-Americans, are the largest group of people of color we interviewed. This group includes people from the United States, Africa, and the Caribbean Islands. The groups of Hispanics, Asian-Americans, and Native Americans were quite small, despite our attempts to include them. Hispanics include managers who identified themselves as Chicano, Latino, Mexican, and Mexican-American. The "other" category includes an Asian Indian, an Armenian, and a person of color whose ethnicity was not apparent from information contained in the interview.

In only seven cases (including some already mentioned) was the interviewer's judgment regarding ethnicity used in lieu of data directly from the interviewee. There were only three cases of "unknown" ethnicity, which we could not determine.

The number of foreign-born people of color is unclear. We did not directly ask the interviewees if they were born in the United States, but we did ask where their parents were born. From this and other interview information, we are reasonably sure that five nonwhite managers were born outside the United States. The vast majority of people of color and whites appear to have been born in this country.

As Table A.2 shows, white men tended to be older as a group than others. Hispanic women, Asian-American women, and those in the small groups of "other" ethnic backgrounds tended to be younger.

In terms of marital status (based on information from 191 managers), approximately three-fourths of the managers we interviewed were married. The single and divorced groups each accounted for 10.5 percent of the sample. The remainder reported that they were either separated, cohabiting, or remarried. More women (31 percent) than men (12 percent) were single or divorced.

Table A.2. Age in Years of Managers Interviewed.

Sex and ethnicity	Number of managers	Average age	Age range
White men	58	49	35–67
White women	55	42	30–58
Black men	29	43	27–60
Black women	25	43	27–56
Hispanic men	10	43	35–54
Hispanic women	3	36	36–37
Asian-American men	2	45	42–48
Asian-American women	5	36	29–40
Native American women	1	40	40
Other men	1	34	34
Other women	2	38	33–42
Total and average	191	44	27–67

Note: Figures are based on data from 191 of the 196 managers interviewed for whom we had information on age and ethnicity.

Table A.3. Education Level of Managers Interviewed.

Sex and ethnicity	Less than a bachelor's degree		Bachelor's degree		Graduate degree		Group total	
	Number	Percent	Number	Percent	Number	Percent	Number	Percent
White men	4	6.9	23	39.7	31	53.4	58	30.5
White women	7	12.5	15	26.8	34	60.7	56	29.5
Black men	5	17.9	10	35.7	13	46.4	28	14.7
Black women	4	16.7	5	20.8	15	62.5	24	12.6
Other men of color	1	10.0	5	41.7	6	50.0	12	6.3
Other women of color	2	16.7	5	41.7	5	41.7	12	6.3
Total	23	12.1	63	33.2	104	54.7	190	100.0

Notes: Figures are based on data from 190 of the 196 managers interviewed for whom we had information on ethnicity and education; some ethnic groups were combined because of their small numbers.

Graduate degrees include forty-five master's degrees, twenty-seven M.B.A.s, nineteen Ph.D.s (one was all but dissertation), eight J.D.s, and six combined advanced degrees. More white women had obtained Ph.D.s than any other ethnic group of women or men (nine of nineteen). More men than women had J.D.s (six of eight).

Level of education does not appear to determine management level. That is, managers in our study seem to be fairly evenly distributed among all management levels regardless of their educational background.

Career and Occupational Characteristics. This section includes information on the level, function, salary, span of control, and tenure of the managers interviewed.

Overall, 104 managers (54 percent of the sample) were in line positions at the time we interviewed them. In terms of level, the largest group in our sample consisted of those at the middle level, designated "managers of managers" (43 percent); about half of those were in line functions. Top-management or executive-level positions were held by 37 percent of our sample; the two top managers in staff positions were in strategic planning and human resources. The ethnic and sex distribution of our sample across management levels reflects the actual distribution that exists in many organizations: white men tend to be at the highest levels, and nontraditional managers tend to be concentrated in staff positions.

Based on the data we have, the average base salary was $111,000; the minimum was $32,000, the maximum was $750,000, and the midpoint was $85,000. The average total cash compensation was $120,000, with a range of $32,000 to $700,000. Unfortunately, our information is incomplete; no data were reported by some managers, and some managers reported their base salary but not their total compensation and vice versa.

The average *known* bonus for interviewees reporting less than an $85,000 base salary was $9,000; for those reporting a salary of $85,000 or more, the average bonus was $49,000. One-third of the interviewees reported a base salary of between $50,000 and $85,000, and one-fourth had total compensation in that range. Only 6 percent of our sample reported a base salary of less than $50,000. Of the fifteen managers interviewed who reported a base salary of at least $200,000, thirteen were men, and all were white.

Managers in private business reported higher base salaries and total compensation than those in public organizations.

Table A.4. Level and Function of Managers Interviewed.

Sex and ethnicity	Group total		Top management Line		Top management Staff		Executive Line		Executive Staff		Manager of managers Line		Manager of managers Staff	
	Number	Percent	Number	Percent	Number	Percent	Number	Percent	Number	Percent	Number	Percent	Number	Percent
White men	59	30.6	9	15.3	2	3.4	21	35.6	8	13.6	5	8.5	8	13.6
White women	56	29.0	1	1.8	-	-	9	16.1	5	8.9	6	10.7	19	33.9
Black men	29	15.0	1	3.4	-	-	8	27.6	1	3.4	11	37.9	4	13.8
Black women	25	13.0	1	4.0	-	-	-	-	2	8.0	6	24.0	10	40.0
Hispanic men	10	5.2	-	-	-	-	3	30.0	-	-	5	50.0	1	10.0
Hispanic women	3	1.6	-	-	-	-	-	-	-	-	1	33.3	-	-
Asian-American men	2	1.0	-	-	-	-	-	-	-	-	2	100.0	-	-
Asian-American women	5	2.6	-	-	-	-	-	-	-	-	3	60.0	1	20.0
Native American women	1	0.5	-	-	-	-	-	-	-	-	-	-	-	-
Other men	1	0.5	-	-	-	-	-	-	-	-	1	100.0	-	-
Other women	2	1.0	-	-	-	-	1	50.0	-	-	-	-	-	-
Level total	193	100	12	6.2	2	1.0	42	21.8	16	8.3	40	20.7	43	22.3

Sex and ethnicity	Group total		First level supervisor Line		First level supervisor Staff		Individual contributor Line		Individual contributor Staff		Consultant Staff	
	Number	Percent	Number	Percent	Number	Percent	Number	Percent	Number	Percent	Number	Percent
White men	59	30.6	-	-	4	6.8	-	-	1	1.7	1	1.7
White women	56	29.0	1	1.8	9	16.1	1	1.8	2	3.6	3	5.4
Black men	29	15.0	-	-	1	3.4	2	6.9	-	-	1	3.4
Black women	25	13.0	3	12.0	3	12.0	-	-	-	-	-	-
Hispanic men	10	5.2	-	-	1	10.0	-	-	-	-	-	-
Hispanic women	3	1.6	1	33.3	-	-	1	33.3	-	-	-	-
Asian-American men	2	1.0	-	-	-	-	-	-	-	-	-	-
Asian-American women	5	2.6	-	-	-	-	-	-	1	20.0	-	-
Native American women	1	0.5	-	-	-	-	1	100.0	-	-	-	-
Other men	1	0.5	-	-	-	-	-	-	-	-	-	-
Other women	2	1.0	-	-	1	50.0	-	-	-	-	-	-
Level total	193	100	5	2.6	19	9.8	5	2.6	4	2.1	5	2.6

Note: Figures are based on data from 193 of the 196 managers interviewed for whom we had information on ethnicity.

The average salary for managers in the private sector was nearly twice that of public sector managers ($126,629 compared with $65,139). Seventy percent of the private sector managers reported salaries of $85,000 or more (the midpoint) compared with only 13 percent of the managers in the public sector.

The number of direct reports ranged from 0 to 200, with an average of 10 and a midpoint of 6. The number of total subordinates was as high as 75,000; the average was 2,075 subordinates, and the midpoint was 65. One manager whose title and level of responsibility fit the "manager of managers" category had no direct reports (6.6 percent). Moreover, two managers classified as first-level supervisors indicated that more than one level of subordinates reported to them. These apparent inconsistencies occurred because level was assigned on the basis of our judgment of each manager's responsibility within his or her organization's structure while we also adjusted for consistency across the organizations in our study.

The average tenure of the managers in our sample was fifteen years, with a range of a few months to forty years. The vast majority of white men we interviewed had been employed for more than ten years at their organizations. Eighty-nine percent of the sixty-three managers who had tenure of ten years or less were nontraditional managers.

The Interview Process

Once the managers in our sample consented to be interviewed, they were sent the interview questions at least a week in advance of the actual interview. A number of managers did make notes and gather relevant materials before they were interviewed.

Interview Questions and Techniques

The first interviews were conducted in late 1988, with an initial set of questions developed for the study. On the basis of what we learned from interviewing at the first organization, we added, deleted, and reworded some questions. We continued to refine the interview format even after we had started interviewing

Table A.5. Average Span of Control (Direct Reports and Total Subordinates) of Managers Interviewed.

Sex and ethnicity	Ethnic group total		Top management				Executive				Manager of managers				First-level supervisor			
			Line		Staff		Line		Staff		Line		Staff		Line		Staff	
	Dir[a]	Tot[b]	Dir	Tot	Dir	Tot	Dir	Tot	Dir	Tot	Dir	Tot	Dir	Tot	Dir	Tot	Dir	Tot
White men	51	45	13	32,159	5	38	10	2,951	39	426	17	474	7	93		-[c]	13	13
White women	45	44	NA		-	-	14	2,991	6	76	7	283	5	76	8	8	9	8
Black men	27	26	45	160	-	-	8	1,139	6	1,100	10	667	5	10	17	64	4	34
Black women	22	22	4	400	-	-	-	-	6	6	23	597	5	83	17	64	1	1
Other men of color	13	12	-	-	-	-	8	830	-	-	10	694	4	8			2	-
Other women of color	10	10	-	-	-	-	NA		-	-	5	434	0	0	12	12	3	3
Number of managers[d]	168	159	10	9	1	1	36	31	13	13	38	37	37	38	5	5	16	13
Percent	100%	100%	6%	6%	0.6%	0.6%	21%	20%	8%	8%	23%	23%	22%	24%	3%	3%	10%	8%

Notes: Figures are based on data about direct reports from 168 managers and on data about total subordinates from 159 managers; some ethnic groups were combined because of their small numbers.

[a]"Dir" stands for the average number of direct reports, line and staff, for each level.

[b]"Tot" stands for the average number of total subordinates, line and staff, for each level.

[c]No managers in our study were in this group.

[d]The number of managers from which the average span of control was calculated at each level for line and staff.

Table A.6. Average Tenure in Years of Managers Interviewed.

Sex and ethnicity	Total number in group	Top management		Executive		Manager of managers		First-level supervisor		Professional	
		Line	Staff	Line	Staff	Line	Staff	Line	Staff	Line	Staff
White men	55	24	28	19	22	21	24	-	24	-	36
White women	52	14	-	9	17	12	15	12	11	5	11
Black men	28	22	-	19	20	16	7	-	5	3	-
Black women	25	3	-	-	17	11	12	8	13	-	-
Other men of color	13	-	-	21	-	10	8	-	16	-	-
Other women of color	11	-	-	22	-	11	10	15	3	13	7
Average per level		63	28	90	76	81	76	35	72	21	54

Notes: Figures are based on data from 184 of the 196 managers interviewed; some ethnic groups were combined because of their small numbers.

at a few organizations. For example, we realized after we had conducted about two dozen interviews that we should have asked the managers about their compensation, span of control, and other characteristics, and so we added the appropriate questions in subsequent interviews.

We also modified the content questions somewhat after we had completed several interviews. The final question in each interview was "Is there anything we should have asked you but did not?" One manager told us we should have asked specifically about long-term goals for diversity efforts. We therefore added a question about five-year goals. While not all of our interviewees had the chance to respond to that question, we were able to collect that information from many of the managers we interviewed. The same is true for a few other questions we addressed. However, most of the questions were put to all of the interviewees in the same way. Finally, three additional questions regarding factors of success were included for many of the nontraditional managers and their bosses who were selected for interviews.

Prior to conducting the interviews, the members of the research team were instructed on the purpose of the questions and how to probe for more detailed responses. This training helped ensure that all interviewers would ask the same questions in the same way to get the same level of detailed answers from the managers. The interview questions, along with "probe" instructions for the interviewers, appear in Exhibit A.1.

Exhibit A.1. GOLD Project Interview Questions.

Demographic Data

1. What is your marital status? How many children, if any, do you have?
2. How do you identify yourself in terms of ethnic background?
3. Tell us about your parents—where were they born?
4. What is your age?
5. What is your level of education (degree[s], major, school)?

Exhibit A.1. GOLD Project Interview Questions, Cont'd.

6. What is your career history (length of time with this company, which positions held, length of time as a manager, length of time in current position, previous positions in previous organizations, length of time as manager of [other interviewee])?
7. What is your annual salary or compensation?
8. How many subordinates report to you (directly or indirectly)?

Background and Overview

1. In your organization, has there been a change over the past several years in the way that women and people of color have been treated or have fared, particularly in the management ranks? Can you tell us about important factors inside or outside your organization that you think helped effect that change? [Probe for an organizational profile that gives historical perspectives, trends, or important characteristics of the organization, such as a period of turbulence, change in leadership, key clients, growth, a court case, new legislation.]
2. Do you think there are barriers or special problems for women or people of color in advancing to senior management in general? In your organization? What are the barriers? [Probe for how barriers are similar or different for the various groups and subgroups.]
3. In his 1970 book *Up the Organization,* Robert Townsend says that "stamping out [prejudice] will be a process, not an act." Is there such a process taking place in your organization? If so, which policies or practices (formal or informal) are part of the process? [Probe for which policies or practices benefit which subgroups, and how long each has been used. The goal is to understand the constellation of current policies and practices. Be sure to note any that were not specifically designed to benefit women and people of color but did.]

Key Policies and Practices

1. Of all the policies or practices you've mentioned, which one or two do you think are most significant? Use the following questions to describe each in depth. Then, if you want to, pick another that you think is significant and proceed through the same questions.

    When started?   How does it work?

    Why and how started?   Who may/does/should
                                participate?

Exhibit A.1. GOLD Project Interview Questions, Cont'd.

Who started it/runs it/is   How are participants
responsible?   selected?

2. How effective are these policies or practices? How are they being measured or evaluated? How do you think they should be measured or evaluated? Use specific data and examples related to recruitment, development, retention, promotion, and so on.

3. What do you think makes these particular policies or practices so effective? Name up to three important factors in your organizational culture — such as leadership, demographics, and marketplace — that have helped make them effective.

4. On a scale of 1 to 10, how effective do you think these policies or practices are in advancing women and/or people of color toward senior management?

5. What are the weak points of these policies or practices? How can they be made more effective? [Or, Which improvements were already made? Are more in progress?]

6. Do these policies or practices have any downsides or negative effects? [Probe for backlash from any groups, including nontraditional managers.]

7. Although these policies or practices may have been designed to benefit women and/or people of color, do you think they also benefit any others in your organization? Whom do they benefit? How?

8. What goals do you have for progress on this issue in your organization in the next five years? What will help or hinder you in reaching the goals you have identified?

Recommendations

1. Of all the policies or practices that your organization has used in an attempt to advance women and people of color into management, have any of them failed? Which ones and why?

2. If you had complete authority to advance women and people of color into higher management in your organization, what is the first step you would take toward that end? What other steps would you take? Finally, what would you avoid doing?

3. If we wanted to get more in-depth information about these policies/practices, whom should we speak to?

4. Are you aware of any policies/practices used in other organizations that are particularly effective in terms of diversity? [Probe for contact information.]

Exhibit A.1. GOLD Project Interview Questions, Cont'd.

5. Are you aware of any other organization that is using one of the same policies or practices that your organization is using, but with more success? [Probe for contact information.]
6. Finally, is there anything we should have asked you but did not?

Additional Questions

1. Your subordinate is unusual in that she/he has reached a level in management that many of his/her counterparts have not. What makes this person different in this regard? [Probe for contributing values, pressures, influence of other individuals, key events, "lucky breaks," and the like, as well as for policies or practices.] Do you consider him/her to be "successful?" How do you define success?
2. Now we can talk specifically about any policy or practice with which your subordinate has been involved. Can you identify one or two that you think are most significant? Use the following questions to describe each in depth. Then, if you want to, pick another that you think is significant and proceed through the same questions.

   When started?   How does it work?
   Why and how started?   Who may/does/should
                                    participate?
   Who started it/runs it/is   How are participants
   responsible?   selected?

3. How has your subordinate changed since she/he has become involved in these policies or practices? How has this person benefited from them? [Probe for new skills, abilities, salary increase, promotions, new responsibilities, new contacts or reputation, new prospects or ambitions.] Does any particular benefit or difference stand out? How much time lapsed until the benefits became evident?

Note: The additional questions were asked both of nontraditional managers and their bosses. The questions as they are presented above are worded as they were addressed to the bosses; these questions were worded slightly differently when addressing nontraditional managers directly.

The interviewers were trained to take notes during the interviews because audiotaping was generally not used. In most cases, new interviewers were apprenticed to me or another experienced interviewer, serving as a second or even third interviewer or note taker during a few interviews while the more experienced interviewer observed. Later, we compared our notes to identify how the note-taking process could be improved. All the interviewers quickly became adept at writing verbatim responses and making shorthand notes that they filled in more completely once an interview was completed. While it was not possible to write down every comment made in an interview, the notes tended to capture the essence of the comments made and the confidentiality of managers' responses were better protected than if taping had been used.

Face-to-face interviews were conducted with all except 5 of the 196 managers, usually in their own office or an adjoining conference room. We felt it was important to make it as easy as possible for managers to participate in this research and easy for them to develop a comfortable rapport with their interviewer(s). The interviews took slightly less than two hours each, averaging 107 minutes.

Interview Bias

The literature indicates that interviewer bias may occur in research such as this, particularly when respondents are questioned about their own feelings and opinions. Since the vast majority of our questions were about the interviewees' organization or managers as a group rather than about the interviewees themselves in particular, it is less likely that they felt the need to disguise their honest reactions. The literature on interviewer bias also suggests that bias can occur even with same-sex or same-ethnicity pairs. Whites interviewed by whites about race relations, for example, may tend to modify their responses to be more conservative than they really are. (See Shirley Hatchett and Howard Shuman, 1975–1976; Nora Cate Schaeffer, 1980; and Michael Weeks and R. Paul Moore (1981) for more information on this and other research on interview bias.) While our study is probably not completely bias free, there are no indications that managers' responses were significantly affected by the interviewers' personal characteristics.

We tried to pair each of our diverse team members with as diverse a group of managers as possible. Table A.7 shows the mix of interviewer-interviewee pairings, excluding interviews in which more than one interviewer was involved. (The com-

Table A.7. Interviewer-Interviewee Pairings in the Study.

Interviewee	Interviewer						
Sex and ethnicity	White women (4)	Black men (1)	Black women (1)	Hispanic men (1)	Asian-American women (1)	Other women of color (1)	Row totals
White men	14	7	3	5	9	5	43
White women	19	4	3	3	3	5	37
Black men	13	5	3	2	2	1	26
Black women	11	2	3	1	4	-	21
Hispanic men	1	4	1	-	2	-	8
Hispanic women	1	1	-	-	-	-	2
Asian-American men	-	-	-	-	-	1	1
Asian-American women	1	1	-	-	2	-	4
Native American women	1	-	-	-	-	-	1
Other women	-	1	-	-	-	-	1
Other men	1	1	-	-	-	-	2
Column totals	62	26	13	11	22	12	146

plete interview team included seven women and three men — four whites, three blacks, one Asian-American, one Latino, and one born and reared in the Middle East.

We then conducted some basic analyses of these 146 pairings to determine whether responses to the question about advancement barriers differed when the interviewer was a white instead of a person of color. We found no differences in the barriers cited, suggesting that the ethnicity of the interviewer was not a significant influence on managers' responses.

Confidentiality

A number of the managers and executives we interviewed made a point of saying that confidentiality was not an important issue for them, that they would share their views and experiences with anyone in or outside the organization. However, an equal number of managers answered our questions only because of our assurance that their comments would not be attributed to them as individuals. One black woman, for example, specifically cautioned me against even describing her position and appearance for fear that her comments could be traced to her. Another woman of color told me that she had been instructed to focus only on the positive side of a program in her interviews with the press but that she could speak to both the positive and negative aspects of the program in my interview because her comments would not be attributed to her or to her company by name.

Because we relied on some "savvy insiders" to help us identify the key policies and practices used in their organization and to identify other managers familiar with these diversity activities (and even to arrange interview appointments with the other managers), some of these insiders in some of the sixteen organizations do know who was interviewed for this research. The savvy insiders sometimes chose to let all of the interviewees from their organization know who else was also involved, but the use of that information is at the discretion of the insiders and the others they informed. Moreover, when we interviewed boss-subordinate pairs, clearly the boss knew that the subordinate was one of the interviewees and vice versa. I believe, however, that the precautions taken by the research team to preserve the anonymity of the interviewees and the confidentiality of their responses has added a level of accuracy and thoroughness to the results that would not otherwise have been possible.

Analysis of Interview Responses

Because our research materials consisted largely of handwritten notes from interviews, our challenge wsa to turn this information into quantifiable data. For many of the questions, I was able to devise a coding scheme after reading through all of the responses and then to code each response into the proper category. Barriers to advancement, for example, were first categorized on the basis of one or two readings of all managers' responses, and then each of the 563 responses was coded into one of those categories. To check my judgments, I asked another research team member to code some responses independently, and the categories seemed to work well. After the preliminary descriptive analyses were completed, some of the smaller categories were collapsed for more meaningful statistical analyses.

The responses concerning barriers, key elements, and demographic variables were analyzed on the basis of individual responses. The practices, however, could be meaningfully analyzed only at the organizational level. The analysis of responses related to organizational practices involved an additional step of "weighting." This weighting process allowed us to determine not only the frequency with which a practice was used but also its importance as a diversity activity within an organization. An "importance" value was calculated for each practice. A practice that was mentioned by one or only a few managers from an organization and did not seem to be central to the overall diversity effort was given an "importance" value of 1, indicating that the practice was present or used in that organization. When a number of managers described the same practice or when one or more managers emphasized the importance of a practice, it was weighted by a factor of 2 (as a more important, or "priority," practice). When there was considerable consensus among the managers from an organization that a practice was central or critical to the overall diversity effort, the practice was weighted by a factor of 3 (as a "core" practice). The tables in the final section of this appendix therefore show both frequency (the number of organizations in which a practice was at least present) and the weighted "importance" value. The ranking of practices in the tables was done on the basis of "importance" rather than on prevalence alone.

Supplementary Tables

In Tables A.9 through A.12, practices are ranked in order of importance rather than simply by prevalence. Practices that were tied have been given the same ranking. As already explained, the "importance" value was calculated by totaling (1) the number of practices an organization uses that are neither "core" nor "priority" practices, (2) the number of "priority" practices times a weighting factor of 3. Also in Tables A.9 through A.12, the

Table A.8. Barriers to Advancement.

Category	Barriers	Responses	Percent
1	White men already in place, keep others out	**187**	**33.2**
	1. Greater comfort with one's own kind	37	6.6
	2. Prejudice	70	12.4
	3. Threatened by nontraditionals	19	3.4
	4. Insensitive or arrogant	8	1.4
	Other[a]	53	9.4
2	Cannot find qualified nontraditional candidates	**149**	**26.5**
	5. Less education	16	2.8
	6. Lack of organizational savvy	46	8.2
	7. Lack of or resistance to mobility	22	3.9
	8. Difficulty in balancing career and family	33	5.9
	9. Poor recruitment	21	3.7
	Other	11	2.0
3	10. Poor selection or promotion	**18**	**3.2**
4	11. Poor career planning	**51**	**9.1**
5	Poor environment	**54**	**9.6**
	12. Poor work environment	47	8.4
	13. Poor social environment	7	1.2
6	14. Lack of accountability or incentives	**21**	**3.7**
7	15. Backlash	**9**	**1.6**
8	16. Infighting	**17**	**3.0**
9	17. Loss of confidence or motivation	**14**	**2.5**
10	18. Business restrictions such as downsizing	**10**	**1.8**
11	19. Inertia, risk-averse culture	**7**	**1.2**
12	20. Sexual harassment	**4**	**0.7**
13	21. Pay differentials	**3**	**0.5**
	Subtotal	544	96.6
	"No barriers exist"[b]	19	3.4
	Total	563	100

[a]These responses cover a variety of barriers that fit the category but could not be further classified within it, often because they were too vague.

[b]Respondents indicated that no barriers exist for white women, or for members of certain ethnic groups, or for nontraditional managers overall.

Table A.9. Diversity Practices Ranked by Importance.

	Diversity practices	Rank	Importance	No. of sites	Type
1.	Top management's personal intervention	1	40	16	Acc
2.	Targeted recruitment of nonmanagers	2	21	13	Rec
3.	Internal advocacy groups	3	17	10	Acc
4.	Emphasis on EEO statistics, profiles	4	17	9	Acc
5.	Inclusion of diversity in performance evaluation goals, ratings	5	16	12	Acc
6.	Inclusion of diversity in promotion decisions, criteria	6	14	11	Acc
7.	Inclusion of diversity in management succession planning	7	14	10	Acc
8.	Diversity training programs	8	12	10	Dev
9.	Networks and support groups	9	11	9	Dev
10.	Work and family policies	9	11	9	Acc
11.	Key outside hires	11	11	8	Rec
12.	Development programs for all high-potential managers	12	11	7	Dev
13.	Policies against racism, sexism	13	10	9	Acc
14.	Internal audit or attitude survey	14	10	8	Acc
15.	Extensive public exposure on diversity (AA)ₓ	15	10	6	Rec
16.	Informal networking activities	16	9	8	Dev
17.	Active AA/EEO committee, office	17	9	7	Acc
18.	Job rotation	17	9	7	Dev
19.	Formal mentoring program	19	8	7	Dev
20.	Informal mentoring program	19	8	7	Dev
21.	Inclusion of diversity in determining managers' compensation	21	8	6	Acc
22.	Entry development programs for all high-potential new hires	22	8	4	Dev
23.	Board of directors members, activities	23	7	6	Acc
24.	Internal training (such as personal safety or language)	23	7	6	Dev
25.	Recognition events, awards	23	7	6	Dev

#	Practice				Type
26.	Development programs for high potential nontraditionals	26	7	5	Dev
27.	Corporate image as liberal, progressive, or benevolent	27	6	6	Rec
28.	Personnel resources	27	6	6	Acc
29.	Grievance procedure or complaint-resolution process	29	6	5	Acc
30.	Child-care resources	30	5	5	Acc
31.	External training, seminars	31	5	5	Dev
32.	Partnerships with educational institutions	31	5	5	Rec
33.	Career planning	33	5	4	Dev
34.	Recruitment incentives such as cash supplements	33	5	4	Rec
35.	Programs to interest employees in management jobs	35	5	3	Dev
36.	Internships (such as INROADS)	36	4	4	Rec
37.	Selection of nontraditional vendors	37	4	3	Acc
38.	Inclusion of diversity in mission statement	38	3	3	Acc
39.	Miscellaneous accountability practices	38	3	3	Acc
40.	Publications or PR products that highlight diversity	38	3	3	Rec
41.	Targeted job assignments for nontraditionals	41	3	2	Dev
42.	Targeted recruitment of managers	41	3	2	Rec
43.	Customer satisfaction or complaint audits	43	2	2	Acc
44.	Exit interviews	43	2	2	Acc
45.	Noncash benefits for attracting nontraditionals	43	2	2	Acc
46.	Miscellaneous development practices	43	2	2	Dev
47.	Partnerships with nontraditional groups	43	2	2	Rec
48.	Structured survey feedback to managers, promotion candidates	43	2	2	Dev
49.	Community involvement	49	1	1	Rec
50.	Entry development programs for high-potential nontraditionals	49	1	1	Dev
51.	Inclusion of diversity in selection decisions, criteria	49	1	1	Acc
52.	Inclusion of nontraditionals in special awards	49	1	t	Acc

Note: Practices are grouped into three types: accountability (Acc), development (Dev), and recruitment (Rec).

Table A.10. Accountability Practices Ranked by Importance.

Accountability practices	Present (1)	Priority (2)	Core (3)	Importance	No. of sites
1. Top management's personal intervention	1	6	9	40	16
2. Internal advocacy groups	5	3	2	17	10
3. Emphasis on EEO statistics, profiles	2	6	1	17	9
4. Inclusion of diversity in performance evaluation goals, ratings	8	4	*	16	12
5. Inclusion of diversity in promotion decisions, criteria	8	3	*	14	11
6. Inclusion of diversity in management succession planning	6	4	*	14	10
7. Work and family policies	7	2	*	11	9
8. Policies against racism, sexism	8	1	*	10	9
9. Internal audit or attitude survey	6	2	*	10	8
10. Acive AA/EEO committee, office	5	2	*	9	7
11. Inclusion of diversity in determining managers' compensation	4	2	*	8	6
12. Board of directors members, activities	5	1	*	7	6
13. Personnel resources	6	*	*	6	6
14. Grievance procedure or complaint-resolution process	4	1	*	6	5
15. Child-care resources	5	*	*	5	5
16. Selection of nontraditional vendors	4	*	*	4	4
17. Inclusion of diversity in mission statement	3	*	*	3	3
18. Miscellaneous accountability practices	3	*	*	3	3
19. Customer satisfaction or complaint audits	2	*	*	2	2
20. Exit interviews	2	*	*	2	2
21. Noncash benefits for attracting nontraditionals	2	*	*	2	2
22. Inclusion of nontraditionals in selection decisions, criteria	1	*	*	1	1
23. Inclusion of nontraditionals in special awards	1	*	*	1	1

Table A.11. Development Practices Ranked by Importance.

Development practices	Present (1)	Priority (2)	Core (3)	Importance	No. of sites
1. Diversity training programs	8	2	*	12	10
2. Networks and support groups	7	2	*	11	9
3. Development programs for all high-potential managers	3	4	*	11	7
4. Informal networking activities	7	1	*	9	8
5. Job rotation	5	2	*	9	7
6. Formal mentoring program	6	1	*	8	7
7. Informal mentoring program	6	1	*	8	7
8. Entry development programs for all high-potential new hires	1	2	1	8	4
9. Internal training (such as personal safety or language)	5	1	*	7	6
10. Recognition events, awards	5	1	*	7	6
11. Development programs for high-potential nontraditionals	3	2	*	7	5
12. External training, seminars	5	*	*	5	5
13. Career planning	3	1	*	5	4
14. Programs to interest employees in management jobs	1	2	*	5	3
15. Targeted job assignments for nontraditionals	1	1	*	3	2
16. Miscellaneous development practices	2	*	*	2	2
17. Structured survey feedback to managers, promotion candidates	2	*	*	2	2
18. Entry development programs for high-potential nontraditionals	1	*	*	1	1

Table A.12. Recruitment Practices Ranked by Importance.

Recruitment practices	Present (1)	Priority (2)	Core (3)	Importance	No. of sites
1. Targeted recruitment of nonmanagers	5	8	*	21	13
2. Key outside hires	5	3	*	11	8
3. Extensive public exposure on diversity (AA)	2	4	*	10	6
4. Corporate image as liberal, progressive, or benevolent	6	*	*	6	6
5. Partnerships with educational institutions	5	*	*	5	5
6. Recruitment incentives such as cash supplements	3	1	*	5	4
7. Internships (such as INROADS)	2	1	*	4	3
8. Publications or PR products that highlight diversity	3	1	*	3	3
9. Targeted recruitment of managers	1	1	*	3	2
10. Partnerships with nontraditional groups	2	*	*	2	2
11. Community involvement	1	*	*	1	1

column heading "No. of sites" refers to the number of organizations in which a practice is at least present if not a "priority" or "core practice.

In regard to the column headings in Tables A.10 through A.12, "Present" refers to the number of organizations in which a practice is used; "Priority" refers to the number of organizations in which a practice was judged to be less important than a "core" practice but more important than other practices; "Core" refers to the number of organizations in which a practice was judged to be a keystone, that is, at the core of the overall diversity effort. Also in Tables A.10 through A.12, an asterisk (*) indicates that the practice was judged not to be a "core" or "priority" practice.

REFERENCES

"25 Best Places for Blacks to Work: Black Enterprise Identifies the Leading Corporations That Offer the Best Opportunities for Black Professionals." *Black Enterprise,* Feb. 1992, pp. 71–96.

"1992 Hispanic 100: The One Hundred Companies Providing the Most Opportunities for Hispanics." *Hispanic,* Jan.–Feb. 1992, pp. 49–76.

Alderfer, C. P., Alderfer, C. J., Tucker, L., and Tucker, R. "Diagnosing Race Relations in Management." *Journal of Applied Behavioral Science,* 1980, 16(2), 135–166.

Auster, E. R. "Behind Closed Doors: Sex Bias at Professional and Managerial Levels." *Employee Responsibilities and Rights Journal,* 1988, *1,* 129–144.

"Baldrige Award Winners." *Wall Street Journal,* Dec. 13, 1990, p. 1.

Baskerville, D. M., and Tucker, S. H. "A Blueprint for Success." *Black Enterprise,* Nov. 1991, pp. 85–93.

Beer, M., Eisenstat, R. A., and Spector, B. "Why Change Programs Don't Produce Change." *Harvard Business Review,* Nov./Dec. 1990, pp. 158–166.

Bell, E. L. *The Bicultural Life Experience of Career Oriented Black Women.* New Haven, Conn.: Yale School of Organization and Management, 1988.

"Bias in Promotions at the Very Top Targeted." *San Diego Union,* July 30, 1990, pp. A1–A2.

Birnbaum, P. H. "Integration and Specialization in Academic Research." *Academy of Management Journal,* 1981, *24,* 487–503.

"Blacks in Management: No Progress." Editorial. *Management World,* Jan. 1983, p. 24.

Braham, J. "Is the Door Really Open?" *Industry Week,* Nov. 16, 1987, pp. 64–70.

Brown, B. "Imperial Life." Paper presented at the Niagara Conference, Niagara, Canada, Nov. 13, 1990.

Cabezas, A., and Kawaguchi, G. "Empirical Evidence for Continuing Asian American Income Inequality: The Human Capital Model and Labor Market Segmentation." In G. Y. Okihiro, S. Hune, A. A. Hansen, and J. M. Liu (eds.), *Reflections on Shattered Windows: Promises and Prospects for Asian American Studies.* Pullman: Washington State University Press, 1988.

Cannings, K., and Montmarquette, C. "Managerial Momentum: A Simultaneous Model of the Career Progress of Male and Female Managers." *Industrial and Labor Relations Review,* Jan. 1991, pp. 212–228.

Carli, L. L. "Gender, Language, and Influence." *Journal of Personality and Social Psychology,* 1990, *59,* 941–951.

Carroll, D., and Williams, F. "Women Leave Their Mark on Travel Industry." *USA Today,* Mar. 19, 1990, p. 1E.

Carter, D. J., and Wilson, R. *Minorities in Higher Education.* Ninth Annual Status Report. Washington, D.C.: Office of Minorities in Higher Education, American Council on Education, 1991.

Catalyst. *Women in Corporate Management: Results of a Catalyst Survey.* New York: Catalyst, 1990.

Caudron, S. "Monsanto Responds to Diversity—The Dollars of Diversity." *Personnel Journal,* Nov. 1990, pp. 72–80.

Chin, R., and Benne, K. D. "General Strategies for Effecting Changes in Human Systems." In W. G. Bennis, K. D. Benne, R. Chin, and K. E. Corey, (eds.), *The Planning of Change* (3rd ed.). Troy, Mo.: Holt, Rinehart & Winston, 1976.

Chusmir, L. H., and Durand, D. E. "The Female Factor." *Training and Development Journal,* Aug. 1987, pp. 32–37.

Cook, D. "The Silent Minority." *California Business,* Oct. 1989, pp. 23–27.

Copeland, L. "Valuing Workplace Diversity: Ten Reasons Employers Recognize the Benefits of a Mixed Work Force." *Personnel Administrator,* Nov. 1988, pp. 38–40.

Cox, T. H., and Blake, S. "Managing Cultural Diversity: Implications for Organizational Competitiveness." *Academy of Management Executive,* 1991, *5,* 45–54.

Cummins, R. C. "Job Stress and the Buffering Effect of Supervisory Support." *Group & Organization Studies,* 1990, *15,* 92–104.

"Debate — Affirmative Action Is Doing the Right Thing." *USA Today,* June 29, 1990, p. 10A.

De Meuse, K. P., and Tornow, W. W. "The Tie That Binds — Has Become Very, Very Frayed!" *Human Resource Planning,* 1990, *13,* 203–213.

DiTomaso, N., Thompson, D. E., and Blake, D. H. "Corporate Perspectives on the Advancement of Minority Managers." In D. E. Thompson and N. DiTomaso (eds.), *Ensuring Minority Success in Corporate Management.* New York: Plenum, 1988.

Dominguez, C. M. "A Crack in the Glass Ceiling." *HRMagazine,* Dec. 1990, *65.*

Dreyfuss, J. "Get Ready for the New Work Force." *Fortune,* Apr. 23, 1990, pp. 165–181.

Drucker, P. F. "Don't Change Corporate Culture — Use It!" *Wall Street Journal,* Mar. 29, 1991, p. A14.

Duke, L. "Cultural Shifts Bring Anxiety for White Men." *Washington Post,* Jan. 1, 1991, pp. A1, A14.

Dunbar, L. W. (ed.). *Minority Report: What Has Happened to Blacks, Hispanics, American Indians, and Other Minorities in the Eighties.* New York: Pantheon, 1984.

Edsall, T. B., and Edsall, M. D. "When the Official Subject Is Presidential Politics, Taxes, Welfare, Crime, Rights, or Values . . . the Real Subject is RACE." *Atlantic Monthly,* May 1991, pp. 53–86.

Efron, S. "Japanese-Americans Fear Backlash over Pearl Harbor." *Los Angeles Times,* Nov. 2, 1991, pp. A1, A26.

Eisenberger, R., Fasolo, P., and Davis-LaMastro, V. "Perceived Organizational Support and Employee Diligence, Commitment, and Innovation." *Journal of Applied Psychology,* 1990, *75,* 51–59.

"Ethnic Mix Gives California Its Youth." *Wall Street Journal,* July 12, 1990, p. B1.

Fairchild, H. H., and Fairchild, D. G. "World-Class Tensions: Ethnic Rivalry Heats Up Southern California." *Los Angeles Times,* May 5, 1991, p. M2.

Faludi, S. *Backlash: The Undeclared War Against American Women.* New York: Crown, 1991.

"Feinstein Job Quota for Women, Minorities Decried." *San Diego Union,* June 10, 1990, p. A24.

Fernandez, J. P. *Racism and Sexism in Corporate Life: Changing Values in American Business.* New York: Lexington Books, 1981.

Fernandez, J. P. *Survival in the Corporate Fishbowl: Making It into Upper and Middle Management.* New York: Lexington Books, 1987.

Fernandez, J. P. *Managing a Diverse Work Force: Regaining the Competitive Edge.* New York: Lexington Books, 1991.

Fierman, J. "Why Women Still Don't Hit the Top." *Fortune,* Jul. 30, 1990, pp. 40–62.

"The Fortune 500 — The Largest U.S. Industrial Corporations." *Fortune,* Apr. 23, 1990, pp. 338–365.

Foster, C. D., Landes, A., and Binford, S. M. (eds.). *Minorities: A Changing Role in American Society.* Wylie, Tex.: Information Plus, 1990.

Foster, C. D., Siegel, M. A., and Jacobs, N. R. (eds.). *Women's Changing Role.* Wylie, Tex.: Information Plus, 1990.

Fulwood, S., III. "Rights Bill Will Not Force Quotas, Leading Firms Say." *Los Angeles Times,* June 30, 1991, pp. A1, A16.

Gannett Foundation. "Destroying the Myth . . . Building the Future." Advertisement. *Black Enterprise,* Mar. 1991.

Gerhart, B., and Rynes, S. "Determinants and Consequences of Salary Negotiations by Male and Female MBA Graduates." *Journal of Applied Psychology,* 1991, *76,* 256–262.

Goldin, C. *Understanding the Gender Gap: An Economic History of American Women.* New York: Oxford University Press, 1990.

Gregory, D. *The Light Side: The Dark Side.* Poppy Industries, 1969. Album. Cited in the Racism/Sexism Resource Center for Educators newsletter, Nov. 1983.

Guptara, P. "The Art of Training Abroad." *Training and Development Journal,* 1990, *44,* 13–18.

Hammes, S., and Teitelbaum, R. S. "The Fortune Global 500." *Fortune,* July 29, 1991, pp. 237–279.

Hatchett, S., and Shuman, H. "White Respondents and Race-of-Interviewer Effects." *Public Opinion Quarterly,* 1975–1976, 39(4), 523–528.

Hinrichs, J. R. "Commitment Ties to the Bottom Line." *HRMagazine,* Apr. 1991, pp. 77, 79–80.

Hudson Institute. *Workforce 2000: Work and Workers for the Twenty-first Century.* Indianapolis, Ind.: Hudson Institute, 1987.

Hymowitz, C. "Stepping Off the Fast Track." *Wall Street Journal,* June 13, 1989, p. B1.

Hymowitz, C. "As Aetna Adds Flextime, Bosses Learn to Cope." *Wall Street Journal,* June 18, 1990, pp. B1–B2.

Hymowitz, C., and Schellhardt, T. D. "The Glass Ceiling." *Wall Street Journal,* Mar. 24, 1986, pp. 1D–5D.

Johnston, W. B. "Global Work Force 2000: The New World Labor Market." *Harvard Business Review,* Mar./Apr. 1991, pp. 115–127.

Jones, E. W., Jr. "What It's Like to Be a Black Manager." *Harvard Business Review,* 1973, *51,* 108–116.

Jones, E. W., Jr. "Black Managers: The Dream Deferred." *Harvard Business Review,* May/June 1986, pp. 84–93.

Judge, G. "Shifting Markets, Shifting Structures." In D. E. Thompson and N. DiTomaso (eds.), *Ensuring Minority Success in Corporate Management.* New York: Plenum, 1988.

Kanter, D. L., and Mirvis, P. H. *The Cynical Americans: Living and Working in an Age of Discontent and Disillusion.* San Francisco: Jossey-Bass, 1989.

Kanter, R. M. *The Change Masters.* New York: Simon & Schuster, 1983.

Karr, A. R. "Paying College Expenses for Workers Helps Carl's Jr., a 600-Restaurant Chain, Keep Employees Longer." *Wall Street Journal,* Nov. 12, 1991, p. A1.

Keele, R. "Mentoring or Networking? Strong and Weak Ties in Career Development." In L. L. Moore (ed.), *Not as Far as You Think.* New York: Lexington Books, 1986.

Keller, J. J. "AT&T Will Settle EEOC Lawsuit for $66 Million." *Wall Street Journal,* July 18, 1991, p. B2.

Kennedy, J., and Everest, A. "Put Diversity in Context." *Personnel Journal*, 1991, *70*, 50–54.

Kennedy, R. B. "Preference for Veterans May Impede Women." *Personnel Journal*, Sept. 1990, pp. 124–126.

Kennedy, R. D. "Inroads That Go Beyond Affirmative Action." *Wall Street Journal*, Sept. 10, 1990, p. A14.

Kim, J. "Issues in Work Force Diversity." Panel presentation at the first annual National Diversity Conference, San Francisco, May 1991.

Klimonski, R. J., and Strickland, W. J. "Assessment Centers — Valid or Merely Prescient?" *Personnel Psychology*, 1977, *30*, 353–56.

Koretz, G. "An Acid Test of Job Discrimination in the Real World." *Business Week*, Oct. 21, 1991, p. 23.

Korn/Ferry International. *Korn/Ferry's International Executive Profile: A Survey of Corporate Leaders in the 80s.* New York: Korn/Ferry International, 1986.

Kotter, J. P. "What Leaders Really Do: Good Management Controls Complexity; Effective Leadership Produces Useful Change." *Harvard Business Review*, May-June 1990, pp. 103–111.

Kuiper, S. "Who Helped the Corporation Earn Those Millions? Or, Where Are the Women?" *Proceedings of the 51st Association for Business Communication International Convention.* Los Angeles: Association for Business Communication, 1986, pp. 116–120.

Lee, W. S., and Mark, R. "Family, Minority Motivation Requires Highest CEO Priority." *Financier*, 1990, *14*, 27–31.

Mabry, M., and others. "Past Tokenism." *Newsweek*, May 14, 1990, p. 37.

McCall, M. W., Jr., Lombardo, M. M., and Morrison, A. M. *The Lessons of Experience: How Successful Executives Develop on the Job.* New York: Lexington Books, 1988.

McIntosh, P. *White Privilege and Male Privilege: A Personal Account of Coming to See Correspondences Through Work in Women's Studies.* Working Paper No. 189. Wellesley, Mass.: Wellesley College Center for Research on Women, 1988.

May, L. "Blacks Urged to Unite with Other Minorities." *Los Angeles Times*, July 22, 1991.

Michels, A. J., and Welsh, T. "The 500 Largest Service Corporations." *Fortune*, Jun. 3, 1991, pp. 253–284.

Mooney, C. J. "Universities Awarded Record Number of Doctorates Last Year; Foreign Students Thought to Account for Much of the Increase." *Chronicle of Higher Education*, Apr. 25, 1990, p. A1.

Morrison, A. M., and Von Glinow, M. A. "Women and Minorities in Management." *American Psychologist*, 1990, *45*, 200–208.

Morrison, A. M., White, R. P., Van Velsor, E., and the Center for Creative Leadership. *Breaking the Glass Ceiling: Can Women Reach the Top of America's Largest Corporations?* Reading, Mass: Addison-Wesley, 1987.

Nabbefeld, J. "Insurer Settles Women's Lawsuit: State Farm Faces $100 Million to Discrimination Claimants." *San Diego Daily Transcript*, May 10, 1988, pp. 1A–3A.

Nelson-Horchler, J. "The Best Man for a Job Is a Man!" *Industry Week*, 1991, *240*, 50–52.

O'Dell, C., and McAdams, J. *People, Performance, and Pay: A Full Report on the American Productivity Center/American Compensation Association National Survey of Non-Traditional Reward and Human Resource Practices.* Houston: American Productivity Center, 1986.

Ohlott, P. J., Ruderman, M. N., and McCauley, C. D. "Gender Differences in Managerial Job Demands and Learning." Greensboro, N.C.: Center for Creative Leadership, June 1991 (Photocopied).

Palmer, J. "Three Paradigms for Diversity Change Leaders." *Organizational Development Practitioner*, 1989, *21*, 15–18.

Pelz, D. C. "Some Social Factors Related to Performance in a Research Organization." *Administrative Science Quarterly*, 1956, *1*, 310–325.

Phillips, L. "Quotas Crystallize as an Issue in '90 Senate Election in N.C." *USA Today*, Mar. 27, 1991, p. 5A.

Pollock, E. J. "Law: Better Confrontation Than Discrimination?" *Wall Street Journal*, May 14, 1991, p. B1.

Rebchook, J. "Once Fired, Suing the Boss Comes Easy." *Rocky Mountain News*, Mar. 11, 1990, p. 3B.

Riskind, S. "The New Executive Unemployed." Letter to *Fortune. Fortune,* May 6, 1991, p. 113.

Roman, M. "Women, Beware: An MBA Doesn't Mean Equal Pay." *Business Week,* Oct. 29, 1990, p. 57.

Sachs, R. "The Productive Workforce: The Final Frontier of Competitive Advantage?" *Business Forum,* Spring 1990, pp. 5–7.

Sandroff, R. "Sexual Harassment in the Fortune 500: How Top Policymakers at America's Giant Corporations See (or Refuse to See) the Harassment of Women Employees." *Working Woman,* Dec. 1988, pp. 69–73.

Schaeffer, N. C. "Evaluating Race-of-Interviewer Effects in a National Survey." *Sociological Methods and Research,* 1980, *8,* pp. 400–419.

Schmidt, P. "Women and Minorities: Is Industry Ready?" *New York Times,* Oct. 16, 1988, pp. 25–27.

Scovel, K. "The Relocation Riddle." *Human Resource Executive,* June 1990, pp. 46–51.

Smith, T. W. *Ethnic Images.* National Opinion Research Center, GSS Topical Report No. 19. Chicago: University of Chicago, Dec. 1990.

Smollar, D. "SDSU's Filling of Psychology Post Is Faulted." *Los Angeles Times,* Feb. 3, 1991a, pp. B1–B4.

Smollar, D. "Flyers Prompt Free-Speech Furor at UCSD." *Los Angeles Times,* May 23, 1991b, pp. B1–B6.

Sprout, A. L. "America's Most Admired Corporations." *Fortune,* Feb. 11, 1991, pp. 52–82.

"'Stay Bonuses' Are Used to Keep Key Employees During Mergers or Shutdowns." *Wall Street Journal,* Mar. 12, 1991, p. A1.

Stevens, A. "Anti Discrimination Training Haunts Employer in Bias Suit." *Wall Street Journal,* July 31, 1991, pp. B1–B5.

Sutton, C., and Moore, K. "Executive Women — 20 Years Later." *Harvard Business Review,* 1985, *5,* 42–66.

Tamaki, J. "Award in Sex Bias Case Raised to $17.6 Million." *Los Angeles Times,* Oct. 4, 1991, pp. D1, D5.

Tashjian, V. W. *Don't Blame the Baby: Why Women Leave Corporations.* Wilmington, Del.: Wick and Company, 1990.

Thomas, J., and Scott, M. S. "Studies Show Widespread Bias Against Blacks." *Black Enterprise,* 1991, *22,* 11.

Thomas, R. R., Jr., "From Affirmative Action to Affirming Diversity." *Harvard Business Review,* Mar.–Apr. 1990, pp. 107–117.

Thomas, R. R., Jr., *Beyond Race and Gender: Unleashing the Power of Your Total Work Force by Managing Diversity.* New York: AMACOM, 1991.

Thompson, B. L. "Training's Salary Survey." *Training,* 1990, *27,* 49.

Thompson, D. E., and DiTomaso, N. (eds.). *Ensuring Minority Success in Corporate Management.* New York: Plenum, 1988.

Thornburg, L. "Transfers Need Not Mean Dislocation." *Human Resource Magazine,* Sept. 1990, pp. 46–48.

Townsend, R. *Up the Organization.* New York: Knopf, 1970.

Trost, C. "Firms Heed Women Employees' Needs: New Approach Forced by Shifts in Population." *Wall Street Journal,* Nov. 22, 1989, p. B1.

Tucker, S. H., and Thompson, K. D. "Will Diversity = Opportunity + Advancement for Blacks?" *Black Enterprise,* 1990, *21,* 50–60.

Tumulty, K. "Marshall Says Bush Should Not Use Race as Excuse for Picking Wrong Successor." *Los Angeles Times,* June 29, 1991, p. A22.

U.S. Department of Labor. *A Report on the Glass Ceiling Initiative.* Washington, D.C.: U.S. Department of Labor, 1991.

van den Berghe, P. L. *Race and Racism: A Comparative Perspective.* New York: Wiley, 1967.

Van Velsor, E., and Hughes, M. W. *Gender Differences in the Development of Managers: How Women Managers Learn from Experience.* Greensboro, N.C.: Center for Creative Leadership, 1990.

Watts, P. "School's Out?" *Executive Female,* Jan./Feb. 1991, pp. 16–55.

Weeks, M. F., and Moore, R. P. "Ethnicity-of-Interviewer Effects on Ethnic Respondents." *Public Opinion Quarterly,* 1981, *45,* pp. 245–249.

Weiss, D. E. "The Score on Chores Around the House." *San Diego Union,* Apr. 1, 1991, p. D1.

"White College Graduates Make a Third More Than Blacks." *Los Angeles Times,* Sept. 20, 1991, p. D5.

Wilson, W. J. *Power, Racism, and Privilege: Race Relations in Theoretical and Sociohistorical Perspectives.* New York: Free Press, 1973.

Wynter, L. E. "Business & Race: Minority Grads Remain in Demand Despite Slump." *Wall Street Journal,* Apr. 18, 1991, p. B1.

Zeitz, B., and Dusky, L. *The Best Companies for Women.* New York: Simon & Schuster, 1988.

Ziller, R. C. "Homogeneity and Heterogeneity of Group Membership." In C. G. McClintoch (ed.), *Experimental Social Psychology.* New York: Holt, Rinehart & Winston, 1972.

INDEX